Taiwan New Cinema at Film Festivals

Taiwan New Cinema at Film Festivals

Beth Tsai

EDINBURGH
University Press

Edinburgh University Press is one of the leading university presses in the UK. We publish academic books and journals in our selected subject areas across the humanities and social sciences, combining cutting-edge scholarship with high editorial and production values to produce academic works of lasting importance. For more information visit our website: edinburghuniversitypress.com

© Beth Tsai, 2023, 2024

Edinburgh University Press Ltd
13 Infirmary Street,
Edinburgh, EH1 1LT

Typeset in Garamond MT Std by
Manila Typesetting Company

A CIP record for this book is available from the British Library

ISBN 978 1 4744 9691 9 (hardback)
ISBN 978 1 4744 9692 6 (paperback)
ISBN 978 1 4744 9693 3 (webready PDF)
ISBN 978 1 4744 9694 0 (epub)

The right of Beth Tsai to be identified as author of this work has been asserted in accordance with the Copyright, Designs and Patents Act 1988 and the Copyright and Related Rights Regulations 2003 (SI No. 2498).

Contents

Figures	vii
Acknowledgements	ix

Introduction 1
   Taiwan Peculiarities 3
   Transnational Cinema as a Method 7
   A Roadmap: Historicising Taiwan New Cinema and Focus on
   Filmmakers 9

Part I   Historicising Taiwan New Cinema

1 The Rise of Taiwan New Cinema and the Festival Strategy 17
   Taiwan's Commercial Cinema (1955–80) 19
   Taiwan's Film Industry in Crisis 23
   The Rise of Taiwan New Cinema 26
   The Festival Strategy 29
   Edited, Sealed, Delivered: *A City of Sadness* 32

2 Women Critics and Building the Auteur 38
   The Scandalous Truth behind the Sour Apple 40
   From Exclusion to Acceptance 45
   A Global Slow Take on Film 51
   Conclusion 57

Part II   Filmmakers in Focus

3 Going East: Women Walk the City in Hou Hsiao-hsien's *Le Voyage
   du ballon rouge* (2007) and *Café Lumière* (2003) 61
   Transnational Voyages 64
   Cinematic (Re)Mapping of City Life in *Café Lumière* 66
   Towards a Postcolonial History 73
   The Filmmaker as *Flâneur* in *Le Voyage du ballon rouge* 78
   Conclusion 86

4 Going West: Tsai Ming-liang at the Louvre and Cinema in the Gallery 87
    Journey to the Museum 91
    From the Local Theatre to the Global Stage 94
    Tsai Ming-liang's Movie Theatre 98
    At Home at the Museum 102
    Conclusion 105
5 A Southbound Turn: Dreaming Taiwan in Midi Z's Realist Films 106
    From *Fudaojin* to the World Cinema Fund 108
    Beneath the Film Subsidies and the Southbound Policy 110
    Poverty, the Gaze and the Mode of Production 113
    Into the Soundscape and the Film Industry's Exploitation of Women 119
    Conclusion 126
6 To the Future: Film Festivals as Producers and Sleeping in the Cinema 128
    Festival Co-production and Financing 131
    Festival Film 134
    The Sleepy Spectator 138

Postscript: An American Girl in Taiwan 149
Bibliography 153

Index 163

Figures

1.1	Kueiyuan and Qingmei on a motorcycle in *Dangerous Youth*	22
2.1	The boys take a second and third bite into the apples in Wan Ren's 'The Taste of Apples'	42
2.2	The final title card of *What Time Is It There?*	56
3.1	Yoko taking the Tokyo metro and looking out from the train in *Café Lumière*	68
3.2	Trains moving diagonally in *Café Lumière*	70
3.3	A long crane-shot of trains in *Café Lumière* as the camera tilts down slowly	71
3.4	A snapshot of Tokyo's cityscape in the spring of 1983 from Wim Wenders's documentary *Tokyo-Ga*	73
3.5	A mural stencil of a red balloon in *Flight of the Red Balloon*	81
3.6	Song Fang showing her video work to Suzanne on a laptop in *Flight of the Red Balloon*	81
3.7	A close-up shot of Song Fang's video work, or the film-within-the-film moment in *Flight of the Red Balloon*	82
3.8	*The Balloon* or *Corner of a Park with a Child Playing with a Balloon*, 1899	84
3.9	A scene from *Flight of the Red Balloon*, in which the glass in the picture frame blurs Félix Vallotton's oil painting	84
4.1	Lee Kang-sheng falling asleep with the TV on in *What Time Is It There?*	88
4.2	Installation view of Tsai Ming-liang's *It's a Dream*	92
4.3	The man who steals Hsiao-Kang's clock in *What Time Is It There?*	99
5.1	Shin-Hong's friends wonder where the country of 'Taipei' is in *Return to Burma* (2011)	112
5.2	The scooter taxi scene in *Return to Burma*	118
5.3	The final moment from *Nina Wu*, showing the titular character	121
5.4	The film director keeps over-correcting Nina, from *Nina Wu*	122

5.5	The director forcefully attempts to unlock the emotions of Nina in front of the camera, from *Nina Wu*	124
5.6	In a *Nina Wu* behind-the-scenes featurette, actor Shih Ming-Shuai describes the challenge of shooting a slap scene	124
6.1	The opening credits of Tsai Ming-liang's *Walker*	129
6.2	Installation view of *Sand* at the Dune Gallery in Zhuangwei	140
6.3	Installation view of the exhibition *Walker* at the Dune Gallery in Zhuangwei	140
6.4	Installation view of *No No Sleep* at the Dune Gallery in Zhuangwei	141
6.5	Image showing the Japanese actor Masanobu Ando from *No No Sleep*	142
6.6	Lee Kang-sheng devouring a chicken leg in real time from *Stray Dogs*	145

Acknowledgements

The seminal idea for this project first came in a meeting with JungBong Choi, who was working at New York University at the time, and suggested that I look further into the connections between Taiwan cinema and film festivals. His recommendation became the seed of thought and the idea grew into a doctoral dissertation, completed at Stony Brook University, which later became the blueprint of this book.

While my dissertation was completed in 2017, it wasn't until the summer of 2020 that I began drafting a proposal for this project. The COVID-19 pandemic has upended much of society in an unprecedented manner: disruption to human activities and how the world lives in all possible ways. During the lockdown summer in upstate New York, I found time to put together the first draft of my book proposal in under ten days – an efficiency I never had before. I am profoundly grateful to my women's writing group who read, commented on, and offered suggestions on my proposal: Bonnie Tilland, Laura Jo-han Wen, Martina Koegeler, and, of course, my confidante, Sophia Marguerite Basaldua-Sun. If writing the first draft was a breeze, it was because of the rigorous training I received from my dissertation advisor, mentor, and friend, E. K. Tan, who continued to inspire me, meld my thoughts, handhold me throughout the process, and be the voice of reason whenever I second-guess myself. Without my dissertation committee members signing off the rough version with their approval – Krin Gabbard, Guo-Juin Hong, Jacqueline Reich, and especially Liz Montegary – I wouldn't have had the opportunity to revise a student's work into a book-length project.

Special recognition is given to Nicholas de Villiers, to whom I owe immeasurable gratitude. Nick has been the biggest champion of my work since the beginning. As a junior scholar who struggled to find a voice in the competitive world of academia, I dare say he believed in my work more than I myself did. His generosity, encouragement, support, and remarkable breadth of knowledge propelled me to move the project forward in smooth sailing and continued to serve as a model of intellectual refinement and career aspirations.

Much appreciation goes to Shi-Yan Chao, who kickstarted our friendship at the 2016 annual Society for Cinema and Media Studies (SCMS) conference in Atlanta – I will forever cherish the star-struck moment I first shook hands with Nick, and thus began all the future collaboration opportunities, profoundly built on our mutual admiration for filmmaker Tsai Ming-liang and French philosopher and literary critic Roland Barthes. It was in our little cinephile club that we found comfort in a world of chaos, be it feeling marginalised, queer, or not accepted.

I am also grateful for the critical audiences who patiently listened to and offered suggestions for earlier versions of this book material that I presented at different places. I have met so many wonderful friends and colleagues during the time I was attending conferences at Lund University, Hong Kong University, and University of Cincinnati, and all the annual conferences of SCMS, Northeast Modern Language Association (NeMLA), Association for Asian Studies (AAS), AAS-in-Asia, and New York Conference on Asian Studies (NYCAS): Emilie Yueh-yu Yeh, Maya Nedyalkova, Cindy Hing-Yuk Wong, Chris Berry, Song Hwee Lim, Joseph Mai, Audrey Evrard, Ungsan Kim, Mila Zuo, Ling Zhang, Michelle Bloom, Ellen Chang, Elena Gorfinkel, Jean Ma, Chenshu Zhou, and many more. Brian Hu, I'm singling out your name because I wouldn't have chosen Edinburgh University Press as the imprint I wanted to work with without you sharing your behind-the-scenes publishing story over a glass of champagne (me) and one of whisky (you). Thank you, Michael Gott, for connecting me with the publisher's Film Studies editor (when I first mentioned my book project at the Pullman wine bar in Montreal). I also can't leave out the festival studies comrades I met during the time I served as co-chair of SCMS Film and Media Festivals Scholarly Interest Group: Antoine Damiens, Ma Ran, David Richler, Dorotka Ostrowska, Tamara Falicov, Marijke de Valck, Jon Petrychyn, Ger Zielinski, Claudia Sicon, Eren Odabasi, Matt St John, and Michael Talbott.

I am thankful for the camaraderie of my graduate and postgraduate years (if I haven't already mentioned you above) – these friendships have come a long way: Joy Schaefer, Claire Yu, Ruby Liang, Colleen Chiang, Jaap Verheul, Tanya Goldman, Rochelle Sara Miller, Raúl Feliciano Ortiz, Shira Segal, and Hangping Xu. *Gracias y abrazos* to long-standing friend José Miguel Palacios, who offered feedbacks on my drafts from so many different writing stages. *Bisous et merci* to Frédérick Pelletier for his industry insights and unwavering support over the years.

I was fortunate to have my research supported by the Centre for Taiwan Studies at the University of California, Santa Barbara, shepherded by the interim director Sabine Frühstück. Gillian Leslie, my book editor, has been a solid supporter of my work. I am much obliged to my wonderful, brilliant research assistant Pauline Wong, who took care of all the moving parts of the book, from collecting information on festival funding to obtaining image copyrights.

Fragments of Chapter 1 in this book have been previously published as 'Visible Art, Invisible Nations? On the Politics in Film Festivals, Hou Hsiao-hsien, and Taiwan New Cinema' in the edited collection *International Film Festivals: Contemporary Cultures and History Beyond Venice and Cannes*. This anthology is edited by Tricia Jenkins and was first published on 20 September 2018 with I. B. Tauris, an imprint of Bloomsbury Publishing plc. An earlier version of Chapter 4 first appeared as open-source in the *International Journal of Asia Pacific Studies* 13, no. 2: 141–60 under the title 'The Many Faces of Tsai Ming-liang: Cinephilia, the French Connection, and Cinema in the Gallery'. This article was made available for reuse under a Creative Commons Attribution License. Lastly, all the images I photographed of Tsai Ming-liang's installations at the Dune were given permission to publish by the exhibition's production company, Homegreen Films.

Introduction

Taipei's Golden Horse Awards Ceremony – popularly known as the 'Chinese Oscars' – is a glamorous, high-profile annual industry event that follows the film festival of the same name. Its goal is to recognise excellence in Chinese-language cinema but in 2016 an unscripted moment stole the show, shining a harsh light not just on the divide between the 'first' and 'second' waves in Taiwan New Cinema but also on the fraught colonial and postcolonial histories of Taiwan. During the award ceremony, a recap video was shown in honour of Myanmar-born film director Midi Z (Zhao Deyin in Mandarin), part of the 'second' wave, who was named Outstanding Taiwanese Filmmaker of the Year. In the video clip, the celebrated Taiwan New Cinema auteur Hou Hsiao-hsien (part of the 'first') was asked by someone off screen to comment on Midi ('What makes him stand out from the crowd?'). Hou quipped: 'The difference is that … he [Midi] probably came here as an illegal immigrant!' Hou's punchline – a reference to the plot of Midi's 2012 film *Poor Folk* (and the original title also carries the word for illegal immigrant) – gave Midi no other choice but to defend himself on the podium. 'In response to director Hou's earlier comment,' said Midi, 'I want to clarify that I did not smuggle into the country. I came here legally in 1998 when I was sixteen years old' (53rd Golden Horse Awards 2016). Audiences laughed, but what was supposed to be benign humour was also poorly masked bias.

In his teasing, Hou failed to remember the diverse, pan-Chinese background marking so many Taiwanese directors: Wang Tong, Edward Yang, Tsai Ming-liang, and even Hou himself. The seemingly harmless joke exposes the settler/Han Chinese superiority hidden beneath liberal democracy and multiculturalism, a position that 'obscures the socio-historical contexts of the rise of a transnational migrant filmmaker' (Shen 2018, 3). The implicit racial and ethnic bias is also structural, written into the very awards ceremony itself, as is evidenced by the treatment Tsai Ming-liang had received there fifteen years earlier. In 2001, instead of being named Outstanding Taiwanese Filmmaker of the Year (as the award was renamed the following year), Tsai received, horrifically, a 'Special Jury Prize for an Individual'. In its one-off naming and refusal to acknowledge Tsai as Taiwanese, the award imposed a segregated Taiwanese identity rather than celebrating the migrant director's Southeast Asian diasporic background as part of the Taiwan experience.

In fact, many Chinese diasporic and Southeast Asian directors making films in Taiwan today – such as Tsai Ming-liang, Ho Wi-ding, Lau Kek-huat, and Midi Z – migrated to Taiwan for their education and ended up pursuing a career in their host country. They are 'hyphenated people' (Chow 1993), 'Taiwanese new immigrants' that came to the country not as factory workers or as a result of marriages with Taiwanese spouses to pursue a 'Taiwan dream' (Robinson 2020). If Rey Chow coined the term 'hyphenated people' to counter Orientalism, essentialism, particularism, and geographical determinism in East Asian cultural studies, the hyphen yet does so much more. It invites questions not only about identity politics, but also about the intersection of gender, queerness, migration, mobility, and border-crossing, as well as – for this project – the international funds and transnational players that commission, produce, and present world cinema.

Being 'hyphenated' is just one transnational dimension of Taiwan New Cinema (first wave, 1982–9; second wave, 1990–), whose films explore social tensions and problems in cinematically compelling ways, blending social realism with modernist innovation. The films themselves are the material embodiment of the transnational flows of capital and people: internationally co-produced, globally circulated, and regularly spotlighted at international film festivals, where their reception is appropriated by curators. These international film festivals have not only put Taiwan on the map but also repositioned Taiwan's geopolitics closer to Southeast Asia and renegotiated the island's uncertain and ambiguous national identity. Such interventions transform film histories, subverting monolithic nationalistic narratives in favour of a more multiethnic, multicultural, and personal story. It is also here, on the level of the film festival, that Taiwan New Cinema distinguishes itself from its Western counterparts. While Taiwan New Cinema shares with these films a formalist concern with cinematic modernism (no longer nostalgically romanticising China's image, as in previous modes of Taiwan filmmaking), it also explicitly represents the cultural exchanges and debates on national identity taking place at the level of film production, exhibition, and reception. This book offers accounts of the film festival's role in both commissioning and exhibiting films, thus influencing new cinematic styles for local, regional, and global consumption. The film festival is approached as a theoretical framework, as well an object of study to analyse how New Cinema directors – Hou Hsiao-hsien, Tsai Ming-liang, and Midi Z, specifically – became representatives of Taiwan once their films were circulated internationally.

In situating Taiwan New Cinema in the exhibition context, this book also takes a closer look at the productive roles women have played as discursive mediators of the cultural imaginary of the nation, the auteur, and the art of slow cinema. While the three primary case studies all focus on male directors, there is an unbending feminist calibre in the modes of production, and feminist interventions draw our attention to who is writing the grand narrative in history. These behind-the-scenes forces include Taiwanese women film critics such as Peggy Hsiung-ping Chiao and screenwriters such as Chu T'ien-wen, as well as the women actors and characters in the films: from the female *flâneurs* in Hou Hsiao-hsien's transnational homages to the survivors of sexual abuse and exploitation in the film industry, as depicted in Midi Z's #MeToo thriller *Nina Wu* (2019), based in part on Taiwanese actress Wu Ke-Xi's own experiences. The voices of these women writers subvert the official narrative told by men and display a complex diversity of feminist thought and modes of intersectional political consciousness by allying themselves intimately through their writings and character design in an industry (including the film festivals, particularly Cannes) that remains male-dominated.

Previous scholars (Lee and Stringer 2012; Stringer 2016) have explored the role that international film festivals play in shaping and defining Chinese-language cinema's global image, asking why only certain films and filmmakers benefit from participation at top film festivals. Building on such conversations, this book revisits Taiwan New Cinema's relationship to film festivals from cultural, historical, and geopolitical standpoints. It is both about the ways in which these art house films were circulated and received *at* international film festivals and about their relationship *with* film festivals. This book views the critical formulation of Taiwan New Cinema and its aesthetic of slowness as an expansion of the legacy in which its 'newness' and 'slowness' – consecrated by film festivals and critics writing for them in the 1980s and onwards – were reduced to an exclusive list of representatives, culled from a few canonical films and directors. The book thus seeks to complement the discussion on film festivals not just as ports of entry for alternative exhibition and distribution but also as mediators for the cultural imaginary.

Taiwan Peculiarities

Scholars have already devoted much study to Taiwan New Cinema, examining it, for example, as a cultural currency to speak for Taiwan, as part of the global new wave movements, as a rupture in Taiwan film history, as nation-branding festival films, as exoticism catering to Eurocentric ideals, and as the site of discourse for history and nationalism. In fact, as Taiwanese film critic and chief executive of the Taipei Golden Horse Film Festival

Wen Tian-Xiang (2015, 258) once remarked, Taiwan New Cinema still gets more than its fair share of attention:

> When we talk about Taiwanese film history in the 1980s, we normally think of Taiwan New Cinema as the representative of the time, when in fact New Cinema prevailed in less than 15% of the films produced [in Taiwan] during this period.

Taiwan New Cinema's canonical status has persisted even into the first two decades of the twenty-first century, in the years since the movement lost its coherence and amid the post-2008 rise of a new, commercially viable Taiwan cinema (different from the 'second' wave that also continues today but is not the foremost). This latest strand subverts New Cinema's art house direction and attempts to produce a new cycle of mostly genre and big-budget films appropriate for exploring contemporary Taiwanese society. The newer Taiwan cinema has not had the same lasting impact or visibility in the international arena as did Taiwan New Cinema, but Taiwan film studies has grown to encompass this era just the same, catalysed by the record-breaking box office success and immense popularity of *Cape No. 7* (2008), which marked the directorial debut of director Wei Te-sheng. Wei Te-sheng is an icon of the post-New Cinema generation of film directors, capturing the spirit of youth, of the time, and of history in the same way that Taiwan New Cinema filmmakers were against history. Wei's epic action saga *Warriors of the Rainbow: Seediq Bale* (2011) tells the true story of Taiwan's Indigenous people, who were almost annihilated in the Japanese occupation of the 1930s. The epic generates a revisionist look at Taiwan's history to formulate a more inclusive, culturally diverse, non-Han-centric consciousness of Taiwanese identity. The scholars who have analysed Wei Te-sheng, however, cannot seem to escape a past haunted by Taiwan New Cinema. Their claim for a radical break with the previous movement is clouded by a compulsive need to justify their discussions of post-*Cape No. 7* genre films with or against the New Cinema framework.[1]

Festival programmers, curators, film libraries, and archival institutes run into the same problem. Amid their efforts to showcase a broader range of Taiwan cinema to domestic and international audiences, their positionality remains anchored in the framework of New Cinema. They either tread too

---

[1] See Kuei-fen Chiu, Ming-yeh Rawnsley, and Gary Rawnsley, eds (2017), *Taiwan Cinema: International Reception and Social Change* (Abingdon: Routledge); and Paul G. Pickowicz and Yingjin Zhang, eds (2020), *Locating Taiwan in the Twenty-First Century* (Amherst, NY: Cambria Press).

carefully in their justification ('no one is arguing that Taiwan New Cinema of the 1980s–1990s left no legacies'; Pickowicz and Zhang 2020, 2) or leverage the term as a promotional strategy. For instance, an exhibition that aims to spotlight the recent artistic trend of Taiwan cinema seesawed its programme naming between 'A Transition from Taiwan New Cinema' and 'Beyond Realism' (Taiwan Culture Portal, n.d.). What the exhibition was intended to screen was a list of films well balanced between artistic explorations and populist tendencies, a blend of realism and escapist fantasy. However, the naming of the exhibition ended up overshadowing the central focus. The unfortunate choice of words speaks to Taiwan cinema's central dilemma: scholars and curators are eager (and rightfully so) to move beyond the legacy of New Cinema but are instead stuck in a quagmire of historical narrative that cannot do *without* acknowledging New Cinema. So why does Taiwan New Cinema receive such privileged status? And why continue to centre it in this project, if its heyday has passed?

The answer to these questions is wrapped up with Taiwan's unique status as a nation and a culture, a particularity that is felt not just at film festivals but in the international arena too – both in the way that this particularity manifests and in the way that it is too frequently subsumed into or engulfed by conversations on China. In film history and festival programme catalogues, films from Taiwan are often filed under 'non-Western cinema', 'Third Cinema', 'Asian cinema', or 'Chinese cinema' (Hu 2017, 69). Relegated to the historiography of global cinema by Western scholars and critics, Taiwan cinema is rarely taken on its own terms (Hong 2011). Moreover, it is often obscured by the academic pursuit of Chinese cinemas, which privileges studies in China (for example, Chinese independent film) over cinema outputs from Hong Kong and Taiwan. The range of topics in cinema studies on China waiting for discovery, analysis, and exploration is extensive – especially now, considering the present juncture between the Communist regime and its soft power ambitions to overtake the Hollywood film industry. But Taiwan cinema certainly deserves not to be lost in this shuffle.

Taiwan – a de jure sovereign state not officially recognised by most countries on the international stage – is at the heart of a geopolitical struggle, facing an ongoing existential threat from the government of the People's Republic of China (PRC).[2] The latter does not recognise Taiwan's sovereignty

---

[2] J. Michael Cole's (2020) book *Cross-Strait Relations Since 2016: The End of the Illusion* surveys current China–Taiwan relations, offering a comprehensive reading of political conflict, interactions, and economic integration at the domestic level, as well as the triangular international relations among the United States, China, and Taiwan.

but rather claims the territory as its own, as can be glimpsed from the administration's insistence on the global use of diplomatic (read: ambiguous) names to refer to Taiwan at international events (Taiwan is forced to compete under the moniker of Chinese Taipei at the Olympics, for example). Amid rising tensions between the United States and China, the US–Taiwan relationship has reached a never-before-seen height of diplomacy on multiple fronts, including bilateral cooperation in technology and trade and the possibility of renaming the island country's de facto embassy as 'Taiwan', not 'Taipei or Chinese Taipei' (Martina 2022). In comparison, US–China relations have reached an all-time low. Tensions flared up following House Speaker Nancy Pelosi's recent visit to Taiwan, which was seen as a symbolic gesture and a reassurance of the US security partnership with Taiwan. China overreacted in retaliation, cancelling talks with the US on military issues and suspending several bilateral cooperation programmes on topics ranging from climate change to illegal immigrants.[3] Worse, during Pelosi's visit, the Chinese military fired missile tests around and over Taiwan. These unprecedented military exercises foreshadowed a possible invasion and demonstrated the Beijing leadership's voracity to take the country by force. If referring to Taiwan as a country makes one a de facto separatist – someone who advocates the formal declaration of Taiwan independence and defies the One-China principle upheld by the Xi Jinping administration – is now the time to poke the bear by tapping Taiwan cinema?[4]

And this is only a sliver of the full scope of issues Taiwan faces in its challenge for international status. Given that geopolitical context, which directly affects the cinema of the nation, Taiwan New Cinema represents a struggling configuration of the 'nation' brought forth by Taiwan's multi-layered colonial and postcolonial histories. If the way that current international

---

[3] Ministry of Foreign Affairs of the People's Republic of China. 2022. 'The Ministry of Foreign Affairs Announces Countermeasures in Response to Nancy Pelosi's Visit to Taiwan'. 5 August. Available at: <https://www.fmprc.gov.cn/mfa_eng/xwfw_665399/s2510_665401/202208/t20220805_10735706.html> (last accessed 16 August 2022).

[4] Of course, it is not taboo to refer to Taiwan as a country in academia, at least in Anglophone academia; nor has there been a shortage of literature dedicated to studies of Taiwan cinema. However, it is peculiar that US scholars sometimes adopt a linguistic ambiguity towards Taiwan. For example, in the introduction to one recent anthology on Taiwan cinema, never once did the editors address Taiwan as a country or a nation; instead, they replaced the term with the descriptive words 'island mass' and 'region' whenever possible (Pickowicz and Zhang 2020, 1–17).

relations operate is comparable to a crowded global marketplace, Taiwan has fostered various kinds of entrepreneurship to increase its visibility or otherwise be stranded in isolation. Applying this competitive identity model of nation-building to film festivals, this study is rooted in the belief that cinema is indeed a vantage point for the study of a small nation's soft power (Lim 2013; Lim 2018a; Zhang 2020). This book offers a study of national cinema and cultural exchange propagated by festival programming to counterstrike the political tension and solidify cinephile culture simultaneously.

Transnational Cinema as a Method

Internationally, while major film festivals have often denied Taiwanese filmmakers their national identity by labelling them instead as 'Chinese', the festival circuit has established and promoted Taiwan (if not as a nation, at least as a discourse; Hu 2017, 74) via New Cinema. This book argues that rather than perceiving New Cinema of the 1980s as a sudden emergence of the 'new wave' dealing with the identities and the problems of Taiwanese life, we can and should situate such films in the global circulation to understand the cultural exchange and political interventions behind them: these films, I argue, were overt attempts to develop a new type of national cinema. This is evident in the emblematic relationship between the major prizes won and the milestones achieved by Taiwan New Cinema directors at film festivals outside Asia – namely, Cannes, Venice, Berlin, and Rotterdam. After the festival exposure, New Cinema, now crowned with laurels, instigated among domestic film critics long-running debates over popular cinema and auteur theory.

A distinctive point explored in this book is the role that film festivals as producers play in lending a platform to help filmmakers attract financial capital (including public subsidies from their home countries) and promote opportunities for directly commissioned work. These opportunities highlight multiple intertextual links and invite comparisons of New Cinema to the work of other directors and artists: François Truffaut (France), Apichatpong Weerasethakul (Thailand), Buster Keaton (US), Hélio Oiticica (Brazil), Wim Wenders (Germany), Satoshi Kon (Japan), Luis Buñuel (Spain/Mexico), and Jia Zhangke (China). The intertextual, metacinematic, and funding opportunities illustrate how, in turn, Taiwan New Cinema directors have produced films for a global market, deploying stylistic influences and thematic concerns about transnationalism. In essence, international film festivals perform an instrumental role in triggering debates about national cinema and serve as producers for funding new transnational projects.

This book situates transnational cinema as a larger framework to study the global circulation of film as a cultural and industrial art form while introspectively examining the multitude of transnational film theories. Juxtaposing film festival studies with transnational cinema, the book's theoretical perspective ascribes central importance to Dina Iordanova's and Marijke de Valck's previous works on the festival circuit, as well as more recent works that are critical of the politics of programming and film selection, written by scholars such as Nikki J. Y. Lee, Julian Stringer, Dorota Ostrowska, Miriam Ross, and Ran Ma. Against the common conception, programming for film festivals does not necessarily follow a top-down approach to cultural gatekeeping; the programming is dependent on who the audiences are. Curators who know their target audience and have the opportunity to contextualise the entirety of a national cinema, handpicking films for 'an informed, curious audience of insiders, outsiders and those in between', are knowing agents of the culture and bring a fresh perspective to it (Hu 2017, 72). Because Taiwan New Cinema criss-crosses transnational labour, financing, appreciation, and distribution, its selection and framing at film festivals cannot be reductively equated to cultural gatekeeping: in Brian Hu's (2017, 78) brilliant observation, '"Taiwan" is never a stable, whole and positivist entity to begin with, and so a film programme cannot be taken for granted in the same way Taiwan itself cannot.'

While this book specifically focuses on Taiwan-based directors, it uses their films as vehicles through which a conceptual framework for studying transnational cinema as a whole is formulated. Transnational film theories emerged in the 1980s in response to globalisation and postcolonialism. This book proposes that additional criteria are required for a film to be considered transnational today. As Austin Fisher and Iain Robert Smith (2019) point out, this is especially the case as film scholars enter the second phase of transnational cinema studies, moving away from definitions or competing traditions in world cinema and recognising that transnational cinema is most productive as both an approach and a methodology.[5] This book not only enriches the

---

[5] *Transnational Screens*, previously named *Transnational Cinemas*, a journal inaugurated in 2010 as a response to a rapid shift in global cinema and television consumption, would be a great place to start for those interested in following the latest conversation and debates about transnational film studies. A few critical articles worth highlighting and particularly relevant to the topics covered in this book would be Chris Berry's (2021) 'What is Transnational Chinese Cinema Today? Or, Welcome to the Sinosphere'; Will Higbee and Song Hwee Lim (2010), 'Concepts of Transnational Cinema: Towards a Critical Transnationalism in Film Studies'; Deborah Shaw (2017), 'Transnational Cinema: Mapping a Field of Study', in *The Routledge Companion to World Cinema*; Leon Hunt and Wing-Fai Leung's (2008) Introduction to *East Asian Cinemas: Exploring Transnational Connections on Film*.

Introduction 9

existing debates about the formation of national cinema but also engages in and challenges the geopolitics of film festivals. Despite most film festivals' board members insisting that film selection is based on artistic value and content, festivals continue to profile cinema, by and large, using national and art cinema criteria. Thus, the international film festival circuit is not a neutral site of events but comprises networks of highly differentiated power structures.

A ROADMAP: HISTORICISING TAIWAN NEW CINEMA AND FOCUS ON FILMMAKERS

This book begins by mapping out the postwar history of Taiwan cinema, from the Golden Age of commercial Taiwanese-language cinema (*taiyupian*) to films favoured by the Kuomintang (KMT, or Nationalist Party), which looked at Taiwan from a Nationalist-oriented, anti-Communism Chinese perspective, and explores the various degrees of reception in the international (Chapter 1) and domestic (Chapter 2) contexts. While New Cinema has sporadically made its way into festival competitions, it was not until 1989, when Hou's *A City of Sadness* won the Golden Lion award at the Venice Film Festival, that Taiwan New Cinema was granted much visibility and recognition in Europe. At home, criticism was polarised. Some critics believed that the prestigious status that Taiwan New Cinema was awarded as a canonical art form was imposed by international film festivals; others became so fixated on the allegorical interpretation of film styles that they insisted that any reading of the films should be grounded in Chinese paradigms. To align with either side of the criticism is to become reductive, bypassing the global connections and textual complexity particular to Taiwan New Cinema. Tracing the roots and routes of how Taiwan cinema is situated in the international film festival circuit, the first two chapters argue that earlier Taiwanese cinema was already transnational and intertextual in its genre references. These chapters introduce archival findings to unpack both global and local political dynamics – from cultural discovery to cultural diplomacy, from rejection to acceptance.

Benefiting from technological advancements in film preservation and digital restoration and the government's involvement in sponsoring and expediting the process, *taiyupian* have been rediscovered and have resurfaced in recent years. English subtitles have also been newly added, allowing them to circulate outside Taiwan for the first time. Because of the easier accessibility of these films, Chapter 1, 'The Rise of Taiwan New Cinema and the Festival Strategy', takes a fresh look at this history and contextualises the realist tendency in Taiwan New Cinema, drawing a lineage from its predecessors – both the nativist concerns in *taiyupian* and the realist aesthetic in Healthy Realism (films favoured by the Nationalists). In consideration of the foreign reception and with the goal of increasing international visibility, the festival strategy was prompted by what the New Cinema cohort wanted, needed, and desired. It was a push-and-pull process between challenging traditions and working with the system.

Chapter 2, 'Women Critics and Building the Auteur', turns to the domestic reception of Taiwan New Cinema during and after festival circulation to reflect on film criticism's discourses and transformation. The debates between domestic critics and their shifting attitudes towards Western art cinema's paradigms – exemplified by news reporter Yang Shi-chi, screenwriter Chu T'ien-wen, and film critic, producer, and festival programmer Peggy Hsiung-ping Chiao – played a decisive role in mediating the canonical status of New Cinema. This chapter spotlights writings from the invisible and often-overlooked women in the workforce to chart how Taiwan New Cinema represents local/global encounters, as well as the domination of and resistance to paradigms of Western-induced film criticism, ideologies, and modernist aesthetics.

Much of the debate about New Cinema is grounded in the conflict between the older generation and the newer generation of critics, populist tendencies, and art house preferences. At the core of the divide, it is also a debate about Western auteur theory, where the older generation with the perspective of popular cinema rejects the director-as-author principle. In a way, the auteur theory introduced in the 1960s and 1970s movie magazines *Theatre Quarterly* (*Juchang*) and *Influence* (*Yingxiang*) predicated the New Cinema movement. The East–West paradigms show that a theory, although it may originate from a specific context in a specific time, can be reduced, appropriated, and institutionalised depending on where, when, and how it is deployed. This circulation of ideas, whether consciously acknowledged or unconsciously influenced, takes the form of reading, borrowing, interpreting, localising, and domesticising. While the debates and conversations surrounding the paradigms were mostly held in the 1980s, Chapter 2 repositions Taiwan New Cinema in a broader theoretical space – the notion of slow aesthetics – while mapping out the past and present slow cinema movement worldwide that has been prompted by the festival scene.

The recognition of Taiwan New Cinema on the festival scene led to subsidies, festival funding, and multimedia art exhibitions at museums and galleries for New Cinema filmmakers. These individuals gained extended freedom to make films and explore cinematic forms and social problems, producing a new type of radical cinema distinctly on the broadly construed Taiwan experience. Chapters 3, 4, and 5 in this volume examine the work of three of these directors – Hou Hsiao-hsien, Tsai Ming-liang, and Midi Z – who produced films for a global market and deployed themes and cinematic techniques influenced by world cinema. While these are not the only Taiwan New Cinema directors to have won major prizes at film festivals in Venice, Berlin, and Cannes (Edward Yang, for example, received the Best Director award at Cannes in 2000),[6] I have chosen them in part because Hou and Tsai were members of the New Wave who continued to win awards, nominations, and film competitions as representatives of Taiwan well beyond the 2000s, at the same time that Midi was gaining recognition as part of the new generation. Additionally, Tsai Ming-liang and Hou Hsiao-hsien both transitioned to the museum space, obtaining film commissions from the Louvre and the Musée d'Orsay, a trend that reflects developments in marketing and branding (on the part of the auteurs and the museum itself) to increase visibility and capitalise on visitors' engagement. For his part, Midi Z, while not part of the New Cinema movement initially, should be regarded, as Song Hwee Lim (2018b) notes, as extending the tradition of Taiwan New Cinema with long takes that are yet more action-driven and accentuate the power of soundscape.

Chapters 3, 4, and 5 spotlight these individual case studies. Inspired by the concepts of 'travelling theory' (Said 1982) and 'travelling cultures' (Clifford 1992) – which suggest, respectively, that ideas are transformed by new situations and that we must pay attention to routes, roots, and the connection between home and abroad – I frame these three chapters in terms of the cardinal directions of east (Hou Hsiao-hsien), west (Tsai Ming-liang), and south (Midi Z). Doing so highlights the transnational connections of Taiwan New Cinema as multidirectional, complex, interactive conjunctures that are temporally and spatially bounded. I begin these travels with Chapter 3, 'Going East: Women Walk the City in Hou Hsiao-hsien's *Le Voyage du ballon rouge* (2007) and *Café Lumière* (2003)'. Charles Baudelaire's archetype of the *flâneur* is the masculine figure of modernity who strolls through the metropolitan city with privilege and leisure. Hou's transnationally co-produced films transpose this archetype into the figure of a woman who walks alone and idly through a city (Paris and Tokyo, respectively), taking in the urban spectacle. The way

---

[6] Edward Yang, who died in 2007 while still at the peak of his career, is skipped here because of his growing dissent against the film industry in Taiwan, especially with the Golden Horse Film Festival and the film distribution networks. Yang blamed the latter for preventing the commercial distribution of his last film, *Yi Yi* (2000), in Taiwan; the film was not screened in Taiwan's cinemas, except for limited releases at festivals, until 2017 (Anderson 2005; Berry 2005). Ang Lee, whose films, especially *Crouching Tiger, Hidden Dragon* (2000), were once hailed as the quintessential transnational cinema (Lu 2005), is also left out from the case study, on the whole because he largely transitioned to Hollywood, making mostly English-language blockbusters.

Yoko traverses the Tokyo metropolis in *Café Lumière* – retracing the historical footprint of her research subject, a Taiwanese composer – is allegorical of a woman who seeks to trace the colonial relationship between Taiwan and imperialist Japan. This *écriture féminine* (Lupke 2016) is to female screenwriter Chu T'ien-wen's credit. It is not just a woman's experiences but also her gender expression that disrupt masculinity in film.

Hou's francophone film *Le Voyage du ballon rouge*, conversely, is the only feature-length film in his oeuvre for which Chu was not the principal screenwriter. However, strong female voices are still mobilised in the Sino-French film. In it, a Chinese film student living in Paris is seen casually videotaping red balloons and related murals with her camcorder, almost equivalent to a remake of the 1956 *Le Ballon rouge*, directed by Albert Lamorisse. Song's *flâneur* status is more complicated than a stand-in for the director's alter ego; the making of Song's film-within-the-film and her fascination with red balloons provide viewers with a *mise en abyme* (image within an image) and a reflexive glimpse into an already convoluted world. The layers of intertextuality – from the remaking of *Le Ballon rouge* to its reflexive moments – epitomise transnational exploration and imagination.

Chapter 4, 'Going West: Tsai Ming-liang at the Louvre and Cinema in the Gallery', offers a case study of the emerging trend of Southeast Asian filmmakers crossing over to museum exhibition. I use the westbound framework here because of the curious position the director holds within the cinephile consciousness due to his undying love for the French New Wave and the largely European funds that have supported his films. Tsai's feature-length films (lauded at international film festivals but loathed by domestic audiences) and video installations have been perceived as efforts to return to their pure form as cinematic art. Such was the case with *It's a Dream* (2007) and *Visage* (2009), commissioned by the Cannes Film Festival and the Louvre, respectively. This chapter explores the relation between Tsai's films and the French New Wave, which demands a reassessment of his thematic continuation. Rather than being merely local adaptations of hegemonic European aesthetics, Tsai's films represent a strong intersection between the moving images and the alternative viewing experiences, as well as between global and regional film cultures, taking place in a theatre-within-a-gallery site.

Chapter 5, 'A Southbound Turn: Dreaming Taiwan in Midi Z's Realist Films', explores how a Myanmar-born director became a representative of Taiwan and why the dominant group rejects his ethnic minority. Midi Z is most notable for his 2014 film *Ice Poison*, which was selected as the Taiwanese entry for Best Foreign Language Film at the 87th Academy Awards. Working in a guerrilla style of digital filmmaking as a result of censorship in Myanmar as well as frequent exclusion from the Taiwanese government's *fudaojin* subsidy policy, he makes films that are largely concerned with the harsh economic and social circumstances in the authoritarian regime, along with issues relating to neighbouring countries, such as Laos and Thailand. Midi, who arrived in Taiwan at the age of sixteen to pursue what Southeast Asians perceive as the 'Taiwan Dream', represents displacement and identity in Taiwan, even as his work has been criticised in his home country for not being 'Myanmar enough' (Bernards 2021). Midi's films are aesthetically connected to Taiwan New Cinema, but they also expand the style within the urban soundscape. After discussing his southbound Homecoming Trilogy in light of Taiwan's Southbound Policy, this chapter focuses on *Nina Wu* (2019), which shifts the thematic concerns of economic exploitation to sexual exploitation and the filmmaking style from risky, covert videography to surrealism, flashbacks, and dreams. The bleak ending of *Nina Wu*, like that of so many of his films, conveys hopelessness regarding the character's inability to improve the situation. Configured by the disjunctive and chaotic consequence of global flows, Midi's filmic subjects are fundamentally impeded by the larger political and capitalist forces obstructing their decision, whether it is migratory, economic, or gender related.

Lastly, Chapter 6, 'To the Future: Film Festivals as Producers and Sleeping in the Cinema', traces the function of festival funding and assesses what makes a project such as Tsai Ming-liang's *Slow Walk, Long March* series (also known as the *Walker* series) contribute a new meaning to the label 'festival film'. These short experimental films are commissioned by and distributed across different platforms – from the Hong Kong International Film Festival to the Venice Biennale, from public television to co-production between France and Taiwan. Scholars have previously focused their attention on the festival film, particularly the way festival funding tends to support a filmmaker's artistic vision over the film's marketability (Ostrowska 2010; Ross 2011; Falicov 2016). The existence of these funds raises questions about how film festivals shape contemporary art cinema at large and how these projects become part of the global film festival establishment. Springing off from these new practices, this chapter explores the notion of sleep – both onscreen sleep and offscreen spectatorial sleep – and its contribution to an aesthetic practice of the Anthropocene. The intention here is to conduct a broader enquiry into the relationship between artefacts, affects, tiredness, duration, spectatorship, and site-specific video installation at museums and elsewhere. In Tsai Ming-liang's shift from the cinema to the art gallery, his work benefits from the global economy and hierarchy of curatorial practices lifted from film festivals while also rebelling against the unforeseen consequence of an accelerating world. To relocate, reproduce, and distribute cinematic work in the art gallery space is an act of resiting, a form of effective recycling.

The aesthetic practice of the Anthropocene is predicated upon turning cinema into a reusable, repeatable object (Fay 2018). By emphasising the connection between cinema and the deliberately transported natural surroundings seen at these exhibition sites, resited (or repurposed) cine-installation furthers a contemplation of the conscious observer and a world of artifice and human worlding.

* * *

To close this Introduction, these Taiwanese, Taiwan-based, and Taiwanese diaspora filmmakers' works invite readers to think about exhibition practices, transnational co-production, and the global impact of the new wave movements. As the chapter breakdown here demonstrates, an investigation of the institutionalised European film festivals and their relation to Taiwan cinema traces the changing modes of production, exhibition, and consumption, from co-option (admitting Asian filmmakers to the exclusive club of Euro-American auteurs) to reconfiguration (revealing how film festivals influence, reshape, and initiate practices in the global realm). If the objective of festival co-production and financing is to facilitate the creation of new works by filmmakers from local regions or by new talents who will, in turn, help raise the event's profile and consolidate cultural hierarchies of taste, then this support also signifies the mutual dependency of film festivals and filmmakers. Filmmakers need the festival platform to brand their styles, reinforce their authorial presence, and facilitate their entry into the global film industry. Likewise, film festivals need to cultivate new ways to ensure a continual supply of fresh materials, preferably films that are exclusive to them or have some type of niche market value. When we look forward to the future of cinema, we will continue to find film festivals at key moments of transforming the cinema landscape and exhibition formats. If the current world we live in is at its most catastrophic, unnatural, self-annihilating time, then let us suppose that the future is sleeping in the cinema,[7] where one surrenders to the dreamers, as surrealist André Breton would suggest. We dare dream of sleeping in (with) the cinema to help us find the familiar in an estranged world.

---

[7] For more comprehensive coverage of the histories and theories of the disembodied spectator, see Jean Ma's (2021) 'Sleeping in the Cinema', in *October* 176: 31-52.

Part I

Historicising Taiwan New Cinema

CHAPTER 1

The Rise of Taiwan New Cinema and the Festival Strategy

For the longest time, the cinema of Taiwan has been synonymous with Taiwan New Cinema (*tai wan xin dian ying*), a movement many film critics and scholars recognise as a new direction in filmmaking in the country. From this movement, several world-class directors have emerged, including Hou Hsiao-hsien, Edward Yang, Ang Lee, and Tsai Ming-liang, and have produced a series of films that explore social tensions and problems in cinematically compelling ways, blending social realism with modernist innovation. The success story of Taiwan New Cinema is a familiar one – it is often recognised and juxtaposed as part of the global new wave movement in film history. David A. Cook (2016), in *A History of Narrative Film*, describes these films as 'low- to medium-budget films that dealt with day-to-day reality in Taiwan but were often stylistically experimental' (618). In Kristin Thompson and David Bordwell's (2010) account, Taiwan cinema appears only to exist or be worthy of attention after 1982, when the New Wave started. By their definitions, these films cultivated an 'elliptical approach to storytelling, using flashbacks and fantasy sequences, and dedramatized situations' (652), all reminiscent of European art cinema of the 1960s (namely, films of Italian Neorealism and the French New Wave – *la nouvelle vague*). Apart from sharing the spirit and several aspects of the cinematic form with the French New Wave, this new direction in Taiwanese filmmaking exhibits an evasion of governmental censorship under martial law, on the one hand, and a fresh, modernist exploration of Taiwanese cultural identity not overshadowed by the exiled experience of Chinese mainlanders, on the other hand.

There are many factors behind the canonisation of Taiwan New Cinema on the world stage. One of the most common constituents is that Taiwan cinema is written as part of the Western historiography of global cinema and rarely on its own terms (Hong 2011). Many Euro-American film historians' treatments of Taiwan cinema assign too much prestige to Taiwan New Cinema, to the point that there is an apparent lack of history before and after the discovery. The brief coverage of Taiwan cinema in Thompson and Bordwell's *Film History*, for example, is somewhat ahistorical: the authors jump right into the New Wave by spotlighting two directors, Edward Yang and Hou Hsiao-hsien, and mislabelling the movement as the 'Taiwanese' New Wave. While the term 'Taiwanese' is grammatically correct, the name is typically reserved for the Taiwanese Hokkien cinema (*taiyupian*) produced between 1955 and 1981. In *A History of Narrative Film*, Cook sketches the pre-New Wave history of Taiwan cinema not mentioned in Thompson and Bordwell's (2010) narrative. Nevertheless, Cook (2016) incorrectly describes the film industry during this gap period as 'develop[ing] slowly and … long dominated by Hong Kong' (618). This statement lacks an awareness or an acknowledgement of the vibrant culture of Taiwanese-dialect films at a time when *taiyupian* was predominantly popular genre films and hugely successful at the box office (Yeh 2017).

From a practical standpoint, issues related to film preservation, distribution, and accessibility, in terms of both film reels and language fluency, are some of the reasons why international film scholars have, up until recently, been unable to identify and fill the gap in the history of Taiwan cinema. The emphasis on Taiwan New Cinema is not because film historians deliberately eschew parts of the past; nor do they want to tell an uncomplicated story about New Cinema and the dichotomy with the government-funded, studio-produced Healthy Realism films that New Cinema was trying to revolutionise. Instead, film historians' warm embrace of Taiwan New Cinema concerns the framework of the global New Wave in which they are so invested.

Guo-Juin Hong (2011) is one of the few pioneers in the English-speaking world to take an interest in recovering the missing histories of Taiwan cinema before 1982. In *Taiwan Cinema: A Contested Nation on Screen*, Hong (2011) proposes the importance of approaching Taiwan cinema as a 'nexus of internal and external contentions' (4), yielding a productive revision of Taiwan's national film history under transnational influences. By putting Taiwan cinema into a larger historical scheme, Hong (2011) maps out the forgotten history of Taiwanese-dialect films, as well as revisiting the historiography through the well-known figures of the New Cinema group.

Taiwan New Cinema is both local and global. It is local because it is often regarded as a grassroots movement closely connected to Taiwanese literature (*hsiang t'u* literature) – as many scholars, predominately June Yip (2004), have already explained. It is global because the filmmakers themselves, alongside local screenwriters and international film critics, festival curators, and programmers, worked together to assimilate themselves and their films into the global 'new wave' movement by using the rhetoric of the term. Taiwan New Cinema is intrinsically transnational, and this degree of transnationalism carried the legacy of *taiyupian* with their aspirations and appropriations of world cinema. The legacy of *taiyupian* was first observed by Taiwanese scholar

Gene-Fon Liao (2001) and picked up two decades later by Chris Berry (2020), who considered the film production of this period 'Taiwan's Hollywood'.

In this chapter, I will first map out a brief history of Taiwan cinema – from the Golden Age of commercial cinema *taiyupian* to pro-KMT propaganda films – and contextualise the growing international reputation of the New Cinema movement through the eyes of Euro-American film critics, such as Tony Rayns, Marco Muller, Olivier Assayas, and Caryn James. Taiwan New Cinema bears local specificities, but it also entered the global sphere when the very concept of the 'new wave' – a term that originated in France with the journal *Cahiers du Cinéma*'s promoting of a set of French films from the late 1950s and early 1960s – had become a marketing term to promote fresh entries into the international cultural market.

This chapter uses Hou Hsiao-hsien's *A City of Sadness* (1989) as a case study to demonstrate how the evaluative criteria shared by many film festival professionals successfully advanced Taiwan New Cinema within the rhetoric of national cinema, new wave, and authorship. Filmmakers' push for festival submission (sometimes, they had to bypass governmental approval) and international exposure did not simply stem from their political agenda to raise the country's profile; nor was the festival success of New Cinema accidental or unexpected. It was a combination of grassroots efforts propelled by the lack of Taiwanese governmental support, the directors' aspiration to establish a greater international presence (which indirectly questions the long debate about 'What is national cinema?' and 'Whose national cinema are they serving?'), and their eagerness to connect to the global film production and distribution industry.

Taiwan's Commercial Cinema (1955–80)

The term *taiyupian* refers to low-budget black-and-white films in the Taiwanese language, which had their heyday in the 1950s and well into the 1960s. Between 1955 and 1981, 1,114 *taiyupian* were produced, marking the real beginnings of a sustainable film industry in Taiwan (Lu 1998). As a few pioneer scholars (Huang 1994; Liao 2001; Hong 2011) have pointed out, this part of history has long been forgotten, neglected, or left fragmented. By the time film scholars and archivists started exploring *taiyupian* in 1989, prompted by an invitation to curate a programme for the Taipei Golden Horse Film Festival, they could not recover most titles. Many film prints were missing, unsalvageable, or blurry, or had incorrect aspect ratios. Many copies exist only in VHS format and are not subtitled, making them less accessible for non-dialect speakers (Liao 2020). At the same time, even though surviving films of *taiyupian* were rediscovered in the late 1980s, it was challenging to locate the master film reels (or negative prints) needed for preservation and restoration purposes. The film prints initially found had been kept in poor storage conditions that lacked climate control. Most were severely scratched and damaged, and had seriously deteriorated, and some were even missing their audio soundtracks (Huang 2020).

Availability certainly has played a role in the limited understanding of *taiyupian*. Even though the Chinese Taipei Film Archive (now renamed Taiwan Film and Audiovisual Institute) started paying more attention to these films in the 1990s, the technological shift to digital film preservation and restoration expedited the process. Beginning in 2014, the film institute typically restores two to four films per year. In the same year, the Taiwanese government's Ministry of Culture launched the Taiwan Cinema Toolkit project. This platform allowed restored film versions with new English subtitles to circulate outside Taiwan for the first time. Most recently, there has been a surge of festivals and events showcasing *taiyupian*. From the symposium of Taiwan's Lost Commercial Cinema at King's College London and the first Taiwan Film Festival in Edinburgh to a curated programme at Harvard Film Archive dedicated to Taiwanese-dialect cinema, these events all signal a pivotal moment of renewed interest in Taiwan cinema on the global stage.

Analysing the history of the *taiyupian* era, many wondered why these films strayed away from the grand narrative and for a long time remained off the radar for local cinephiles. It even prompted the question of why the KMT government 'tolerated *taiyupian* at all' (Berry 2020, 2). This exclamation refers to the cultural policy mobilised by the Nationalist government to designate and promote Mandarin as the 'national language' (*guoyu*) when the dominant spoken language on the island is the local variant of the Minnan language known as 'Taiwanese', or *taiyu*. Before the mid-1960s, the Nationalist government was unconcerned about the film industry, leaving most production companies in the private sector. This contrasted with the government-backed, star-studded Mandarin cast films of Healthy Realism (*jiankang xieshi dianying*) of the 1970s, from their early depiction of genteel farmers in rural areas to portrayals of young urbanites venturing out into city life. These are considered state-sanctioned politicised films blatantly agenda-pushing a new understanding of the nation under the logic of 'model' Chinese – where class, ethnic, or individual-level conflicts do not exist or are eventually resolved. While Healthy Realism films were never explicitly created with propaganda in mind, they carried strong ideologies of anti-Communism and didactic Han Chinese culture, embodied in the prescriptive use of the Mandarin language and moral instruction.

The cultural war of the languages had a long-lasting negative impact on the Taiwanese dialect, and Heritage speakers of Hokkien were affected.

Moreover, by extension, the cultural war promoted a discriminatory attitude towards those with accented Mandarin or 'Taiwanese Mandarin' (*Taiwan guoyu*), referring to people who speak Mandarin with a Hokkienese accent. This language bias is a direct consequence of the 'Mandarin unification campaign' (initiated in 1946 by Governor Chen Yi), which recognised only Mandarin as the official language and prohibited the use of all dialects, including Hokkien, Hakka, Japanese, and Indigenous languages. Faced with the existence of Healthy Realism films, young filmmakers and newcomers were compelled to return to Taiwanese consciousness and their version of the lived experience in Taiwan New Cinema. It was not until 1996 that the government began adopting inclusive policies towards Hokkien and Hakka in education and elsewhere.

This leads to an intriguing chicken and egg problem: did the language bias and the unfavourable cultural conditions limit *taiyupian*'s availability, or did the lack of availability (prints, circulation, subtitles) result in limited interest from scholars and the general audience? The recent discourse has reconceived the *taiyupian* era as the Golden Age of Taiwan cinema (Yeh and Davis 2005) or Taiwan's Hollywood (Berry 2020). This reclaiming points to a time when there was not only an outpouring of new films produced but also an aspiration to establish a film industry like Hollywood to produce big-budget cinema of high technical quality. Because *taiyupian* are mostly low-budget black-and-white films, they have been dubbed 'Hollywood on a budget', to underscore the limited resource situation (Berry 2020, 2). Most importantly, the era is considered Taiwan's Hollywood because these are, unmistakably, genre films. The many types of genre range from screwball comedies, suspense, thrillers, musicals, romances, and fantasy to radical experimentation with aesthetics and themes of sexual behaviour and youth rebellion.

In reviewing *The Bride Who Has Returned from Hell* (1965, dir. Hsin Chi), for example, Niina Doherty (2020) describes the film as a Taiwanese-language classic, even with its misleading title (it did not live up to the horror genre that one might expect from the word 'hell'). The film 'delivers a unique take on the gothic romance genre with mystery, romantic entanglements, murder and even a hint of supernatural' (Doherty 2020). *The Bride Who Has Returned from Hell* adapts its story from a gothic romance novel, *Mistress of Mellyn* by Victoria Holt. The film reminds modern audiences of similar stories before it, such as *Rebecca* by Daphne du Maurier and the subsequent film adaptation by Alfred Hitchcock. The story of the original novel is set in nineteenth-century Cornwall, in the UK. The film transplanted the settings to 1960s contemporary Taiwan – which, in turn, displays a collage of Victorian literature themes that meet in the semi-rural countryside of Taipei. The cinematography of the film gives an impression of shadowy German Expressionism.

Weirdly enough, the film juxtaposes the iconic James Bond theme song in the climax scene, which is both strange and comical. At the same time, the inclusion of the Bond music score is evidence of Hollywood's influences on global culture.

The intrinsic quality of *taiyupian*'s transnationalism can be seen in another example – *Dangerous Youth* (1969, Hsin Chi). This work of dark socialism explores the theme of sexual exploitation and depicts how young people are willing to use sex as leverage for money to pursue a luxurious lifestyle. *Dangerous Youth* reminds viewers in many ways of the iconic 1969 American independent road movie *Easy Rider*, directed by Dennis Hopper. Both films share certain traits: an excessive use of the soundtrack, a portrayal of carefree youth, and the thrill and masculinity associated with motorbikes, a symbol of freedom (Figure 1.1). At the same time, the theme of sexual exploitation references early works from the Japanese auteur Nagisa Oshima, particularly his 1960 film *Cruel Story of Youth*. There is also a scene in *Dangerous Youth* where a young man rides his motorcycle, making multiple loops for no apparent purpose. This strange, exhaustingly long take of a motorcycle can be recognised as exploring avant-garde aesthetics akin to those of the French New Wave, in which a painstaking tracking shot does not add much to the story but serves to challenge or alienate audiences. In the same film, the montage inserts of neon signs and bright city lights are reminiscent of filler scenes used in Japanese director Akira Kurosawa's films. There is also a surprising amount of black jazz, soul music, and R&B used on the soundtrack. An attuned viewer can quickly identify King Curtis's version of 'Spooky' and 'Sittin' on the Dock of the Bay' in the background, along with music from Booker T & the MG's and 'The Memphis Blues' by Louis Armstrong. At this time music licensing was a

Figure 1.1 Kueiyuan and Qingmei on a motorcycle in Dangerous Youth *(1969), directed by Hsin Chi. Still frame.* © *Taiwan Film and Audiovisual Institute (TFAI).*

very grey area and global regulations on using copyrighted music in films were non-existent, to say the least, thus giving *taiyupian* filmmakers the impression that they had free rein to copy or adopt works as they wished.

When one analyses Hsin Chi's *The Rice Dumpling Vendors* (1969), it is nearly impossible to ignore the opening scene and the bathroom killing sequence, which is almost a shot-by-shot remake of Hitchcock's *Psycho* (1960). The pastiche style here, including film form, thematic explorations, and music, corresponds to what Emilie Yueh-yu Yeh (2022) calls 'bricolage', highlighting the 'make-shift' and 'making do' (Certeau 1984) quality as a response to production restraints. Further, to avoid film censorship, any wrongdoings or criminal activities in the story are placed overseas (such as in Hong Kong), even though the entire film was shot in Taiwan (Yeh 2022). *Taiyupian*'s borrowings from Hollywood and Japanese cinema, as well as the appropriation and transplantation of global music and cityscapes, suggest a deeper transnational connection among different cultures and filmmaking practices in the 1960s.

Taiwan's Film Industry in Crisis

What caused the decline of *taiyupian* and why did these films disappear from the public eye? Previous understanding of *taiyupian* considers the 'low-brow' quality of dialect films the reason why they were unable to compete with the KMT government-supported, big-budget colour films of Healthy Realism (Chiao 1994). The *taiyupian* movies themselves demonstrate aspirations of what they hope to become, despite the sometimes offbeat, awkward, and clumsy acting. However, these experimentations have also worked to garner a cult appreciation today (Berry 2020, 6). As Chih-Heng Su (2020) argues, the real reason behind the decline of *taiyupian* primarily concerns the social, political, and economic policies of the state in promoting Healthy Realism films, mainly at a time when *taiyupian* dominated the box office market before the first Mandarin-language colour film *Oyster Girl* (*Ke nu*, directed by Lee Hsing) was released in 1963. New regulations and production codes implemented by the government favoured the rise of Mandarin cinema, pushing dialect filmmakers out of the motion picture industry and into television. Further, the movie-going experience in the 1950s and 1960s was segregated between Hokkien and Mandarin speakers (Chiao 1994).

The relationship between Taiwanese-language and Mandarin film production was not always antagonistic, however. Instead, the two joined forces in terms of personnel and equipment sharing. Lee Hsing, for example, directed more than thirty Mandarin-speaking films and is best known for his Healthy Realism films *Beautiful Duckling* (1965), *He Never Gives Up* (1979), and *The Story of a Small Town* (1979), to name but a few. Yet, as Chris Berry (2020, 4) points out, few recognised that Lee Hsing also directed the big *taiyupian* comedy hit *Brother Wang and Brother Liu Tour Taiwan* (1959). In fact, it was his debut film. Further, as Ming-Yeh Rawnsley (2013, 446–7) has observed, private-sector *taiyupian* filmmakers often rented cameras and facilities from the well-equipped but under-used Mandarin-language film studios. They also shared a film crew and staffing team.

Ultimately, a combination of conditions was the true culprit behind the sudden downfall of *taiyupian*. The first is the fluctuation of motion picture film stock supply. *Taiyupian* were able to thrive in production between 1961 and 1969 because of cheap black-and-white film stock (Lu 1998). Unfortunately, they were later unable to procure the finance for colour films, which drastically reduced the number of *taiyupian*. Second, state laws and regulations for film production in Taiwan initially favoured *taiyupian* filmmaking. In 1956, the government lifted the import tax on film stocks and facilities, hoping to lure Hong Kong filmmakers to shoot in Taiwan. In return, Taiwanese filmmakers partnered with film professionals from Hong Kong to take advantage of the tax exemption. Things went south when the KMT government established a Department of Culture in 1967 to monitor and regulate all cultural affairs, including the arts, radio, television, and motion pictures. The administration not only reversed its previous stand on minimum government involvement in the film industry but also announced that it planned to start 'incubating a healthy and powerful domestic film industry' (Su 2020, 4). The administration issued a new definition of what it considered to be 'national cinema' (*guochan dianying*). Not surprisingly, *taiyupian* was excluded on this narrow definition. To the KMT government, Taiwan cinema is 'clearly and exactly defined as films that use Mandarin and are filmed in Taiwan. Taiwanese is a local dialect and is, therefore, "not included"' (Su 2020, 5).

This new policy resulted in two significant roadblocks for *taiyupian* and their future sustainability. First, Mandarin filmmakers continued to work with Hong Kong film professionals. They enjoyed tax exemptions on film stock while receiving subsidies for colour film and state-of-the-art studio equipment and facilities. *Taiyupian* filmmakers were denied the same access because they were excluded from the designation of 'national cinema'. They also had more difficulty in having their work approved for theatrical release under the new censorship system unless they were willing to dub it into Mandarin. Subsequently, *taiyupian* companies were prevented from obtaining local distribution rights for Japanese films, losing a profitable side revenue. Second, the market for *taiyupian* sank even lower when the KMT government stopped exporting dialect films overseas – such as to Southeast Asian countries, where the demand for Hokkien cinema was much greater at that time than the market for Mandarin-language films. The unfavourable conditions the KMT created imposed further tighter restrictions on non-Mandarin film production. However, the final stroke was the global shift to colour films. Eastman Kodak, Fujifilm, and Agfa-Gevaert discontinued their 35 mm black-and-white film in the late 1960s, which played a significant role in the sudden disappearance of Taiwanese-language cinema.

The KMT government's renewed interest in the film industry is linked to the understanding that motion pictures can serve a political agenda – the 'campaign machine', as they called it (Su 2020, 10). To them, film is a medium that is susceptible to prescribed Nationalist ideology. As mentioned earlier, Mandarin films produced during this period (1964–80) were represented by Healthy Realism. These are vernacular social realism films 'full of hopes', with an aspiration to 'tell stories that are healthy, bright, and lively' (Zhang 1994, 19). To the KMT government, these films were meant to convey a positive outlook on life through stories about the rural working class. This filmmaking style is inspired by a reinterpretation of Italian Neorealism – which typically features location shooting, non-professional actors, subdued acting, and attention to the surroundings to deliver a sense of realism, as advocated by French film critic André Bazin. The actual production of Healthy Realism films, however, is heavy-handed in terms of screenwriting, studio shooting, artificial sets, star casting, and colour cinematography. In addition, everyone in the films' universe speaks Mandarin (even where the language does not fit the setting; Liao 1994). With the intervention of the government, as well as the expansion of the state-owned Central Motion Picture Corporation (hereafter Central Motion Picture), Healthy Realism films have always been presented as a success story. What was little known to the public was that Central Motion Picture, at the time, was on the brink of bankruptcy (Su 2020). It was only 'saved' on the orders of the government and at the taxpayers' expense, the money being used to absorb its outstanding debts. Without Central Motion Picture, there would not have been an upsurge in Mandarin-language cinema.

In the grand scheme of things, Healthy Realism films are a product of governmental policies – a new exploration of aesthetics in the service of politics. Guo-Juin Hong (2011) is right to point out the ambiguity of such films. The existence of Healthy Realism films reflects new modes of production and changed filmmaking techniques – including the standardisation of colour film – and should be celebrated as such. These films also provide an ideological reimagination of a modernised nation, as seen in director Lee Hsing's work. Films such as *Oyster Girl* and *Beautiful Duckling* envision 'an agricultural paradise where nature and culture harmoniously coexist' (Hong 2011, 77). It is somewhat anachronistic, though, for previous scholars to downplay identity conflicts and state intervention in cultural production because these films exemplify a modern national (or pan-Chinese) identity. Earlier scholars have claimed that 'Healthy Realism is a successful alternative to Taiwanese-dialect films because it approximates the epitome of what the dominant politics wish to see' (Hong 2011, 81). It is precisely the prescriptive claim of the 'dominant' view that is problematic here, but undeniably, this has long been the mainstream version of the history of Taiwan cinema.

Even though the KMT government did not openly prohibit or suspend the production of Taiwanese-language films, its reluctance to assist is itself a form of suppression. To recap, the following fundamental policy changes sealed the fate of *taiyupian*: first, reduced tax or tax exemptions on film stock for Mandarin film production; second, reduced revenue for *taiyupian* companies due to their ineligibility to distribute Japanese cinema; third, film subsidies and movie production incentives reserved for Mandarin films only; fourth, new regulations on exports and international co-production; and fifth, a global reduction in manufacturing and distributing colour film stock (Su 2020). Without a doubt, the policies created by the KMT administration were meant to boost Mandarin-language cinema and gradually eliminated the relevance of *taiyupian*.

While this part of history is currently being revised by many scholars devoted to revisionist and archival research, much work is still required to challenge the grand narrative. Nevertheless, the critical perspective here takes issue with how the history is framed – particularly with the smooth transition from Taiwanese-language film to Healthy Realism. Revisiting this part of the history demonstrates that there was once a viable motion picture industry in Taiwan and that the legacy of *taiyupian* continues to be found, albeit more in spirit than in cinematic form, in later trends or movements, such as the exploitation films of the early 1980s (Taiwan Black Movies) or Taiwan New Cinema. This aspect of the history reminds us again of the political and ideological force the KMT embodies. Reclaiming a fragmented narrative of Taiwanese-language cinema tells a different story that provides meaningful change to reinterpret the Nationalist past. To make sense of the present, Taiwanese history has to be rethought.

THE RISE OF TAIWAN NEW CINEMA

Taiwan New Cinema arose in the early 1980s, when Taiwan's film industry was facing serious challenges from films from foreign markets. The first sign was the waning interest in *qiong yao* cinema. These are romantic melodramas based on the novels of the same name, which attained great popularity throughout the late 1970s. While this type of genre film once did well in the domestic and regional markets, it was deemed old-fashioned when the overall budgets and production values plummeted. The unchanging formula of over-sensationalised melodramas no longer appealed to the audience in the same way, and the Taiwan industry plunged into the realm of exploitation films – also known as Taiwan Black Movies – for a series of B-movie crime films and ultraviolent avenging women roles. The formulistic melodramas could not compete either with cheap, fast-turnround Hong Kong action movies, as well as the disruptive culture of bootleg videos and video rental stores. To revitalise the declining movie industry, Central Motion Picture began an initiative to support several fresh, young, go-ahead directors – including Edward Yang, Hou Hsiao-hsien, and Chen Kunhou, who kickstarted what is known as the first wave of Taiwan New Cinema.

By narrow definition, Taiwan New Cinema is a short-lived movement that started around 1982 and ended in 1987. The 'new' here suggests a breakaway from what came before. Still, Taiwan New Cinema's realist tendency draws a lineage from its predecessors – both the nativist concerns in *taiyupian* and a reconsideration of a realist aesthetic from Healthy Realism. The films produced at this time, on the one hand, constituted political resistance to Nationalist rule and, on the other hand, displayed a concern with revolutionising cinematic conventions that many global New Wave directors had shared since the 1950s. Taiwan New Cinema is known for its realistic and sympathetic portrayals of Taiwanese life, departing from Healthy Realism's modes of filmmaking aligned with Nationalist mandates and the genre cycle of *qiong yao* melodramas. The significance of Taiwan New Cinema insinuates not just their success at film festivals or their new direction in style but also a complex dynamic between cultural policy, public opinion, taste making, and the changing economics of the film industry.

A look at Taiwan New Cinema produced between 1983 and 1984 shows that, stylistically, these films were smart enough to adopt the standard widescreen ratio despite their low budget and were shot on 35 mm instead of the more affordable 16 mm format. Because they were inexpensive to produce, they brought in a substantial profit if they proved successful. For example, Hou Hsiao-hsien's *The Boys from Fengkuei* (1984) was created on a budget of approximately NTD 6,000,000 (USD 1.5 million) and generated a profit from distributor rentals[1] of NTD 4,700,000 (USD 1.1 million). A significant portion of the film's earnings came from international sales. These films also experimented with different narrative techniques to break the conventions of mainstream Mandarin cinema. Actors tended to deliver more reserved performances, particularly in contrast to the star-studded casts of Healthy Realism. Taiwan New Cinema directors favoured non-professional talent and replaced

---

[1] The rentals are the revenues returned to the studio after the theatres have taken their percentages of gross ticket sales.

close-up shots of dramatic acting with long shots and long takes. Characters were no longer restricted to speaking in Mandarin, showing a blend of different dialects and accents. Thematically, these films employed rich local and historical materials from nativist literature and were often concerned with national identity. Japanese film critic and historian Tado Sato (2015, 147–8) points out that one of the main peculiarities of Taiwan New Cinema is its underlying theme of national identity, as, unlike in Japan or other neighbouring countries, Taiwan's national sovereignty was very much in question and was unsettled in these films.

Prior to these changes came the establishment of a sustainable economy in Taiwan that led to the downfall of the state-controlled film production system, forcing filmmakers to seek funding beyond the state. Legislators were given a chance to set up new policies aimed at both revising film censorship codes that were outdated and encouraging new directions in cinematic production. The film *In Our Time* (1982) is generally acknowledged as the forerunner of the New Cinema movement because it was the first to receive extensive media attention and subsequently propelled Central Motion Picture to invest in then-unknown directors and screenwriters, such as Hou Hsiao-hsien, Chu T'ien-wen, and Wu Nien-Jen.[2] *In Our Time* also prefigured a movement devoted to the postwar generation and the local history of Taiwan. The quadripartite film debuted four directors who would be part of the internationally acclaimed film movement: Tao Te-chen, Edward Yang, Ko I-cheng, and Chang Yi. Other acclaimed professionals of the movement include Chen Kuo-Fu, Mark Lee Pingbing (photographer), Liao Qingsong (editor), Du Duzhi (sound recording engineer/sound effects director), Wan Ren, and Wang Tong. The first wave ended around 1990 and gave way to what could informally be called the second wave, featuring directors such as Tsai Ming-liang and Ang Lee.

However, the rise of Taiwan New Cinema did not stem just from its economic context. Taiwan New Cinema has a unique history that includes significant moments at film festivals, particularly how these films circulated at major European film festivals. If success on the film festival circuits led Taiwan New Cinema towards the international stage, vernacular filmmaking also left traces of global culture, forming an increasingly transnational dialogue. To further a revisionist perspective, it is imperative to reconsider Taiwan New Cinema with respect to film festivals from cultural, historical, and geopolitical

---

[2] While the general conception is that Taiwan New Cinema began with *In Our Time* (1982), earlier attempts at exploring new film techniques were already evident in Wang Chu-chin's *The Legends of Six Dynasties* (1979) and *Those Days in the Heaven* (1980), as well as Lin Ching-chieh's *Student Days* (1981).

standpoints. Many discussions (Lee and Stringer 2012; Stringer 2016) have asserted the role that international film festivals inevitably play in shaping and defining Chinese-language cinema's global image, entertaining the question of why certain films and filmmakers benefit from participation at top film festivals (namely, A-list events, sanctioned by the International Federation of Film Producers' Associations). Building on such observations, the rest of this chapter focuses on considering the formulation of Taiwan New Cinema and its realist aesthetic as a kind of nation branding in which the 'newness' or 'new wave' – consecrated by film festivals in the mid-1990s and onwards – have too often been reduced to an exclusive list of representatives culled from a few canonical films and directors.

THE FESTIVAL STRATEGY

The reality was that Taiwan New Cinema remained bereft of funds and state support and had to develop on its own. The lack of financial support led directors to concentrate their efforts on securing Taiwan New Cinema's presence at international film festivals. The consensus was that Taiwan New Cinema had first to enter smaller, mid-tier festivals to build a reputation, which was a prerequisite for being accepted at major international film festivals, such as Cannes, Venice, and Berlin. As Chang Shih-Lun (2002) observes,

> These attempts began with mid-tier film festivals […] partly out of government encouragement (to raise the visibility of the Republic of China), but more importantly, out of consideration that frequent participation in mid-tier film festivals could earn a certain degree of acclaim, upon which New Cinema could gradually establish awareness and a reputation in the global film community and eventually aim for places in the three major European film festivals. (22)

The festival strategy to 'raise the visibility of the Republic of China' (the official name of Taiwan) was evidently initiated by New Cinema filmmakers themselves. In 1987, Government Information Office (GIO) director Shaw Yu-Ming received an open letter from Hou Hsiao-hsien and Edward Yang, calling on the government for more active support in local film production, as well as for official endorsements on the film festival circuit. Their plea was urgent, Hou and Yang claiming that 'As China fever sweeps the West, each film festival is turning attention towards films by filmmakers in the People's Republic of China. We [Taiwanese] can't afford to lose out on this rare opportunity' (Hsiao 1988, 126).

New Cinema filmmakers understood that having exposure to the world market would attract foreign distributors and investors, yielding more profits and potential transnational investment in production. They also felt the Taiwanese government would, in return, establish a greater international presence by openly supporting New Cinema directors and their films. The significance of this festival strategy was twofold. First, it recognised that Taiwan New Cinema had to operate within the logic of film festivals to obtain better recognition and marketing strategies that would otherwise doom the films to just domestic film distribution. Second, given the country's lack of recognition in the international arena (and the unstable political status of Taiwan), winning awards at major international film festivals meant these films would be a way to represent and legitimate Taiwan as a self-governing democracy on a global scale. This film festival strategy was ultimately backed when the KMT government retrospectively gave full financial and moral support to the New Cinema movement after *A City of Sadness* (1989) first entered film festivals without state permission.

In the earlier stages of Taiwan New Cinema, much of its international exposure and festival visibility was influenced by European film critics, including the United Kingdom's Tony Rayns, Italy's Marco Muller, and France's Olivier Assayas. Rayns is a frequent contributor to British film magazine *Sight and Sound*. He is known for introducing Hong Kong cinema to the UK before the emergence of Taiwan New Cinema and was also the first international critic to term the movement the 'new wave in Taiwan', drawing connections to Hong Kong and other global counterparts (Rayns 1984, 24–9). This also indicated that Taiwan New Cinema was part of a worldwide discourse from the very beginning – a collective action with a counterhegemonic purpose against conventional narrative cinema. Indeed, New Wave cinema typically refers to movies made by younger independent filmmakers with formal innovations and political and cultural connotations, launching a new generation of auteurs and new stars, and reform on the level of film budgets and exhibition platforms.

Comparably, without Italy's Marco Muller, there is no guarantee that *A City of Sadness* – the quintessential film of Taiwan New Cinema – would have been able to enter competition at the Venice Film Festival and subsequently win the highest prize given there – the Golden Lion for Best Picture. Muller, nicknamed the 'Marco Polo of Chinese cinema' by Edmond Wong (former director of the Taiwan Film Archive), is a long-time observer and translator of Chinese-language films. He was enlisted by the esteemed Hong Kong critic Shu Kei – who was, at the time, overseeing all advertising and publicity campaigns for *A City of Sadness* – to work as the film's Italian translator, facilitating the process of selling it to the Venice Film Festival's international jury. With Muller's help, Taiwan cinema was able to broaden its horizons in the film market with a roster of films and line-ups. Referring to Marco Muller as

'Marco Polo', of course, serves as a double-edged sword; on the one hand, the cultural significance of Marco Polo stands for a group of explorers, suggesting that Muller's influence and contributions represent Western film critics' discovery of Taiwan cinema. On the other hand, Marco Polo and the West's discovery characterises an unequal relationship between East and West, and between 'the centre' and the 'margins' on the map of global art cinema, thus reinforcing the gatekeeping practices of Western critics.

Aside from Rayns and Muller, Olivier Assayas of *Cahiers du Cinéma* played an indispensable role in introducing Taiwan New Cinema to French cinephiles. Assayas's influence was instrumental: he was single-handedly responsible for bringing Hou Hsiao-hsien's film *The Boys from Fengkuei* to the Nantes Three Continents Festival in France, paving the way for Taiwan New Cinema's subsequent awards, success, and international recognition (Hsiao 1988, 146–8). The story goes as follows: in 1984, Assayas was on assignment in Hong Kong. There he met Taiwanese critic and director Chen Kuo-Fu, who convinced him to detour to Taiwan and check out the new films they had made there. Assayas was impressed by what he saw, but he was most impressed with *In Our Time* and *The Boys from Fengkuei*. Back in France, he began telling everyone about what he had seen in Taiwan. At the end of that year, *Cahiers du Cinéma* released a special issue that spotlighted Taiwan cinema, in which Assayas wrote a seven-page article to introduce New Cinema and the Taiwanese film industry. Ever since, France has been a huge advocate and a major market for Hou Hsiao-hsien and other Taiwanese directors. Assayas's involvement was monumental because, back then, no one even knew if New Cinema would ever catch the eye of people outside of Taiwan. Yet for Chen Kuo-Fu and his New Cinema cohorts, the encounter was not entirely coincidental; rather, it is best described as carefully orchestrated. They knew, in 1984, that Chinese-language cinema was almost unheard of in the West, and even if it was seen, the films were limited to kung fu movies. Upon being given the opportunity to meet a French critic, Chen and Hsiao Yeh carefully chose the two films for Assayas to see in hopes that the latter would, in return, open the door to the French audience for Taiwan cinema. With Assayas's stamp of approval, Taiwan New Cinema was fully linked to the global New Wave movement.

Each of these examples reveals the indispensable role played by film festivals and film criticism in helping film movements gain momentum both inside and outside of their home countries. However, while local Taiwanese critics appreciated outsiders' praise of Taiwan cinema, not all of them approved of the Euro-American support and questioned the reports' historical inaccuracies. In return, defenders of New Cinema argued that the only way for Taiwan cinema to survive was for it to enter the global market, illustrating how national cinema and cultural identity are bound up in film festivals.

Indeed, it seems that once a film enters a festival such as Venice as a competitor, the film lends itself to being constructed as a national allegory. Such is the case with Hou Hsiao-hsien's *A City of Sadness*, which is discussed below.

EDITED, SEALED, DELIVERED: *A CITY OF SADNESS*

With *The Boys from Fengkuei* and *A Summer at Grandpa's* (1984) both receiving the highest award of the Golden Montgolfière prize at the Nantes Three Continents Festival, Hou Hsiao-hsien became a festival darling in Western Europe. His next film, *A Time to Live, A Time to Die* (1985), caught the attention of major festival-goers at the 1986 Berlin International Film Festival, followed by *Daughter of the Nile* (1987) at Cannes. However, it was *A City of Sadness* that established Hou's status as a world-renowned art house auteur by winning the Golden Lion at Venice. This recognition effectively expanded Taiwan New Cinema's visibility in Europe and North America.

On 8 August 1989, Hou Hsiao-hsien had just finished the post-production for *A City of Sadness* and was ready to order release prints when he realised the deadline for submission to the Venice Film Festival was due in ten days. So as not to miss the deadline, Hou sent a copy of the film prints directly to Italy, bypassing the regulation that the film needed to be first sent to the KMT government to obtain its permission before being released. When the government learned of this, the director of the GIO openly criticised Hou's distributor, stating that film law clearly stipulates that motion pictures must receive a certificate of approval before they can be shown in public (*Central Daily News* 1989). They added that before the law could be amended, the GIO had to carry out the inspection work in accordance with the law; otherwise, they were not doing their job right. During the process, the media also reported a rumour that *A City of Sadness* had been edited and censored, and was missing two minutes of a critical scene (*China Times Express* 1989; *Central Daily News* 1989). The GIO's spokesperson denied this charge. Facing pressure from the local and international communities,[3] the government decided to make a special case for *A City of Sadness*. The director of the Motion Picture Division said they would allow the film to participate at Venice if Hou's distributor sent another copy to the office for immediate review (*United Daily News* 1989). The GIO retrograded the violation claim that would otherwise have resulted in banning the film.

---

[3] In 1989, both the Toronto International Film Festival and the Venice Film Festival requested world première rights for *A City of Sadness*. The rights ultimately went to Venice because *A City of Sadness* was selected in the competition for the Golden Lion Award, outshining the prestige a Toronto première could potentially bring.

A City of Sadness is a historical film that explores the long-time taboo subject of the White Terror and the 28 February massacre[4] in Taiwan, perpetrated by the KMT government after it arrived from mainland China in the late 1940s. The film was the first to deal with the KMT's authoritarianism and the civil conflicts in the period 1945–9. Using voiceovers, personal letters, radio announcements, small talk between characters, and even scribbled notes, *A City of Sadness* recounts, and subtly generates public awareness of, a part of history that the KMT government has long censored.

Scholars (Lin 1995; Li 1998) have typically read *A City of Sadness* as a national allegory, constructing the Taiwanese experience 'as a monolithic, unified, abstracted, and seemingly objective national history' (Berry and Farquhar 2006, 37). The film is about the everyday lives of ordinary people and how traumatic historical events shake up society. The story depicts the Lin family's experiences during the White Terror and how the brothers, old and young, able and disabled, were forced to deal with KMT oppression. However, by using memory as a primary trope, the film gives tangible form to the imagination of the subaltern's experiences, resisting the complete fusion of individuals into the collective body of national history. Additionally, Western critics' focus on the film's style worked to establish it as symbolic of a nation's struggle.

Press reviews in European film magazines often inscribed Hou's films as belonging to a distinctive national cinema – separate from Western models, particularly in style. One review of *A City of Sadness* in *Cahiers du Cinéma* reads: 'Inscribed in Hou Hsiao-hsien's mise-en-scène is a nearly experimental project of reconstruction – the reconstitution, from a few ordinary moments in

---

[4] The 28 February massacre in 1947 happened during the transition between the end of Japanese rule (1895–1945) and the time when Chinese Nationalist troops, led by Chiang Kai-shek, were exiled to Taiwan after their defeat by the Communist Chinese. The incident began in Taipei when a woman selling cigarettes was arbitrarily detained, leading to several large-scale public protests against the new authority's repression and corruption. In the following days, Governor Chen Yi kept up a pretence of negotiating with the leaders of the protest movement but secretly ordered troops to move in and start shooting people. Most of the civilians who were fatally shot were, in fact, unarmed. The massive massacre totalled roughly between 18,000 and 28,000 people. Thousands of others were arrested and imprisoned in the following decades, and many of those remained in prison until the early 1980s. The event marked the beginning of forty years of repressive martial law on the island, termed the 'White Terror', imposed by Chiang Kai-shek's dictatorship. It ended in 1987, when martial law was lifted and Taiwan started moving towards rapid modernisation and democratisation.

the lives of his characters, of the epic birth of a nation' (Rauger 1993, 18). Philip Kemp (1994, 51) from *Sight and Sound* writes in his review that

> The welter of characters and relationships in *A City of Sadness* [...] often left the uninstructed Western viewer struggling to keep track ... Hou's indifference to Western tastes also shows in his inclusion of several long, unbroken extracts from Li [Tian-lu]'s puppet shows. Beautiful, stylised and remote, they have all the charm of the half-understood – what's happening is clear enough, but why is tantalizingly opaque – so there's a real sense of culture shock.[5]

If reviewers were unable to take historical references into account, they ascribed Hou's formal and narrative devices to being part of a universal film language:

> By presenting the lack of understanding between Chinese people, Hou made a film not about the Lin family and its four sons, not about a small port town on the island of Taiwan, not about the nationalist crisis that shook the country between 1945 and 1949, not about a movement of Chinese civilization, but about universal values [...] It is not a cultural difference that separates us from the Taiwan of the film, but the artistic desire of the director not to give himself entirely, to retain a degree of mystery – this universal way of interrogating the world. (de Baecque 1990, 24)

In North America, Hou's films were frequently screened at the New York Film Festival but critics struggled to understand them. When *New York Times* film critic Janet Maslin (1986) saw *A Time to Live, A Time to Die*, she called it 'slow and muted', stating that it was 'unpretentious' but 'largely unremarkable'. Other critics were generally excited about the new discovery in Chinese-language cinema, particularly Hou and China's Fifth Generation filmmaker Zhang Yimou. Vincent Canby frequently compared Hou's films to those of the French New Wave directors. Canby (1988) describes the characters in *Daughter of the Nile* as being like the vivid individuals portrayed in Jean-Luc Godard's films of the late 1960s and early 1970s, adding that Hou's coming-of-age film *A Summer at Grandpa's* is a curious combination of works by Truffaut, Godard, and Yasujiro Ozu. Very seldom would a critic demonstrate their political awareness of the historical context or awareness of how much a film was indebted to its literary source by Chu T'ien-wen. The exception here is American film critic Caryn James. She thought that while Hou does not make the viewing experience easy, with his 'languid' and 'motionless' camerawork, *A City of Sadness* is worth the long wait for 'that crucial moment when

---

[5] Philip Kemp (1994) is referring to Li Tian-lu, Taiwan's most celebrated puppeteer, from Hou Hsiao-hsien's *The Puppetmaster* (1993).

politics and personal suffering blend' (James 1989). Furthermore, she states that *A City of Sadness* 'compresses a chaotic period of Taiwan's history into the story of a single family' and that the characters become an embodiment of Taiwan itself, a symbol for Taiwan's helplessness (James 1989).

A preliminary overview of these texts indicates that the reviews functioned as a terrain for suggesting specific modes of watching Hou's films. One consideration that should have been given to these reviewers is the number of reviews they produced and the film's lack of visible circulation in Europe and North America. Despite the various festival awards, none of Hou's major films was given a theatrical release in Europe or the US. Hou's films circulated almost exclusively at film festivals, film societies, museums, and art house cinemas, where they were granted limited showings. Alternatively, the screening of Hou's films could be part of a thematic or retrospective understanding of Chinese cinema. In the circumstances, the near absence of screening of Hou's films on European and American exhibition circuits made these reviews even more influential on the public, be it Taiwanese, European, or American.

A closer look at the reviews brings a different set of interpretations. Valentina Vitali (2008) is quite critical of the European press, mainly the British and French reviews that rest on articulating formalist concerns only. She argues that the reviews strongly suggest to the reader–viewer that historical references are either unnecessary or optional, thus reducing any sense of historicity to a universal formal language (Vitali 2008). Nonetheless, under the film-author framework, these reviews successfully established Hou Hsiao-hsien as an auteur in the eyes of the European spectator, especially the French cinephile. In this context, European and American reviews of Hou's films act as an instrumental way of reading films and generate a discourse on how Hou bears a tangible relation to art house cinemas, ignoring the national and complex history of Taiwan itself.

Hou Hsiao-hsien is considered to be part of a global *'nouvelle vague'* movement because the reviews read his films based on the New Wave paradigms that have been customarily brought to European cinemas. More precisely, Hou's films act as a site that evokes nostalgia for the French New Wave or, more generally, global art cinema, which weaponises them to defend themselves against mainstream Hollywood. To begin with, witness the way Olivier Assayas (1997) describes his attachment to Taiwanese filmmakers:

> I often tell other people about my first encounter with Hou Hsiao-hsien: it was in 1984, I also met Edward Yang and his cinematographer, Christopher Doyle there [...] This encounter evoked in me an unprecedented feeling of becoming a part of a group. Although I cannot stand the concept of

'cinema family', at some moments I feel that I am a European cousin of these people. (26)

While Tony Rayns (2014) did not initially see Taiwan New Cinema as a movement, he noted the following in an interview about its predecessors' efforts to create a style more in tune with world cinema:

> I never really thought of it much as a movement in the first place [...] it was a scattered and dispersed group. What they had in common was the desire to do different. They wanted to make a different kind of film, in a different way, different style, more in tune with international cinema. They wanted something that can be shown internationally and can actually hold its head up internationally; something that was over-standard that could match the best out there in the world. At the same time, to be assertively Taiwanese in a way that would force the world to recognise, there was something happening in Taiwan.

The focus on style, or the poetics of modern visuality, is also closely connected to the politics of the nation-state. According to Chia-chi Wu (2007, 76),

> The historiographical significance of Taiwan New Cinema lies in its dual tendency in inscriptions of the 'nation'. On the one hand, it attempts to portray the living experiences of the communities that are differentiated by social, historical, cultural/linguistic, and ethnic terms ... On the other hand, Taiwan New Cinema represents, with its modern visuality, a coming to terms with the heterogeneity and a re-visioning of the nation that hopefully could resolve historical injustice and accommodate differences.

The texts presented here all address the idea that the nation-building process in Taiwan New Cinema was based on modes of modern visuality and the international high-art voices that inevitably gave rise to controversy and political contestation. Taiwan New Cinema's visibility on the festival scene reflects the culture of the marginalised group instead of being a representative of the national culture curated by the state. Conversely, New Cinema voluntarily contributed to the imaginings of a homogeneous national identity through the Western gaze.

For the first time in history, Taiwan New Cinema filmmakers produced works that offered possibilities for serious political discussion. Many of the modern techniques in New Cinema borrowed from, but were not limited to, Italian Neorealism: the use of long takes, long shots, real location shooting, and working with non-professional talent. There was also the lineage of *taiyupian*: the filmmakers' ambition to do something differently, to bring back an awareness of nativists' concerns and portray the common daily language of Taiwanese Hokkien was consistent with what *taiyupian* was trying to achieve. Further, Taiwan New Cinema directors' tenacity and their festival strategies speak to the importance of situating Taiwan cinema in a global context, which is in tune with the inherent transnationalism *taiyupian* brings as part of its legacy. The local audience, however, had a hard time understanding New Cinema modernism; these films came out during a time when local economic development and modernisation had just begun. Nevertheless, the domestic defenders of Taiwan New Cinema were composed of a group of cultural critics who were trained in Western literary theories and film criticism, as is discussed further in the second chapter. They often applied Western aesthetics and its philosophy of film in defence of New Cinema, including Peggy Hsiung-ping Chiao (film scholar and critic), Huang Jianye (director of the Chinese Taipei Film Archive), Hsiao Yeh (novelist, writer, and producer at Central Motion Picture), Chu T'ien-wen (novelist and screenwriter), and Alphonse Youth Leigh (film critic and journalist). These critics evaluated the films through the framework of European auteurs to validate Taiwan New Cinema, referencing auteurs such as Truffaut, Godard, Alain Resnais, and Michelangelo Antonioni, to name just a few. It was also the first time in history that these domestic film critics, well versed in international film history, successfully placed Taiwan cinema on the world map by exercising the very criteria shared by many European film festivals.

CHAPTER 2

Women Critics and Building the Auteur

Just a year after *In Our Time* (1982) was released, Taiwan's critics were divided. Many, especially the older generation, tended to be reactionary rather than embracing new directions. Even though the government-backed Central Motion Picture had partially initiated New Cinema, local audiences had not fully welcomed the movement. These films remained elusive and rather difficult for domestic audiences to accept, despite the directors' insistence on using film as art to look at the humble, day-to-day lived experience of the Taiwanese and the nation's modern history. The older generation of critics, dominated by those who identified as Chinese Civil War victims exiled from the mainland, complained that New Cinema was anti-commercialist, anti-populist, and designed to appeal only to foreign audiences. Even though the legacy of Taiwan New Cinema provided great sustenance and inspiration for the next generation of filmmakers around the world, including Barry Jenkins (US), Apichatpong Weerasethakul (Thailand), Olivier Assayas (France), Jia Zhangke (China), Wang Bing (China), Hirokazu Kore-eda (Japan), and Bong Joon-ho (South Korea), Taiwan New Cinema in its formative period did not achieve the same traction domestically as it enjoyed at international film festivals. Even today, many people continue to believe New Cinema to be responsible for the collapse of Taiwan's film industry – a myth that has been debunked by scholars (Chiao 1988; Lu 1998) many times but somehow remains an unstoppable narrative that is continually being retold.

Younger critics, meanwhile, praised the filmic style of the New Cinema and advocated on the side of change. The very reason used by older reviewers for despising New Cinema – catering to foreign audiences – was considered powerful leverage for New Cinema by the younger critics. New Cinema represented the internationally minded, modernist (and postmodern) cinema they envisioned. It provided resonances of Taiwan life with a fresh look and aesthetic innovations imbricated with the necessary vernacular modernism. However, this is not to say that the group of young critics and film professionals spoke with one voice. There is a distinction between sharing a vision to do things differently from the past and prescribing a Western paradigm; the very same concept of a new wave was associated with other national film movements, not least the French New Wave.

When the Taiwan New Cinema movement emerged, the term 'New Cinema' was first seen in the promotional materials for *In Our Time* and *The Sandwich Man* (1983, directed by Hou Hsiao-hsien), which were drafted by Hsiao Yeh. This sentiment was echoed by Assayas (1984) in an article describing the films as 'une nouvelle vague à Taïwan' (58). But this designation was met with reservations and scepticism from within the group itself, seen, for example, in screenwriter Wu Nien-Jen's rejection of such labelling: 'I am basically against making distinctions between "old" and "new" cinema ... Such divisions are made by others. I am opposed to these categorisations' (Lee and Peng 1987, 9). The hesitation is understandable, given that New Cinema was a 'movement of unintended consequences' (Udden 2013). Or, as British critic Tony Rayns (2014) sees it, it was not so much a movement as a scattered and dispersed group. What its members had in common was a desire to challenge the existing rules and restraints of studio production and to seek a discursive way of reflecting on modernity in the way that international film festivals demand.

The full recognition of Taiwan New Cinema as an influence in cinema history, then, was first prescribed and fashioned by film critics within the discourse of the public debates and accepted in retrospect by the filmmakers themselves. Chang Shih-Lun (2002) went so far as to argue that film professionals would have initially rejected the term New Cinema if it were not for the 'sensationalisation' by film critics, headed by renowned film scholar Peggy Hsiung-ping Chiao, who sought to defend the movement from the mainstream media's vitriolic attack especially the objections raised by the older generation of film critics. The term is used by Peggy Chiao essentially to reimagine Chinese-language cinema and to advocate for a pan-Chinese utopia by considering New Cinema an apparatus.

This chapter surveys the domestic reception of Taiwan New Cinema during and after festival circulation to reflect on film criticism's discourses and transformation. The debates between domestic critics and their shifting attitudes towards Western art cinema's paradigms played a decisive role in mediating the canonical status of New Cinema. The locus of this chapter is to spotlight writings from the invisible and often overlooked women in the workforce, such as news reporter Yang Shi-chi, alongside acclaimed and better-known female screenwriters and festival programmers: namely, Chu T'ien-wen and Peggy Chiao. Before the institutionalisation of film studies in universities in the mid-1990s, movie reviews published in newspapers played a powerful role in guiding and shaping public opinion about New Cinema. Examples include the columns 'Peggy Chiao at the Movies' and 'Cinema Forum' by Huang Jianye, featured in the *United Daily News* (*Lian he bao*). All were followed and championed by a wide readership.

Conversely, articles on auteur theory published in the 1960s and 1970s movie magazines *Theatre Quarterly* (*Juchang*) and *Influence* (*Yingxiang*), prior to the New Cinema movement, bolstered the trend towards recognising directors as creators who stamp their signature style on their filmmaking. This type of non-academic film review led to the establishment of film criticism culture in Taiwan; reviewers moved beyond the past trend of focusing on celebrity gossip and contributed to a string of serious discussions on new wave films at a time when film studies were not even considered worthy of academic attention. While the debates and conversations surrounding the paradigms occurred primarily in the 1980s, this chapter repositions those debates in a broader theoretical space – the notion of slowness in cinema – while mapping out both the past and the contemporary slow cinema movement across the globe, prompted by the festival scene.

THE SCANDALOUS TRUTH BEHIND THE SOUR APPLE

We must first go back to the very scandal that led to the decade-long debate. The 'Apple Peeling Incident', as it is widely known, was a major media controversy that reinforced the divide between the two groups of critics, who remained fierce opponents well into the 1990s. The controversy began in 1983 when reporter Yang Shi-chi, after receiving a tip from director Wan Ren, leaked the news that higher officials in Central Motion Picture intended to censor *The Sandwich Man*. This tripartite project was adapted from three stories by Taiwanese nativist (*hsiang t'u*) writer Huang Chun-ming's work – 'The Sandwich Man', 'Vicki's Hat', and 'The Taste of Apples' – which were directed by Hou Hsiao-hsien, Tseng Chuang-hsiang, and Wan Ren, respectively. The incident refers to Central Motion Picture's attempt to edit out certain scenes from Wan Ren's segment of the film, 'The Taste of Apples', because its tone was considered offensive to some.

In Yang Shi-chi's exposé, 'Our Son Almost Lost His Doll', which was published in the *United Daily News* on 15 August 1983, Yang disclosed Central Motion Picture's plan to cut several scenes from 'The Taste of Apples' because the vignette was deemed in 'poor taste' and 'defamatory' of the nation. The title of the exposé is a wordplay on the Mandarin title of 'The Sandwich Man', which literally translates to 'The Son's Big Doll'. Evidently, someone, presumably from Film Critics China (or a delegate), the only 'official' society of film critics at the time, filed an anonymous complaint with Central Motion Picture and accused Wan Ren's 'The Taste of Apples' of being a disgrace to the country. In 1983, Taiwan had not yet lifted martial law, and major newspapers and television stations were owned and controlled by the KMT administration. Yang's exposé was an unusual act of resistance at a time when Central Motion Picture could have easily shut down production of the film.

'The Taste of Apples', faithful to its literary source, offers a comical if bittersweet story of a happy accident involving a poor working-class Taiwanese family and US military personnel stationed in Taiwan. The opening sequence consists of a car accident montage: a black US Embassy flag car, a shoddy bicycle, the yellow dividing line of a two-lane road, a pickaxe and smashed white rice on the ground, and a salted egg rolling down the street. This is followed by a shot of a pool of blood over a chalked outline of where a dead body would have been, first emerging in black and white and slowly transitioning to colour to reduce the impact. The montage sandwiched in a sequence of an assistant to the US Ambassador shouting over the phone and explaining the sticky situation: 'Listen. This is an Asian country with which we have the closest cooperation and friendship. So, I don't think there should be any problem. However, the President would be very unhappy if there was any trouble with any of the local people or the government.' With this dialogue, the film adaptation is insinuating that the story takes place during the Cold War, during which the United States extended its imperialistic power by stationing military personnel on the island from 1954, following the Taiwan–China crisis.

In Yang's report, the censorship was not limited solely to moral concerns; Central Motion Picture requested revisions to the dialogue in the final scene. That language is a jab at the characters' attitudes towards the United States, shifting from ambivalence (as originally depicted in the literary source) to rejection of America's economic and material support. In both the original text and its cinematic counterpart, the ending depicts the father, a worker who has been hit by an American colonel's car, being whisked to a US hospital for treatment. Not only does he receive top-quality medical care and generous compensation, but his entire family are also offered additional assistance, such as sending their mute daughter for special education abroad. This warm treatment, of course, includes the sumptuous fruits – apples – neatly piled up on an end table in the hospital room. Apples in the 1970s not only had to be imported because they were not native to the island country of Taiwan but also were a symbol of wealth and the easy life, although the import trade was not regarded as an obvious tentacle of US imperialism.

Figure 2.1 *The boys take a second and third bite into the apples in Wan Ren's 'The Taste of Apples', a segment from* The Sandwich Man *(1983). Still frame. © Central Motion Picture Corporation.*

In Huang Chun-ming's story, the family finally bites into the shiny red apples that have been lurking in the background, waiting for attention:

> The silence of the room was broken by the crisp sound of apples being bitten into, gingerly, one after another. As they took their first bites they said nothing, although they felt that the apples weren't quite as sweet as they had imagined; rather, they were a little sour and pulpy, and when chewed they were frothy and not quite real. But then they were reminded of their father's comment that one apple cost as much as four catties of rice, and with that the flavour was enhanced. (Huang 2001, 156)

The man and his family, reacting candidly, are surprised that the taste of an actual apple is different from what they had imagined. However, given the monetary value of the fruit and the fact that the car accident was a blessing in disguise, they swallow their feelings and force themselves to believe that apples are just as delicious as everyone claims (Figure 2.1). This ambiguity is symbolic of the mixed feelings of the Taiwanese towards US global influence and military power, even as the country continues to rely on economic and material assistance from the Americans (in the form of nutritional support like powdered milk, grains, and produce). The purpose of the US aid to bolster Taiwan's postwar economic development during the Cold War was to reinforce the small nation's military capabilities against a possible invasion by

Communist China. Clearly, then, Central Motion Picture's attempt to change the scene (they wanted the characters to say the apples were inedible, 'sour and pulpy') reveals more about the political stance of the production company than any coded meaning. Central Motion Picture's inclination to change the ending, prompted by the anonymous complaint from Film Critics China, was an extension of its residual bitterness over the US decision to sever formal diplomatic ties with Taiwan just a few years earlier.

But just who was this brave news reporter named Yang Shi-chi? She was a journalist for the right-leaning *United Daily News* (second in circulation among Taiwan's newspapers at the time) and a frequent contributor to the entertainment news section. Her unwavering support for New Cinema as a pushback against mainstream cinema, especially after she published the exposé, has been heralded as a 'godsend' by those who championed the movement. Veteran film critic Alphonse Youth Leigh,[1] known for his eccentric personality, once called Yang the Godmother of New Cinema because of her outspoken support, but also because Central Motion Picture dropped its demand for editing changes after its request had been exposed in the media and sparked a backlash against the censorship plans (Zhan 1984, 18). Yang Shi-chi's fame was short-lived and her connection to New Cinema is largely limited to the Apple Peeling Incident because of her untimely death that same year, after she had been working for the *United Daily News* for only nine months. A media award was established in her memory in 1986 to recognise distinguished members of Taiwan's film industry for their outstanding contributions to the profession. To this day, it is the only award in the industry that is named after a journalist.

There is no denying that Yang Shi-chi's report was a turning point in cinema history, and her brief time in the media industry should certainly be lauded. But it is also worth pointing out that the paradoxical side of her intervention was the transgressive nature of her writing – a corrosion of journalism's ethical code. Zhan Hongzhi (1984) disagrees with his fellow film critic Leigh's characterisation of Yang, arguing that Leigh's praise is exaggerated. In Zhan's view, Yang was ill equipped for film appreciation; her understanding of world cinema was flawed and she often made factual mistakes

---

[1] The widely known film critic, writer, and cinephile Alphonse Youth Leigh has gone by many names over the course of his career. In his early days, he used Li Youxin. He is a vegetarian and animal welfare advocate who loved his pet birds so much that he changed his legal name to Alphonse Perroquet/Parrot Caille/Quail Youth Leigh in 2006. He is also known for sporting long, wavy white hair everywhere he goes.

in her writing. This is especially evident during her early days reporting for *Min Sheng Bao*, a tabloid newspaper. While recognising Yang Shi-chi as one of the biggest New Cinema enthusiasts and a vanguard journalist, Zhan simultaneously calls her out for breaking the ethical code by offering commentary and personal opinions rather than taking an objective stance. The way Zhan (1984) sees it, 'She didn't do her job as a reporter, and her film reviews were not very good, either' (18). Zhan's condescending tone may be unnecessary and even cruel, but his fault-finding does have value. The significance of Yang's intervention in the industry has less to do with the content of her commentary – although that was helpful – and more to do with her attempt to use the platform to offer a kind of industry overview and analysis. Instead of worrying about her accountability as a non-trained film critic, Yang used her exposé and commentary to speak for unheard voices and resistance to the state-imposed censorship that was sanctioned during Taiwan's martial law period. By extension, her very existence and the conflicts she faced in a journalist's role speak to the infrastructure (or lack thereof) of film criticism at the time.

Following the Apple Peeling Incident, members of the conservative group continued their polemic against the New Cinema group and were especially antagonistic towards director Zhang Yi's *Jade Love* (1984) because it featured a simulated sex scene. The film was an easy target for the older generation of critics to lash out against and essentially to blame the New Cinema movement for the fall of the local film industry. In a *Min Sheng Bao* op-ed, 'Please Don't Play to Kill Our Cinema!'[2] (*Qing buyao [wan wan] guopian!*), Du Yunzhi (1984) disparaged *Jade Love* as slow and uninteresting. Du's rejection stemmed from his belief that because the motion picture industry is essentially a business, New Cinema should have been obligated to cater to a mainstream audience. He blamed New Cinema for forcing people to witness the downfall of movie-going, and suggested that New Cinema filmmakers should instead learn from the Hong Kong New Wave and model themselves after its success.

---

[2] There are a variety of English translations of Du Yunzhi's title that arise from the difficulty of translating the puns from Mandarin. The word 'wan' shares the same phonetic sound of the word that follows; the two words mean 'play' (or meddle) and 'terminate', respectively. Peng Hsiao-yen's translation of the title, 'Please Don't "Terminate" Our National Cinema', is probably the closest to its literal meaning in Mandarin. To showcase the intended pun and wordplay effectively, I have adopted the phrase 'play to kill' to describe the dilemma, akin to the ways cats play with their prey and subdue their victim before delivering the killer blow.

In Du's justification, Hong Kong directors deserved respect because they juggled stylistic and ideological advances while working within the confines of the commercial system. However, Du's short-sighted attack not only neglects but also completely ignores the vibrant history and commercial success of genre films that preceded Healthy Realism and escapist cinema – none other than Taiwanese films – while continuing to marginalise voices and social changes beyond the popular art form.

We now return to the debate over New Cinema that was grounded in the conflict between old and new, between populist tendencies and art house preferences. This division was not merely generational; it was also very much about the discourses of film criticism. Most of the older generation, exemplified by Liang Liang, Tsai Kuojung, and Jing Xiang, who were particularly outspoken against New Cinema, were members of Film Critics China. However, those of the younger generation were typically not associated with, or refused to become members of, that organisation, the only legitimate film society then in existence. Many younger critics took on roles beyond writing film reviews. They worked closely with the film industry as programmers, curators, or even writers-turned-directors, as in the case of Chen Kuo-Fu. The core of the divide was very much a debate over auteur theory, with the older generation coming from the perspective of popular cinema and its rejection of the director-as-author principle. For instance, in her best effort to counter auteur theory, Chinese literature scholar Peng Hsiao-yen (2012) fundamentally reduced the principle to a director who is simply 'repeating himself', completely misreading writings from Truffaut and American film critic Andrew Sarris, whom she ironically discussed at length. The validity of the older generation also relied on a thinly veiled political bias and the question of gatekeeping. With Film Critics China having been effectively established by the KMT government, its members' opinions should be treated as a single voice that was already in retreat, rather than representing the collective voice of the wider public.

FROM EXCLUSION TO ACCEPTANCE

After Yang Shi-chi's exposé was published, film critic and newspaper columnist Peggy Chiao published an article in the competing newspaper *China Times* to protest against the presumed censorship. Chiao was indisputably one of the most significant behind-the-scenes progenitors of the Taiwan New Cinema movement. An esteemed film scholar, critic, and educator who also worked extensively as a festival programmer and producer across Sinophone film industries, Chiao is best known for her edited collection *New Taiwan*

Cinema (*Taiwan Xindianying*), published in 1988. Working closely with film professionals, she acquainted herself with other international festival writers such as Tony Rayns, Shelly Kraicer (International Film Festival Rotterdam), Wimal Dissanayake (Hawaii International Film Festival), Sato Tado (Fukuoka International Film Festival), Bérénice Reynaud (the French film critic, historian, and curator), and Shu Kei (Hong Kong International Film Festival). These writers were (and still are) the dominant force in introducing films from Taiwan, Hong Kong, and China to Western audiences, even as they simultaneously take on roles as festival programmers, jurors, exhibition curators, translators, and scholars.

Chiao began writing and publishing essays and film reviews in Taiwanese newspapers and magazines in the early 1980s. When *In Our Time* (1982) debuted, Chiao was a full-throated supporter despite the emerging criticism of the styles of New Cinema. Hostility towards New Cinema did not end at exhibition and reception; it bled into meetings and deliberations at the Golden Horse Awards' festival screenings and award sessions. At one point, the animosity became so intense that some veteran film professionals refused to work with directors from the New Cinema group. This prompted Chiao and fifty other film critics, directors, film professionals, authors, and screenwriters to publish a manifesto in 1987, calling for an 'alternative cinema' (*lingyizhong dianying*) and greater subsidies from the government to support marginalised, non-mainstream work. The list of co-signers included Edward Yang, Hsiao Yeh, Wu Nien-Jen, Chu T'ien-wen, and Huang Chun-ming. The manifesto was a reaction to a series of controversies that swirled around New Cinema filmmakers, criticising the media industry's unsupportive attitude and defending the new style to the public.

While Peggy Chiao was a key figure among local film critics whose aggressive efforts helped shape and develop Taiwan New Cinema, she was also emblematic of the group of critics who first rejected Western art cinema's paradigms but later adopted that epistemology in their critiques to justify the New Cinema movement. If we look at Chiao's writings between 1984 and 1989, we can see that she was initially critical of Eurocentric film theory:

> The news media and local film critics have taken a biased, Western-infused lens, overpraising the existence of Taiwan New Cinema. Every statement they make, including the philosophy behind it and the terms they use – nativist literature, realist films, observation of people's lives – are just the application of Western theory ... If we don't deal sufficiently with the discursive conditions [that gave rise to these films], we are simply a poor imitation of Western culture. (Chiao 1984; my translation)

Paradoxically, for someone who later enjoyed a prolific career as one of New Cinema's propagators, she was rather sceptical of New Cinema's festival strategy and its success abroad:

> The critical opinion of foreign film critics often results in the skewing of public opinion. Claiming to speak for the West, some people declare that local films are under-appreciated in Taiwan, except for foreigners like them. Thus, [these people conclude that] local films must be shown first abroad in Europe before returning to Taiwan on the momentum of their popularity abroad. (Chiao 1985, 23)

In the same article, Chiao (1985) even condemns Assayas's piece in *Cahiers du Cinéma* for being 'crude and shallow'. The French critic's questionable view results from his 'insufficient knowledge or first-hand experience' of Taiwan cinema (23).

Peng Hsiao-yen (2012, 135) argues that Chiao's opposition to Assayas's 'Orientalising' of Taiwan New Cinema has something to do with the only translated version available at the time: the two-page excerpt in Taiwan's movie magazine *Sibaiji* (*400 Blows* – clearly an homage to Truffaut's film) suffers from several mistranslations into Mandarin that mislead readers. However, one could equally speculate that Chiao's latent bitterness towards Assayas's framing of identity politics in his coverage has more to do with her self-identity as a Chinese exile in Taiwan. For example, Assayas calling Taipei the 'real China' (*vraie Chine*) and being sympathetic to Chen Kuo-Fu, who blamed the KMT regime for making Taiwan an outcast from the international community, could easily be interpreted as irksome – to say the least (Assayas 1984, 58), as could the point at which Assayas accuses Chinese exiles (*chinois de l'exil*) on the island of publicly shunning films made in Taiwan in favour of the action-packed, martial arts-infused cinema of Hong Kong. Perhaps the most triggering and damning comment, in Chiao's view, is Assayas's opinion that Taiwanese films before New Cinema are all hackneyed; Healthy Realism films such as Bai Jing-rui's are mediocre and pretentious (Assayas 1984, 57).[3]

To counter Western models during this time, Chiao (1987) makes use of the principles of Chinese art traditions in her analysis. For example, in her review of *Dust in the Wind* (1986, dir. Hou Hsiao-hsien), she compares the shots and framing to Chinese watercolour landscape painting, highlighting the spatial tropes that enable empty space to take centre stage. Chinese

---

[3] The original French text goes like this: 'Les genres privilégiés du cinéma de Taiwan sont les genres traditionnels ... Ils ont produit le pire avec des cinéastes comme Bai Jingrui, exemplaire de continuité dans la médiocrité prétentieuse et "artistique".'

paintings are composed primarily of brush lines and grey scales of ink and pigment that organise the entire drawing. The empty spaces in between correspond to the Confucian concept of emptiness and nothingness as something palpable, concrete, and meditative. The treatment of ethos and humanistic spirits in these paintings is further explored in the ways that landscape drawings personify mountains, rivers, animals, plants, and even objects. In Chiao's account, *Dust in the Wind* borrows this technique in its cinematography, offering a holistic view like that of a soaring eagle looking down on the world below it. This kind of overview is unlike the mechanical eye of the crane-shot but is an embodiment of Confucian philosophy and Chinese art traditions, focusing on the coexistence and interdependence of nature and the human world.

In another instance, Chiao (1989) refers to Hou Hsiao-hsien's *A City of Sadness* (1989), an epic film that spans the time frame of classical Chinese poetry. More precisely, she considers Buddhist philosophy, in which 'the poet views objects in terms of himself, and so everything takes on his own colouring', to be a useful lens to apply to Hou's filmography. Chiao means that Hou plays with perspective, as in the form of an unreliable narrator. This is a common trope in classical Chinese poetry, where the writing is prone to a dangling modifier (the subject is missing from the syntax), and the words, which come from an observer's viewpoint, are really a façade for subliminal emotions, of which the subject may or may not be aware. In Chinese poetry, personal emotions and perspectives are often presented in a less direct, even convoluted, way. Using a scene from *A City of Sadness* to illustrate the point, Chiao observes that Hinome, one of the female protagonists, uses her diary to record her subjectivity rather than a list of chronological events. Hinome lends her feelings to the way she describes the natural surroundings, encoding one pictorial signifier after another: mountains – autumn – spectacular scenery – blissfulness. In her final letter to Ah-shue, Hinome writes, 'It's getting chilly in the town of Jiufen right now. The mountains are covered in plumelike silvergrass flowers; they look fluffy and white, like snow.' This picture postcard description of Jiufen in the autumn is really Hinome's implicit way of expressing her sorrow and loneliness.

As the 1990s approached, Chiao (1988) had reviewed enough films from the New Cinema group – especially those by Hou – to argue that they were the frontiers of 'a new narrative language, a new sensitivity, and a new experience' (315). The main stylistic features and the anti-climactic effect separated Taiwan New Cinema from genre films and Hollywood conventions. To achieve this, New Cinema effectively employs long shots and long takes that allow deep focus and prolonged duration to capture 'reality' from a distanced view, elliptical and non-linear storytelling that allows (or perhaps requires) the viewer to fill in the narrative gaps, and understated – even quiet – acting (or non-acting) performances that avoid unnecessarily exaggerated unnatural expression (Chiao 1988, 315–17).

By the beginning of 1990, both Hou Hsiao-hsien and Edward Yang had become cultural ambassadors for Taiwan cinema, frequently attending international film festivals with their work and enjoying the prestige that came with regular wins and nominations. Chiao's writing of the period shows her slowly coming to terms with the Western paradigm that she had once vehemently rejected:

> Hou Hsiao-Hsien, the most important figure in Taiwan cinema, has been named one of the world's most important directors in many surveys of world film critics. Thanks to his diligence (including his films and commentary), the cinema of Taiwan finally rose to enter the realm of 'art' cinema in the mid-1980s, claiming a rightful place in world cinema. [Hou] is a conceptual leader and a pioneer in the cinema movement, not just a director. (Chiao 1993, 21)

In her *China Times Weekly* review of Ang Lee's *The Wedding Banquet* (1993), Chiao uses the Olympic Games as an analogy for the impact of film festivals; she calls festival entries an indispensable game plan to 'elevate the country's status' and to remain culturally viable on the world stage (Chiao 2018, 48). Apart from congratulating Lee for winning the Golden Bear (for best picture) at the Berlin International Film Festival, a pivotal moment for Taiwan cinema, Chiao (2018) laments the Beijing government's interference, which requires Taiwanese entities to operate under the name 'Taiwan, China' (47). The hostility of the government of the PRC towards Taiwan was hardly intermittent. Edward Yang's immersive four-hour epic *A Brighter Summer Day* (1991) was forced to enter the Tokyo International Film Festival under the false pretence that the film was a 'US–Japan co-production' (Chiao 2018, 47), which was far from the truth, given that the film was financed and produced by Central Motion Picture and Edward Yang's production company, Yang & His Gang Filmmakers.

Chiao continued to write extensively about Taiwan New Cinema; by this point, however, she was fixated on the 'misunderstanding' displayed by American film critics rather than French ones. The list of names of which she disapproved included Jim Hoberman from *The Village Voice* and Janet Maslin and Vincent Canby of the *New York Times*. Most of all, she noted the critics' and film festivals' massive interest in cinema coming from the PRC, potentially presenting internal competition among Chinese-language films. If French critics were more impressed by Hou Hsiao-hsien and Edward Yang, then their US counterparts paid more attention to Chinese filmmaker Zhang Yimou of the Fifth Generation at the New York Film Festival. Some elements of 'China fever' can be explained by the distribution strategies used by Miramax and the retrospectives of Chinese cinema curated at Sundance in the early 1990s.

To increase Taiwan cinema's competitiveness, Chiao suggested the following innovations in domestic production: first, replace state subsidies for movie production from taxpayers' money with tax exemptions for investors; second, create a more attractive and lucrative environment for 'soft money' sources, including tax credits and tax shelters available to foreign companies – particularly those from Hong Kong – to expand co-production opportunities; third, as China has one of the fastest-growing film markets in the world for Chinese-language cinema, do not underestimate its importance and potential impact; and fourth, prepare for a film distribution revolution and new models of global marketing and consumption, brought forth by emerging digital technologies (Chiao 2018, 69). The last two points are not merely astute but prophetic: her insights also predicted the pan-Chinese, transnational co-productions that would appear in years to come. Her role as a film producer with her company, Arc Light Films, has since led to many commercially viable, festival-winning films, including *Beijing Bicycle* (directed by Wang Xiaoshuai and runner-up for the Golden Bear at the 2001 Berlin International Film Festival), *Blue Gate Crossing* (dir. Yee Chin-yen; nominated for Best Asian Film at the 2002 Hong Kong Film Awards), and most notably Tsai Ming-liang's *The Hole* (1998).[4]

Retrospectively, Chiao urged domestic critics to be more critical of Taiwan's film industry and film culture:

> Shouldn't we take a good look at what we're doing this time? The Western world – especially all the cultural elite in North America, where practically no Taiwan films have ever been shown – unanimously praise the cultural calibre of Taiwan cinema. Meanwhile, our industry, along with viewers and certain short-sighted media, bitterly attacks Taiwan cinema, reflexively demonstrating their coarse lack of cultural cultivation and taste. (Chiao, 1999)

---

[4] Peggy Chiao shared an interesting anecdote about Tsai Ming-liang in her 2018 anthology. In her postscript to her original 1998 review of *The Hole*, she mentions that Tsai wanted to quit the production halfway during shooting, without finishing the dance scenes. How could they release a film that was supposed to be a musical without any actual musical scenes? It was preposterous, Chiao thought to herself. Fortunately, they had a binding contract with a French investment firm that prevented the director from walking out on set. They completed the production as planned, and this experience inspired Tsai to continue working on many more dances in his subsequent films, including *The Wayward Cloud* (2005) and *Visage* (2009).

With a grasp of the observations made above, it is fair to argue that the success story of Taiwan New Cinema is a result of the orchestration of multiple groups working simultaneously, both on the island and abroad. There is no denying that Taiwan New Cinema was first observed by international critics: the practice of joining the festival circuit certainly helped expose Taiwanese filmmakers to the international labours of art cinema and integrated them into the cultural and political economy of the global art market. The debates among domestic film critics prompted film professionals from the New Cinema group to become further involved in the festival scene and eventually led to the anointing of New Cinema as the representative of Taiwan on the global stage. The festival strategy was prompted by what the directors desired, needed, and wanted, and was part of a dialogue between film critics and the New Cinema group's continuing negotiation over film criticism in the public eye. The fact is that international film festivals continue to play an instrumental role in debates about national cinema.

A Global Slow Take on Film

Before Taiwan New Cinema found itself in the middle of the fierce battle between critics propounding their polarised views, Western academia and paradigms of film theory had already been introduced in the film buff magazines. Now-defunct publications featuring reports on world cinema included *Theatre Quarterly* (*Juchang*, 1965–7) and *Influence* (*Yingxiang*, 1971–9). The former frequently covered famed auteurs like Antonioni, Resnais, Godard, and Kurosawa (Qi 1988, 40–6). Aside from offering translated articles from *Cahiers du Cinéma*, the contributors to these magazines also followed in *Cahier*'s footsteps and reprinted Andrew Sarris's 'Notes on the Auteur Theory in 1962' in one of their issues. Sarris's article (and the subsequent debate with Pauline Kael of *The New Yorker*) is considered to constitute the introduction of auteurism to North American readers and the earliest attempt to offer a theoretical framework for it. Just as the grassroots movement of 1950s *hsiang t'u* literature and literary modernism is often considered the source of, and a contributor to, Taiwan New Cinema, leftist intellectuals in the 1960s, with access to the content of these magazines, also, in a way, predicted the emergence of a movement that emphasised the creative vision of the director. This was at a time when political repression was very much a threat and often a reality. Leftists relied on these magazines to liberate their minds and approached the West as a site of knowledge production. This 'borrowing' or even internalising of Western-induced theory to non-Western cinemas can, of course, be problematic, as it points to the global hegemony of

Western paradigms. However, Taiwan's film critics and professionals can be read as having weaponised Euro-American film theory and criticism to rebuke the attackers of New Cinema, who, to this day, are the same people who mock in their publications anyone who is antagonistic to mainstream cinema as condescending and elitist.

Theatre Quarterly's print life was brief. Publishing its inaugural issue in January 1965 and lasting for only two years, the magazine was a pioneer in introducing auteur theory to Taiwanese readers, which set it apart from the audience-based, fanfare-driven approach to the movie industry that was then the norm seen in entertainment news and trade publications. Following in *Theatre Quarterly*'s footsteps came *Influence* magazine; in one special issue, its contributors presented their own lists of Chinese directors through the application of auteur theory. Although *Influence*'s harsh criticism of Chinese-language cinema was met with a backlash, the existence of both magazines and their niche readership created a ripple effect, inspiring later critics like Peggy Chiao to launch movie review columns in the print media.

Even though the two magazines did not have a decisive impact on the discourses of film criticism at the time, the tide turned when the young critics of the 1980s took on more pivotal roles at state level, after the 1987 publication of the New Cinema manifesto. By 1996, Huang Jianye had accepted a new position as director of the Chinese Taipei Film Archive (now called the Taiwan Film and Audiovisual Institute), while Peggy Chiao was invited by the government to curate a special topic seminar and panel discussion on Taiwan cinema in 1993. Zhan Hongzhi (who had been so critical of Yang Shi-chi's subjective, advocacy-driven journalism) proceeded to expand his cultural empire with online publishing and its offshoots. Much film criticism also shifted from public debates to a more central place in the academy, alongside an increase in film appreciation courses offered on university campuses. The expansion of film education paralleled the global development of film studies as an academic field, but it was also triggered by a partisan feud over how – or even whether – to appreciate New Cinema.

If we return briefly to *A City of Sadness*, we find yet another example of massive debates and surrounding controversies; the film stands for a cumulation of dissension within film criticism circles, as writers fought for influence on public opinion. Among countless journalistic reviews of *A City of Sadness*, none stands out more than the full-page, four-part rebuttal explaining the meanings and behind-the-scenes efforts of Taiwan New Cinema by screenwriter Chu T'ien-wen. Chu, who began working with Hou Hsiao-hsien when she was asked to adapt her story 'The Story of Xiaobi' for the screen, has collaborated on almost every one of Hou's screenplays since that time.

In Chu's newspaper spread in the *Independent Morning Post*, 'Thirteen Questions about *A City of Sadness*', she responds to the repeated attacks on the film and tries to justify the *je-ne-sais-quoi* quality she sees in her collaboration. The key takeaways from her argument are as follows:

1. New Cinema is an alternative to mainstream commercial movies and demonstrates great potential for catering to a niche art film market.
2. To accuse New Cinema of being responsible for the collapse of Taiwan's film industry is simply absurd; these films' box office success was predicated on low-budget production.
3. It is counterproductive to argue whether filmmakers are self-Orientalising their films to please Western audiences.
4. It is more practical to trace the imprints of emotion and sentiment in Hou's cinema from classical Chinese poetry.
5. The film's ambiguous political undertone is not a flaw; it invites multiple possibilities for interpretation. (Chu 1989)

In response to Chu's declaration, the anti-auteur group advocated a Structuralist approach to film analysis, moving away from readings that privilege aesthetics and film authorship. They preferred Michel Foucault, Walter Benjamin, or literary critic György Lukács's Marxist theoretical perspective over the formation of film canons. Critics such as Mi Zou, Liang Xinhua, and Chai Ling-ling condemned existing film criticism practices and decried how auteur theory 'isolates film production from the political, economic, and ideological contexts. Treating film texts as solely the creator's expression, simulating aesthetic styles, and reflections of personal life experiences will not withstand the rapid socio-political changes, and that is the reality' (Mi and Liang 1991, 121; my translation).

To the anti-auteur group, all intellectual deliberations about cinema were linked to social relations and power, and not so much a reduction to the 'long take/long shot, mise-en-scène, poetic realism, and [André] Bazin's realism' (Chai 1989). Calling this framework a much-needed 'epistemological rupture', they demanded that the much-heralded New Cinema subject itself to new scrutiny under the microscope lenses of social sciences and communication, which were considered outside the scope of film studies at that time. Every so often, the way the critics fired off their attacks bordered on oppositional hostility. In Chai Ling-ling's (1989) reading of *A City of Sadness*, the critic characterises the defenders of New Cinema as 'desperate, didactic and patronizing', and dismisses their methods of analysis as 'an attempt to establish superiority over the audience'. Although wanting to recognise film production as a cultural practice to probe questions relating to the formation of knowledge, the tone of their writing nevertheless reveals a distrust of the emergence of a new generation of artists and cultural workers and a grudge against the new forces.

Despite the occasional snide remarks the anti-auteur group let slip in their writings, there is some truth in what they said: the study and appreciation of film can unquestionably be broadened beyond formal elements and geared towards the study of history, culture, and ideology, and repositioning film criticism within the larger media ecology. Taiwan was in a precarious state – disconnected from the world – when the two magazines, *Theatre Quarterly* and *Influence*, introduced auteur theory and André Bazin's cinematic realism to their readers. Political repression under martial law made young intellectuals turn to Western ideology as a tactic to process the internal and external crises. This shift in criticism, from a rigorous enquiry into the relation of rhetoric and aesthetics to the ideological interpretation of society, was not limited to film studies; rather, it was a common trend across many disciplines and sub-fields, including but not limited to literature, theatre, and dance. One cohort of the Structuralist group later labelled themselves as the 'war machine' (Lu 1998, 317), against what Louis Althusser denotes as the state apparatus (they believed New Cinema was part and parcel of the state campaign). This shift marks the moment when the Western discourses of Structuralism as such began spreading widely.

If the insights of *Theatre Quarterly* and *Influence* contributed to the discussion of Taiwan New Cinema and auteurs, later scholars have turned their attention to narrower fields of enquiry in auteurism: namely, the art of slow cinema. This was followed by new theories of postmodernism, globalisation, and transnationalism that have risen to prominence since the 1990s. This shifting interest does not merely concern the new framework of affective slowness but also involves the study of art house figures in Taiwan who are commonly dubbed the Second Wave directors, especially Malaysian-born Tsai Ming-liang. The Hong Kong scholar Song Hwee Lim (2014), in discussing Tsai's signature style in both the literal and the authorial senses of the director's oeuvre, notes that the locus of his study is the 'overlapping area between Tsai Ming-liang *and* a cinema of slowness' (10). Taiwan-based scholar Song-Yong Sing (2014), who shares a career trajectory similar to that of Tsai Ming-liang, also characterises Tsai's entire filmography and video installation series as slow cinema. Sing is a Malaysian-born new immigrant who benefited from the Taiwanese government's support for overseas Chinese students. Both studies posit that the slow aesthetics in Tsai's work are related not just to the long take (as measured by metric time) or long duration (*la durée*), to use Gilles

Deleuze's term, but to the way his work, particularly the 'Slow Walk' moving images and performance art series, conceptualises time and the bodily experience for both spectators and onscreen strollers.

As things transpired, 2014 was a significant year for the study of slow cinema. In Anglophone academia, three single-author books on cinematic slowness appeared: Ira Jaffe's *Slow Movies: Countering the Cinema of Action*, Tiago de Luca's *Realism of the Senses in World Cinema*, and Song Hwee Lim's *Tsai Ming-Liang and a Cinema of Slowness*. These publications signalled an imminent boom in global considerations of the discourses on slow and durational cinema, exemplified by, among others, Tiago de Luca and Nuno Barradas Jorge's (2016) anthology, which enjoyed a wide readership. The term 'slow cinema' is believed to have been coined by French film critic Michel Ciment as early as 2003. Lim (2014) nonetheless points out that many film critics – Jonathan Rosenbaum, Adrian Martin, and Matthew Flanagan, to name just a few – have always recognised the undertone of cinematic slowness in their observation of auteurs like Yasujiro Ozu and Béla Tarr (13). The body of their theoretical texts primarily builds upon Deleuze's seminal *Cinema 2: The Time-Image* and characterises slow cinema as part of postwar, postmodern conditions under the thematic tropes of waiting, boredom, and eventfulness, all underpinned by an intensified sense of temporality and bodily exhaustion. But Lim (2014) also moves beyond the postwar sentiments of Deleuze to 'the triangulated relationship among temporality, materiality, and aesthetics' that is central to 'the understanding of the tension between speed and slowness' (12). This includes the relationship of slow cinema to analogue and digital technologies, cinephile culture, and exhibition practices, including screening in museum and gallery spaces, and the physical limitations and material conditions of filmmaking.

To Lim's credit, he not only examines the cinematic phenomenon of slowness in its multiple facets but also addresses in his new framework some of the criticism levelled against this body of films. In offering an overview of the discursive and theoretical terrain of temporality, defining the aesthetics of slowness, Lim's writing builds on and reaffirms the validity of a director's claim to authorship in the context of Taiwan New Cinema. The Second New Wave director Tsai Ming-liang's long-take style is vividly different from that of Hou Hsiao-hsien, to whom Tsai is often compared. While Hou is championed for his elegant slow rhythms, Lim's observations reveal that Tsai's shots are significantly longer and lethargic. Apart from the inter- and intratextual practices that shape the patterns in Tsai's authorship, a familiarity with Tsai's cinematic corpus on the part of the art house audience is also expected. A distinctive point Lim makes about cinephile culture is the literal signature that Tsai inscribed in the closing credits of his third film, *The River* (1997). This act concerns both the director declaring his authorship and branding schemes. Tsai's handwritten signature can be seen on movie posters, DVD covers, opening or closing credits (Figure 2.2), and so on to market the power of artistic vision with his authorial presence. Under the circumstances, the imprint of his signature seems more like a marketing strategy, the selling of a brand, and the director's claim to authorship can come over as arrogant and opportunist. But Lim (2014) suggests that the auteur model of content marketing is a calculated and much-needed gambit in the face of Tsai's diasporic identity (he is not a Taiwanese citizen), questions of homosexuality, the lack of appreciation by domestic audiences, and the role played by cinema as a cultural ambassador of a small nation in world film markets (45-9).

In the Chinese academy, Song-Yong Sing's monograph *Projecting Tsai Mingliang: Towards Transart Cinema* provides equal weight in repositioning Taiwan New Cinema in the context of time-based moving images, transmedia, and art as a philosophical enquiry. In dissecting Tsai's intratextual practices, Sing (2014) links the bodily stillness, mindless meandering, and durational space

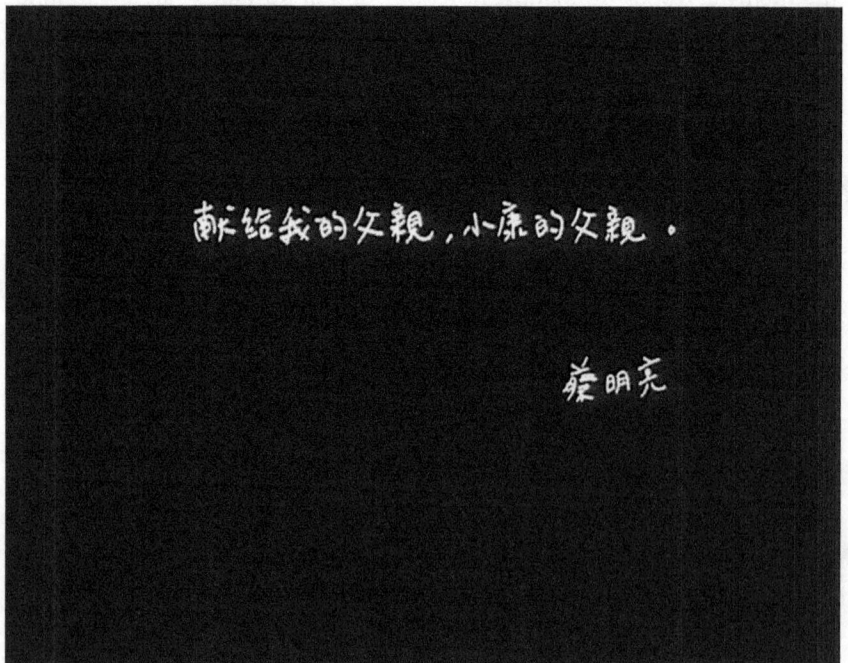

Figure 2.2 *On the final title card of* What Time Is It There? *(2003), Tsai Ming-liang's scribbled signature is seen following the text that reads: 'I dedicate [this film] to my father, and to Hsiao-Kang's [deceased] father'. Still frame. © Homegreen Films.*

in Tsai's films to American underground cinema (such as Andy Warhol's *Screen Tests* and the seemingly never-ending looped footage of *Sleep*) and Euro-American auteurs (Antonioni, Wenders, Roman Polanski, Pier Paolo Pasolini, Sam Peckinpah). Tsai's minimalist approach to sound, which Sing (2014) calls the presence of 'a voiceless body', also contributes to aspects of affective slowness (61). Sing goes beyond the discourse of Italian Neorealism and argues that the use of 'window framing', in both the diegetic and the extradiegetic sense, that is found in *Dust in the Wind*, *The Terrorizers* (1986), and *Daughter of the Nile* (1987) is what connects Tsai Ming-liang's filmmaking style to his New Cinema predecessors Hou and Yang. Tsai's *Goodbye, Dragon Inn* (2003), for example, inherits a narrative structure influenced by society's historical consciousness from the cohorts of Taiwan New Cinema, but it also experiments with a set of new cinematic languages by extending itself into a reflexive, postmodernist film. This is Sing's way of settling the East/West, national/global, realism/metacinema divide that has been central to the old/new critical debates over auteur theory since the 1980s. Perhaps it is plausible to acknowledge that New Cinema has arrived at, or has always been, reflexive postmodernism.

Conclusion

'An auteur is not a brand,' as Richard Brody (2014) says so sternly in his defence in *The New Yorker*. The common conception of the director as creator usually implies a cinema that is resistant to being profit-minded, featuring formalistic genre films that stemmed from the increasing separation of populism from the elite class of auteurs. As this chapter has illustrated, the kernel of the backlash against Taiwan New Cinema and scepticism among Taiwanese film critics involved differences in identity politics. Critics, especially the *sotto voce* women writers, picked up on New Cinema directors' impulse to split from a KMT-oriented Chinese perspective and looked towards Western film theory and paradigms to weaponise their resistance. The core of the rejection of New Cinema by the older generation of film critics has more to do with the way their adversaries downplayed populist cinema, but their rejection also comes over as thinly veiled resentment at the rise of a grassroots identity. This identity was deeply ingrained in Taiwanese cultures that had been marginalised and seen as provincial and less sophisticated, and also in languages that the administration had once tried to suppress. However, this does not mean that they were always supportive of Western influences among the New Cinema group themselves – be it auteur theory, the film festival strategy, or international reception – as seen with Peggy Chiao. As the world continues to sink deeper into the intensification of connectivity that leads to the erosion of spatial barriers through time, both domestic and international scholars are turning to expanded theories of affective slowness in cinema, which offer a third, non-binary way of looking at New Cinema's intrinsically postmodern conditions. To counter the polemic that it is crass to link the auteur to the transformative power of marketing, the act of branding an auteur is sometimes needed as a subversive tactic to proclaim Taiwan New Cinema.

Part II

Filmmakers in Focus

CHAPTER 3

Going East: Women Walk the City in Hou Hsiao-hsien's
Le Voyage du ballon rouge *(2007) and*
Café Lumière *(2003)*

Taiwanese director Hou Hsiao-hsien's non-Chinese-language films, *Café Lumière* (2003) and *Le Voyage du ballon rouge* (*Flight of the Red Balloon*, 2007), stand as pivotal moments of his filmography, as the director raised his status to the level of transnational auteur by making commissioned films outside Taiwan. *Café Lumière*, an invited work from Shochiku Studio, provides a fresh look at the late Japanese master Yasujiro Ozu's recurring theme of cross-generational conflict. *Le Voyage du ballon rouge*, commissioned by the Musée d'Orsay, pays tribute to one of the most beloved children's films in France. Both *Café Lumière* and *Le Voyage du ballon rouge* are more than a Taiwanese director's homage to world cinema auteurs. Like Tsai Ming-liang's *What Time Is It There?* (2001), *Le Voyage du ballon rouge* incorporates a story of a Chinese woman in the French capital and the dialogic relations between Taiwan and France (or Taipei and Paris). In *Café Lumière*, Hou shows how Taiwan shares a modern temporality with Japan, underlining cultural resonances and the attractiveness of the Tokyo metropolis to Asian audiences.

Hou Hsiao-hsien is one of the most discussed filmmakers in Asian cinema today. The main reason for this extensive attention is his subdued aesthetic, which has left an extraordinary mark on world cinema. Many have tried to fit Hou into existing categories and paradigms of art cinema and have sought ready-made explanations for the origins of his filmmaking style. A common, generalised cultural explanation is the textual quality of 'Chineseness' in Hou's work; however, this approach is reductionist, ignoring the specificity and histories of Taiwan that gave rise to Hou's unique career. Another common approach is to emphasise Hou's influences, as film scholars often argue how the director's style resembles, echoes, or recalls certain auteurs of world cinema. Formalist scholarship on Hou often tries to identify the resemblances and affinities between Hou and Ozu.[1] Such approaches are not without merit, but attention must also be paid to the differences between them. Hou, however, claims that he never saw an Ozu film until after he had made *A Time to Live, A Time to Die* (1985), by which time the often-conspicuous comparisons between him and the Japanese master were already proliferating.

Moreover, aside from Jean-Luc Godard's *À bout de souffle* (*Breathless*, 1960) and Federico Fellini's *Amarcord* (1973), Hou rarely publicly spoke about any Euro-American influences. As James Udden (2003) has argued, Hou's style emerged from the social conditions in Taiwan: a confluence of government policies, a youthful and collective rejection of the standard commercial filmmaking of the time, and Hou's own way of improvising and almost non-scripting the actors' performance. Hou's films nevertheless 'stand well on their own and do not need to be somehow "justified" with reference to influences or international standards' (Udden 2003, 121).

As far as cultural particularism goes, neither *Le Voyage du ballon rouge* nor *Café Lumière* can be simply contextualised in the conditions from which Hou arose. The question remains: what makes these two films unique and why do they stand out from Hou's body of work? I argue that Hou offers us one notable example among contemporary East Asian filmmakers that marks the shift from a concern with the national community to the transnational one. Hou's filmmaking never developed in isolation but was also never entirely derived from external influences, which is evidenced by his transnational encounters. Encounters and transcultural exchanges – such as funding schemes, festival platforms, and art house distribution – have allowed Hou's cinematic practice to move beyond state subsidies and expand outside of the Taiwanese film industry.

In this chapter, I argue that through Hou's cinematic rearticulation for local and international audiences, his transnational filmmaking represents an envisioning of a global culture that highlights new modes of East–West connection and imagined communities. Hou's transnational filmmaking since the 2000s thus provides an opportunity to explore questions of transcultural citation and of postcolonial temporality. The films embody transnational aesthetics in terms of the context of production, circulation, and reception, as well as their textual elements. They are rich in intertextuality, which broadens our understanding of the intricate relations among cinemas, nations, and cross-border flows. These films' in-text and metatextual citations of European and Japanese postwar cinema meditate on the influences of global art cinema history and display an ambivalence towards modernisation that has long been regarded as a Western project. By unpacking the film's

---

[1] See the writings of Godfrey Cheshire, I-fen Wu, Tony McKibbin, and Ian Johnston, for example.

modification and exchange of iconography, I show how Hou was able to transform foreign classics into work that is recognisable and perceivable by both foreign and domestic viewers. In particular, as Japan has presented itself as the centre of Asia since the postwar period – in terms of how Japan has continued to practise a kind of cultural imperialism, in the way its popular culture and technology[2] have been exported, circulated, and received within Asia – Hou's films show that the global diffusion shared by transnational filmmaking is not just producing homogeneous East–West communities. Rather, it is intensifying cultural regionalisation across the world. In the case of *Café Lumière*, it represents an emergent regionalised culture of East Asia.

A note is necessary here about the increasing female-centredness of Hou's films over the years. It goes without saying that this has much to do with the long-time collaboration with his regular screenwriter, established literary writer Chu T'ien-wen. Consciously or unconsciously, Chu contributed to many of the female voices and narrative points of view depicted in Hou's films. The director's indebtedness to Chu is referenced by numerous film scholars: for example, Emilie Yueh-yu Yeh and Darrell William Davis (2005), who detail the subliminal autobiographical impulses in Hou's screenplay. Following this observation, Christopher Lupke (2016) posits that it was Chu who brought Hou's cinema an *écriture féminine*, which does not just draw upon women's experiences but disrupts the masculine narrative and cinematic language. Beginning with the screenplay of *Growing Up* (1983) – which was adapted from a short story Chu wrote with the same title (*Xiao Bi de gu shi*) – Chu demonstrated her writing abilities, as she crafted a female first-person narrator who told a boy's coming-of-age story. And Chu's women narrators are not lost in translation on the big screen. As Lupke (2016) observes, the narrative point of view in *Summer at Grandpa's* (1984)

> [moves] back and forth not merely between male and female characters but between experiences and viewpoints that are gender specific, personify a capacity to lay an ostensible framework of patriarchal values and points of view while simultaneously undercutting it with the subversive sotto voce of a female voice. (70-1)

Chu contributed as the principal screenwriter to all of Hou's feature-length films except for, strangely enough, Hou's francophone film *Le Voyage du ballon rouge*. Instead of approaching the films through narrative analysis, I engage in a formalistic reading on the subjectivity of Hou's central female characters.

---

[2] Such as VCRs, karaoke machines, the Walkman, Nintendo Wii, Sony PlayStation 5; cartoons and animation; video games like Super Mario; and the highly versatile semiconductor industry.

In the case of *Café Lumière* and *Le Voyage du ballon rouge*, both female protagonists embody the figure of the *flâneur* (who is traditionally depicted as male) wandering in a global metropolis, as opposed to the docile, drifting woman in Hou's previous work.

TRANSNATIONAL VOYAGES

To illustrate the potential of Hou's films for opening ways to imagine transnational communities, we should begin by interrogating the period of his transnational filmmaking, focusing on how aesthetics and transcultural reception are crucial to such an imagination. The year 1995 marked a transition for Hou, from making so-called national cinema to international co-productions, beginning with *Good Men, Good Women* (1995), a film that attempts to locate the historical trauma in postwar China and Taiwan. In this film, working with two Japanese production companies, Team Okuyama and Shochiku, allowed Hou to redirect his attention from local historiography to take a transnational look at Taiwanese history, which is characterised by the inevitable cultural geometry between Taiwan, Japan, and China. *Good Men, Good Women* focuses on a turbulent part of Taiwan's history – first being colonised by Japan for the fifty years preceding World War II and then being taken over by the Chinese Nationalist Party (KMT), which enacted violent repression. This thematic thread is a continuation of Hou's most acclaimed and critical works, *A City of Sadness* (1989) and *The Puppetmaster* (1993). Together, these films are known as Hou's trilogy of the unspoken history of Taiwan. In a series of elusive and exhausting long takes, the trilogy depicts the history of Taiwan through different individual stories and perspectives in the characters' lives and times. In Dai Jinhua's (2008) observation, 'Hou's Taiwan trilogy violates political taboos and shows a rift in history and emotion' (248). A quick way to summarise Hou's style is that he depicts history by moving away from history: he favours individual memories instead of grand historic moments and prefers to chronicle pivotal events in a circumspect way.

Hou's next international co-production was *Café Lumière*, which was dedicated to the memory of Ozu; it was also his first film outside of Chinese-speaking countries. It follows a pregnant freelance writer, Yoko, and her daily, unchoreographed routine of taking trains, visiting friends, and going to coffee shops in Tokyo. Occasionally, she runs into her rail fan friend, Hajime, who is working on a sound project recording train noise. The fact that Shochiku studios – the home base for most of Ozu's films[3] – was willing to hire a

---

[3] Ozu made a total of fifty-three films in his career, all but three for the Shochiku studio.

Taiwanese director to pay homage is emblematic of Hou's cross-cultural influences and his translational approach to cinema. Not surprisingly, when *Café Lumière* came out in 2003, international film critics were compelled to compare Hou to Ozu and often debated whether Hou could possibly outshine Ozu, one of Japan's and world cinema's great directors. Concerned with such a disadvantage, A. O. Scott (2004) of *The New York Times* poses the rhetorical question 'is it possible to make movies in Ozu's manner?' In answering his own question, Scott (2004) concludes that *Café Lumière* is 'a rigorously minor, faint, diminished echo to Ozu's films, in particular *Tokyo Story* (1953)'. But the film is not a simple formalist echo of *Tokyo Story*; nor is it just the story of a single mother going through a break-up. It is a film that functions as a terrain for the negotiation of cultures deemed suitable for a transnational audience.

Critics and scholars have long compared the idiosyncrasies of Hou and Ozu, concentrating on the formal and thematic qualities shared by the two directors.[4] It is widely accepted that Hou is the only director who has come close to matching Ozu's inimitable style. While some scholars are wary of Anglophone critics projecting ahistorical, Oriental, and imperialistic gazes by engaging only in formalistic readings of these films, Lupke (2016) essentially posits that the point here is not to debate whether Hou was influenced by Ozu. Rather, the discussion should focus on how Hou's films form a dialogue with the Japanese master, not only through his preferences in style and theme but also through the process in which Hou created his films – in particular, how 'the cross fertilization of theme and in some ways technique illuminates not just the understanding of these two important filmmakers but the understanding of East Asian culture in general' (Lupke 2016, 79). If we consider that the distinctive long shot and long take are stylistic traits that have long been Hou's trademark, then, interestingly, in *Café Lumière*, it was not entirely Hou's decision to arbitrate formal qualities so close to Ozu's. During filming, Shochiku Studio laid down many ground rules and restrictions, one of which was to shoot the film only in Japan. Other rules involved maintaining Ozu's editing style and the use of Ozu's signature shots and compositions – such as

---

[4] For reference, see Arthi Vasudevan (2016), 'Café Lumière as Hou Hsiao-Hsien's Own and as a Homage to Yausjiro Ozu', *Frames Cinema Journal* 10 (December), <https://framescinemajournal.com/article/cafe-lumiere-as-hou-hsiao-hsiens-own-and-as-a-homage-to-yasujiro-ozu-2> (last accessed 2 August 2022); and a video essay by Danny Leung (2017), 'Café Lumière: Modernising Ozu's Tokyo Story', 24 March, <https://youtu.be/kQDOJaTdzHw> (last accessed 2 August 2022).

the 'tatami shot', in which the fixed, unmoving camera is placed at a low angle, contrary to the Hollywood conventions of eye-level/medium shot.[5]

Before *Café Lumière*'s initial release in Japan, Hou worried that the film would be poorly received by the local audience for failing to preserve the spirit of Ozu, but the common reaction from Japanese audiences was that they felt the film was actually 'more Japanese than the work done by Japanese themselves' and that 'they seldom saw any Japanese director, virtually none, who made a film like this' (Hou 2004). Many recognised *Café Lumière*'s thematic reference to Ozu's films, such as the central conceit of women and marriages in *Tokyo Story* and *Late Autumn* (1960). In Hou's modern update, however, the film distinctively concerns a pregnant young woman who determines to raise her child out of wedlock. In exploring similar themes through various perspectives and in a cross-cultural context, Hou provides a cinematic meditation on the lives of Japanese people from a detached point of view, not necessarily from a deep understanding of Japanese culture. Recognising the language and cultural barriers as shortcomings, Hou accepted his distance from the culture and worked with it. Shochiku Studio's trust in Hou reaffirms his translational ability to incorporate both Taiwanese and Japanese influences into the film.

CINEMATIC (RE)MAPPING OF CITY LIFE IN *CAFÉ LUMIÈRE*

Café Lumière begins when Yoko has just returned from yet another visit to Taiwan – only this time she finds out that she is pregnant. She nonchalantly informs her parents and close friend Hajime that not only she is pregnant with her Taiwanese boyfriend's child but also she is determined to have this child alone.[6] Although her parents try to express their concern, they eventually

---

[5] Eye-level shots are often done by placing a camera at shoulder height, and are considered to be subjective because the technique is often utilised to imply a character's point of view.

[6] The reason why Yoko considers there to be no future between her and the Taiwanese boyfriend is that her boyfriend is a mother's boy. A mother's boy is a negative term used to describe someone who is too dependent on his mother and allows her to control, if not dictate, most decisions about his life. Often, a grown man who shows signs of being a mother's boy will not only adore his mum but will treat her as the archetype for his ideal spouse, and most women (if heterosexual) will come up short in comparison to his ideal type. While prevalent in Chinese patriarchal society, this sentiment is not specific to Taiwan, although the critique of men like this usually comes from a female sensibility. In a metacontext, it is not hard to imagine that screenwriter Chu T'ien-wen implemented the dialogue as a vehicle to address the gender gap in Taiwanese society.

accept and respect her decision. On the surface, the storyline of *Café Lumière* pits Yoko's independence against the traditional structure of the family unit, where women face the obligations of marriage and procreation. However, many times the camera presents Yoko's point of view and acts as a stand-in for the spectator wandering in the city; it acts as the *flâneur* here, evoking the central figure in Charles Baudelaire's poetry about nineteenth-century Paris. A *flâneur* is a person who walks around the city in a seemingly aimless way, observing the minutiae of everyday life. Much as the anonymity of the crowd in a darkened theatre is part of the formulation of film spectatorship, the streets of the city are home to the *flâneur*, providing 'an asylum for the person on the margins of society' with a heightened sense of spectatorial pleasure where one is observing but rarely interacting with others (Wolff 1985, 40).

The particularity of the *flâneur*, as Janet Wolff (1985) points out, is that whether it is the dandy, the hero, or the stranger,[7] all figures of the stroller in modernist literature 'are invariably male figures' (41). The *flâneuse* (a female *flâneur*) is invisible in the literature of modernity but not because she did not exist – although it is true that, even by the late nineteenth century, women could not go alone to a café or a restaurant in cosmopolitan cities like Paris or London; it has more to do with the way that literature ignores the private sphere of women's domain (Wolff 1985, 44). Yoko, as a female *flâneur*, traverses Japan's modern city via its extensive tram-train public transport network to conduct her work and to keep in touch with her friends and family. Bestowing a privileged observational feel on the viewers, the camera diligently follows Yoko's daily routine of taking the trains and her casual run-ins with Hajime, an antique bookshop owner and a rail fan who spends his leisure time recording train sound. Her experience is that of a freedom to move about in the city, observing and being observed (Figure 3.1). Through the fluidity of camera shots and the moving trains, *Café Lumière* allows a spectator's mind to stroll around the Tokyo streets at a languid pace and in a nomadic way, in the absence of any spectacular, exciting events.

The original film title of *Café Lumière* in Chinese means, as explained by the director himself, 'A time to rest your mind, to adjust your pace, for the long journey ahead of you,' transforming an everyday, casual observation into a mapping of the urban space of Tokyo (Hou 2004). Among all the film directors working in postwar Japan, Yasujiro Ozu established a formidable reputation for crafting realist films that 'simultaneously captured the temporality of

---

[7] See Charles Baudelaire (1995), *The Painter of Modern Life and Other Essays*. Translated by Jonathan Mayne (New York: Phaidon Press); and Walter Benjamin (1973), *Charles Baudelaire: A Lyric Poet in the Era of High Capitalism* (London: New Left Books).

Figure 3.1 *Yoko taking the Tokyo metro and looking out from the train in* Café Lumière *(2003). Still frame.* © *Shochiku.*

everyday life and a society that was being transformed by a new world order' (Chung 2012, 585). The new world order refers to a time when vernacular modernity began to surface; Japan is becoming more urbanised and people are more attuned to their own individuality. What attracted Hou to Ozu was that he does not think that Ozu was trying to recreate an ideal prewar lifestyle that he was nostalgic for; rather, he was trying to observe and document objectively the changing times and the transformation of social values in postwar Japan. For this reason, *Café Lumière* is not just a tribute film but also Hou's cinematic rendering of contemporary lives in dialogue with the epoch of Ozu – that is, a contemporary Tokyo in conversation with a postwar Tokyo of the 1950s.

Plot-wise, the closest comparable film to *Café Lumière* would probably be Ozu's *Late Spring* (1949), a family drama about a widower's daughter who has no plans to marry. Following the same thematic thread, Hou situated Yoko in the same framework but with an updated, feminist approach. For example, rather than the daughter's character getting married, as would happen in most of Ozu's films, the pregnant protagonist is determined not to wed but to raise her child alone. At some point in the story, though, the modern, independent, and self-sufficient Yoko is either doubting her decision or subconsciously fearing losing her baby, as implied by the close-up shots of the illustrated picture book *Outside Over There* by Maurice Sendak. Early in the film, Yoko mentions her weird dream to her friend and secondhand bookshop owner,

Hajime. Hajime recommends that she check out this children's book illustration. The picture book itself is about a pre-adolescent girl's jealousy and sibling rivalry. Seeing through the camera's mechanical eye, the film lingers on specific moments from the book. The passages Yoko recites out loud in English are scenes in which the goblins sneak into the nursery and steal the baby. When the baby's sister, Ida, turns to pick up what she thought was her younger sister, she realises the baby has been replaced by an ice doppelganger, dripping wet and melting away. *Café Lumière* bookends the film with the scene when Yoko's parents are visiting her in the city; they ask her how far long her pregnancy is, and Yoko replies three months. Given that most miscarriages happen in the first trimester, the inclusion of the children's book illustration in this context stands in as a metaphor for the fear of losing a baby – if not consciously weighing her options for the pregnancy other than keeping the baby, meaning abortion.

At the same time, the film is very much about a woman walking in the metropolis, as the spectators follow Yoko's mundane routine: sleeping, eating, talking on the phone, taking trains, going to the coffee shop, meeting friends. Her nomadic movements are encapsulated in many scenes in which trains are shown arriving at and leaving the station, the sound of the train whistle, views of train tracks, and other occurrences. The omnipresent train shots allude to a kind of languid pace, a subliminal faithfulness to Japanese society that, like photographs, freezes the occurrence of action in an instant. Plentiful shots of commuter trains in *Café Lumière* are reminiscent not only of Ozu's *Tokyo Story* or *Late Spring* but also of the Francophone title itself, which is a reference to the Lumière brothers, pioneers of cinema, and their seminal film of a train entering a station: *L'Arrivée d'un train en gare de La Ciotat* (1895), a 50-second actuality film that entered film history as the quintessential origin of the medium. The naming is not a coincidence; it is a deliberate reference to the transversal aspect of trains moving across fields and plains. The film literally opens with train carriages moving across the screen right after the title card that explains Ozu's centenary. This sets the tone and introduces the most prominent character, aside from Yoko and Hajime – trains. We follow Yoko travelling between stations, catching glimpses of train doors opening and closing, and looking out of the windows of a moving train through point-of-view shots. Other shot compositions include trains moving diagonally in opposite directions and characters obscured by fleeting trains passing in front of them (Figure 3.2).

Above all, one scene that stands out significantly is a long crane-shot of trains high on the viaduct, and the camera tilts down slowly. An almost unnoticeable Hajime stands on the platform in the bottom right corner, looking like a miniature figure (Figure 3.3). Along with the open framing and actions occurring off frame – views that are blocked by pedestrians, cars, and moving trains – this is consistent with Hou's preferred use of long shots and immobile camera to achieve a distant observational feel. While critics praised these formal strategies as a kind of cinema of distance (Johnston 2005), Hou himself repeatedly explained that his use of a long shot aesthetic had much to do with economic principles in the shooting conditions:

> The timing of my sequence shots has to do with shooting conditions. I always prefer shooting on location or in interiors that have not been especially set up for the film. Complex camera movements in these conditions are not possible. [...] I like to establish a certain distance from the action so as to position myself on the ground of generalities, that is to say, to adopt a point of view that enables a broader understanding of the action and its weight without following it in all its details. (Mazabrard and Strauss 1990, 27-8)

This strategy is motivated by an attempt to capture the natural movement of people, who are most likely to be themselves when they are not aware of the movie camera, or temporarily forget that they are being gazed at by it. In these often off-centred shots, the characters enter or leave the frame at their own pace, sometimes continuing their action off screen while the camera uninterestedly pans away. Some viewers, however, may feel held back and discouraged from continuing to watch what is on screen because the narrative focus is uncertain.

Figure 3.2   *Trains moving diagonally in* Café Lumière. *Still frame.* © *Shochiku.*

Figure 3.3 *A long crane-shot of trains in* Café Lumière *as the camera tilts down slowly. An almost unnoticeable Hajime stands on the platform in the bottom right corner. Still frame.* © *Shochiku.*

In a similar vein, the train sequences suggest Hou's commitment to experiential verisimilitude. Rather than it following Yoko with conventional tracking shots, the camera is in motion itself like a fellow commuter, suggesting the characters' spontaneous travel routes and bringing a more organic approach to the way the lens documents these journeys. The backstory to filming on location is also an interesting one: in reality, the East Japan Railway Company[8] rejected the film crew's application to shoot in actual train stations, leaving Hou and his crew to use covert filming techniques (much as his protégé Midi Z had to do in his own films, as explained later in Chapter 5). The railway company justified their rejection by citing their concerns: they feared production would block streets and stations and the cameras would disrupt the daily commuters. Determined not to compromise his vision, Hou decided to bypass the bureaucracy after negotiations failed; he adopted guerrilla tactics and secretly filmed in train stations – that is, he used hand-held cameras and hid the equipment from any potential patrollers. By eschewing city rules and abandoning a detailed, pre-planned shooting schedule, cinematic realism can, while built on shorter takes, provide glimpses of unrehearsed moments when the characters react to the city's rhythm of life.

[8] Train transport (or the railway network, both surface and underground) in Tokyo refers to a mix of public and private sectors that operate in and around the metropolitan area. JR East (the East Japan Railway) runs the greatest number of lines and covers the most extensive areas within and between the cities and suburban areas.

What I am suggesting here is that the camera becomes a secondary plot and character, which unfold on screen. Questions of film language and economic principle accentuate the differences between Hou and Ozu. Aside from the prominent feature of the tatami shot, Ozu consistently violated the 180-degree line in his shot/reverse shot and instead opted for a series of 'still frames', which open the film and bridge the narrative at various points (Johnston 2005). In contrast, Hou's cinema shows the subject's perspective but in the next shot the camera pans away, suggesting otherwise. If we return to the scene with Hajime, Hou presents the indicative style of the film with even more uncertainty: why is Hajime pushed into the corner of the frame? Why does the camera tilt and pan in a way that creates a structural layer in composition? Does it leave the viewers to appreciate what is said (centre) and left unsaid (periphery)? Is it a panoramic view of the city mapped by institutional bodies? Or perhaps, above all, the emphasis is on the intersecting lines of passing trains?

These intersectional shots of tracks and moving trains correspond in a way to a similar composition in *Tokyo-Ga* (1985), directed by Wim Wenders, a major figure in New German Cinema. In this documentary, which is ostensibly about paying homage to Ozu, Wenders was in Tokyo because he wished to retrace Ozu's steps to learn more about the Japanese master's filming inspirations. The documentary-cum-video-essay ranges from Wenders interviewing Ozu's regular cinematographer, Atsuta Yuharu, and one of Ozu's favourite actors, Ryu Chishu, to scenes of Japanese pinball machine Pachinko and food replicas in restaurant windows. But most importantly, both *Café Lumière* and *Tokyo-Ga* include crane-shots that show angles and intersecting lines of trains and moving cars (Figure 3.4). In addition, the two films share scenes of train reflections, on bridges and between buildings, in train carriages and window displays. Again, this should not be treated lightly as a mere coincidence. Simply because both films were shot in Tokyo with the same lines of commuter trains it does not necessarily mean that they share the same compositional result with the same inspiration. My point here is not to suggest whether Hou references Wenders's *Tokyo-Ga* in the scene with Hajime because, even if he did, he was not trying to create a replica of the images. Rather, my emphasis is on the recognition that arises out of the visual impression from *Tokyo-Ga*, which potentially predominates and reshapes the same visual expression of *Café Lumière*. As the visual expression intersects between German documentary and Taiwanese art house cinema – and since the title highlights the intersection between national and global film history – the film reformulates its cinematic features for a transnational reception.

Figure 3.4 *A snapshot of Tokyo's cityscape in the spring of 1983 from Wim Wenders's documentary* Tokyo-Ga *(1985). Still frame.* © *Chris Sievernich Filmproduktion.*

TOWARDS A POSTCOLONIAL HISTORY

While there are some parallels with Ozu's films, there is a considerable distance between *Café Lumière* and *Tokyo Story*, just as there are differences between the filmmaking of Hou and Ozu. The major difference lies in an awareness of postcolonial history that runs through the film and separates Hou's cinema from the empty realm of pastiche. On the narrative level, *Café Lumière* presents an obvious case for traversing the boundaries of nation, culture, and temporality. In the film, one of the primary threads is Yoko's research on an actual historical and public figure, Jian Wenye, whose career path epitomises transnationalism. He was a composer who was born in the 1930s in Taiwan, established his fame in Japan, and died in Beijing, China. Because most of his musical creation took place in Japan, he was quickly forgotten by his birth country and was buried in historical documents. Dai (2008) considers the formalist comparison to Ozu less pertinent than the recognition of *Café Lumière* as a film that is about 'a young woman roaming in metropolitan cities searching for historical traces' (249). Through the female *flâneur*, the film serves as a national allegory that is encapsulated in the hinterland of history and reality – a film that occupies the real and the discursive space in contemporary Taiwan. While many international critics tend to hollow out a sense of historicity and reduce the formalist long take to a universal cinematic language consumed by art house cinephiles,[9] the legacy of Japanese colonialism remains critical in the current Taiwanese political discourse and serves as a marker in differentiating contemporary Taiwanese identity from Chinese identity.

Addressing the film as a national allegory, *Café Lumière* complicates its transnational nature by representing the history between Japan and Taiwan. Namely, Hou employs Ozu's form and style as part of a narrative device to link the turbulent history of Taiwan, Japan, and China together. Yoko, who retraces Jian Wenye's footsteps to find out where he spent his days in search of biographical material and historical records, represents a woman who attempts to trace the colonial relationship between Taiwan and imperialist Japan. This narrative epitomises the ambiguity between the two countries, which are separated geographically but not culturally or sentimentally. When Yoko tries to locate a secondhand bookshop or coffee shop that Jian used to visit, she is attempting to recover a forgotten history by remapping the city in its bygone memories – an attempt that represents two cultures coexisting at the same time and in the same space. In the end, the only traces that Yoko can find exist in the past, deeply sunk in historical time. Her failed attempt symbolises her inability to arrive at an understanding of history. Even though Yoko struggles to recover the history, the film transcends the entangled moment and regional conflicts and is able to represent and reflect colonial history in its reflexive filmmaking.

The most reflexive moment occurs when Yoko is given the opportunity to meet up with Jian's Japanese wife and gazes at the composer's actual photo album. In this scene, the camera slowly pans sideways, shifting focus between Yoko and the wife while the two talk about Jian's photos. The photos themselves are first blocked by drink glasses but then resurface once the camera cuts to a close-up of Yoko flipping through the pages. The face of the mysterious figure that has been central to Yoko's research is now revealed, along with Jian's wife in a cameo appearance as well as in the photo album. This diegetic interruption – when Yoko looks at the photos of an actual figure – represents the gaze of the coloniser looking at the imperial subject. But the meaning is also twofold. In the colonial history of Taiwan, Japan is more than

---

[9] See Valentina Vitali's (2008) discussion of the press reviews of Hou's films in a range of European magazines in 'Hou Hsiao-Hsien Reviewed', in *Inter-Asia Cultural Studies* 9, no. 2: 280-9.

a colonial ruler. Between 1915 and 1937, the *kominka* (becoming Japanese) movement was launched. The rhetoric of *kominka* is different from that of Western imperialism because the assimilation process involves not only governing Taiwan in the same way as the home islands but also transforming the Taiwanese into loyal imperial subjects. This process was concurrent with modernising Taiwan's infrastructure: railways, roads, airfields, education, public health, administration, and business management. Policy changes, such as language reform and name changing, were attempts aiming at the total annihilation of Taiwanese culture and consciousness. *Kominka* ultimately meant for the Taiwanese to live and die as Japanese in the name of the emperor. However, it brings to light the doubleness and the in-betweenness of national and cultural identity. Such is the rhetoric of the 'ambivalence of mimicry', a postcolonial theory developed by Homi Bhabha. Leo T. S. Ching (2001) explains Bhabha's concept of the 'mimic man' as a representation of the colonised who, by virtue of his observation and his attempt to 'mimic' the coloniser's culture and identity, transforms the observer to become the observed and 'partial' representation that displaces identity at its essence (133–5). In other words, the observer returns the coloniser's gaze, and the desire for mimicry becomes a cultural resistance. Within this articulation of colonial (mis)representation, colonial power is displaced, if not altogether reversed.

To return to the photo album scene in *Café Lumière*, Yoko's gaze is more than that of the coloniser. By recognising mimicry as a possible act of subversion, Bhabha's mimic man theory allows us to interpret Yoko's attempt to trace the trails left by Jian as an ambivalent act of mimicry – a possible act of subversion that moves beyond the binary between the coloniser and the colonised. This reflexive moment in the film – when Jian's indexical presence emerges and returns the gaze at Yoko – is a subtle interruption to diegesis on the one hand and, on the other, works as the subversive power of mimicry, creating a third space that enables other positions to emerge. Through the third space, the film shows a rift in history and reflects a confused identity. If Yoko's part shows an ambivalence towards postcolonial temporality, an uncertainty in which she was not able to participate in historical time, it reveals a deeper symptom of a tangled relationship between China, Japan, and Taiwan, evoking what Ching (2001) calls the 'triple consciousness' between the Japanese colonial legacy, residual Chinese identity imposed by the KMT, and the formation of Taiwanese consciousness. This ambivalence is a result of the lack of systematic decolonisation in the dissolution of the Japanese empire – a process that would allow Taiwan to address and confront its colonial relationship with Japanese rule, if it were not for a radical anti-Japanese sentiment propagated by the KMT government after their arrival in 1949.

The problem in Taiwan's postcolonial temporality is that, for Taiwanese people, the issue of which colonial state to identify with is central to the discussion; it is an ongoing process of dealing with historical trauma from which the country has never recovered. On the one hand, the majority believe they are descendants of the Han Chinese, sharing a 5,000-year history with mainland China, regardless of whether it was the KMT establishment or the present Communist China. On the other, the Japanese colonial legacy provides cultural resonances that the Taiwanese do not necessarily find in Chinese culture; they seek comfort in imagining a past and a future to subvert Han-centric positionality.

Tensions between the mainlanders and native Taiwanese have risen since the Republic of China's officials set foot in Taiwan. In its international news section 'The Chinese in Formosa', *The Economist* witnesses the conflicts and recounts the chaos in one of their issues from 1949, exhibiting great sympathy for the Formosans (Taiwan was known historically as Formosa):

> The first days of the new era, however, brought disillusionment. As a Formosan put it in reproach to an American officer: 'You only dropped the atom bomb on the Japanese; you have dropped a Chinese army on us'. General Chen Yi, appointed the first Governor of liberated Formosa, and his officers regarded Formosa as a rich spoil of war which was to compensate this fortunate company for all the losses and hardships of the war years. The Formosans were supposed to be so grateful for being freed from Japanese rule and restored to the bosom of the Chinese nation that they should be ready to place all their worldly goods at the disposal of the warrior heroes from the mainland. They were subjected to an orgy of plunder and extortion, combined with an incompetence and disorder of administration such as in the bad old days of Japanese imperialist tyranny they had never imagined. In their innocence they had supposed that they, themselves, as the people of Formosa, would now have the benefit of the various Japanese state and private concerns which had made Formosa a source of so much profit to Japan. But every lucrative business or job was snapped up by the newcomers, while at the same time the productivity of estates and industrial plants declined owing to mismanagement and looting. (*The Economist* 1949, 196)

Above all, during the transition period, the Taiwanese were not allowed to run their own provincial affairs, and they could not understand why the island was governed by mainland Chinese *for* mainland Chinese, as the Chinese exiles who came with the KMT raided everything the Taiwanese had inherited from the Japanese during the colonial period. Without being pro-Japanese, the bitter sentiments of the Taiwanese towards China had become one of the root causes of the rift between the Formosans and the newcomers. Hou certainly recognises that the ambivalence of his own identity – that of being Chinese in Taiwan – largely informs his filmic creation:

> To me, China is the origin of Taiwan culture. But I do not mean contemporary mainland China, that concrete entity separated politically from Taiwan. When I was young, I was educated in classical Chinese, reading classical masterpieces and classical poetry. Later I liked reading classical martial art novels and classical drama. These Chinese classics have formed the background of my life and the basis for all of my creative works. But classical China is entirely different from contemporary mainland China. (Hou 1998, 2)

Between his lived experience in Taiwan and the consciousness of cultural China (or imagined China), the fact that Hou leaves out residual 'Chinese consciousness' in *Café Lumière* is an effect not just of the spatial distance between China and Taiwan but also of the psychological distance. Indeed, the film uses long shots and an immobile camera to display Yoko and Hajime in the corners of the frame, often on a railway platform or on a bridge, to create the impression that they are – literally and metaphorically – marginalised. In contrast to the very little space the main characters have taken up in the frame, such as in the scene with Hajime, almost unnoticeable on a platform beneath trains criss-crossing on higher ground, what remains is a succession of tableaux vividly realised in cinematic terms. The image of the characters walking in the city marks them as displaced, recalling Michel de Certeau's illustration of an ideal city where walking has its own rhetoric – an extension of the purpose of Baudelaire's *flâneur*. The film shows an absence of emotions, sealed off from all other worlds. Just as *Flowers of Shanghai* (1998) depicts historic China, even though it was not actually filmed in China,[10] what Hou is doing in *Café Lumière* is reimagining and re-enforcing a kind of Japan–Taiwan colonial relationship that was originally suppressed under KMT's rule.

---

[10] Many Anglophone critics consider that Hou epitomises Chinese tradition (or exoticised images of China) in a film like *Flowers of Shanghai*. The film, set in late Qing China, was originally scheduled to be shot in Shanghai. But while an attempt is made to render a *fin-de-siècle* Shanghai based on Eileen Chang's novel, the actual China is absent from the film. Partly because the production company was denied permission by the Chinese authorities to shoot on location, the film was shot entirely in the studio in Taiwan. In return, the shooting conditions contributed to the praise for Hou's languid and seductive cinematography, although a distant (or decolonialised) approach to historical Shanghai is evident.

THE FILMMAKER AS *FLÂNEUR* IN *LE VOYAGE DU BALLON ROUGE*

Another case study of the woman *flâneur* – who walks the city but does not exist in Baudelaire's writing – is *Le Voyage du ballon rouge* (to avoid confusion with the 1956 French film, it is hereafter referred to by its English title, *Flight of the Red Balloon*), a film that transcends the boundary between East and West. It is explicitly an outsider's film, presented through Hou's distinctive lens of perspectives and dislocation. The 2007 release of *Flight of the Red Balloon* would have been surprising enough without the additional fact that the film, inspired by the classic French movie made fifty years earlier, was the work of a Taiwanese filmmaker who had never filmed outside Asia or and who did not speak a word of French. Invited by the Musée d'Orsay to participate in a series of films to celebrate the twentieth anniversary of the establishment, Hou pays tribute to Albert Lamorisse's short film and children's classic, *Le Ballon rouge* (The Red Balloon, 1956). Originally, the invitation was for four world-renowned directors each to shoot a segment of their vision of film, at least in part, inside the museum. The Musée d'Orsay selected the following auteurs: Olivier Assayas of France, Jim Jarmusch of the United States, Raúl Ruiz of Chile, and Hou of Taiwan. This collaborative venture was supposed to launch at the end of 2006; however, only Hou's *Flight of the Red Balloon* was completed in time,[11] and it opened the 60th Cannes Film Festival.

Critics often refer to the film as a remake: J. Hoberman (2008) from the *Village Voice* describes *Flight of the Red Balloon* as a work that was commissioned as a remake by the Musée d'Orsay; Leo Goldsmith (2009) calls it a 'pseudo-remake', while Steve Persall (2008) dismisses it as a dull 'snoozer'. The French publication *AlloCiné* (n.d.) also describes the film as part remake and part homage because Hou is 'an admirer of the [Lamorisse] film', who 'considers [*Le Ballon rouge*] to be extremely realistic, and particularly representative of his time', since the film shows the realities of Lamorisse's childhood. But is it simply a French film remade by a foreign director? This is an important question, especially considering that the filmmaker borrows Lamorisse's iconography as an empty pastiche – a boy, a balloon, a Parisian cityscape – without the postwar context.

Although *Flight of the Red Balloon* is inspired by Lamorisse's film, Hou's reiteration is nothing like the original, except for a big red balloon and a young

---

[11] Olivier Assayas's *L'Heure d'été* (*Summer Hours*) – the film he made in partnership with the Musée d'Orsay which tells the story of a family-owned art collection – was eventually completed and released in 2008. The museum originally commissioned the film, only to pull out of financing it later.

boy wandering through the grey streets of Paris. Consistent with the director's auteur style and languid long takes, the film has a slower rhythm than usual; viewers must patiently wait around for a seemingly uneventful story to unfold. The film begins with a young French boy, Simon, who finds a mysterious red balloon near the entry to a metro station on a street in Paris. After Simon unleashes the balloon, it begins to follow the boy around the city as if it has a life of its own, acting like a sidekick to the lonely young boy. Simon's mother, Suzanne (played by Juliette Binoche), works as a professional puppeteer. When Suzanne is at work, Simon spends most of his time with his nanny, Song Fang (which, by the way, is the actress's actual name), a Chinese student who has come to Paris to study filmmaking. In taking care of Simon, Song is making her own version of the 1956 *Le Ballon rouge*, featuring Simon. From time to time, we see Suzanne navigating personal troubles outside her busy work life, problems such as her irresponsible downstairs tenant or her relationship with Simon's estranged father. Apart from the dysfunctional lives portrayed in Suzanne's claustrophobic apartment, a puppet master from Taiwan comes to visit Suzanne's theatre company. Fascinated by this opportunity, Suzanne asks Song to be an interpreter during his stay. Like many of Hou's previous films, *Flight of the Red Balloon* has a nonchalant approach to life: no exciting or dramatic events ever seem to happen. Yet every mundane detail contributes to a story to which we can all relate. The film ends without closure. Instead, a red balloon drifts into the sky, which is a play on the opposition between the freedom of a floating balloon in the sky and a young child confined in tight city spaces – designated to reflect the ambience of the modern city.

Unlike the US reception, French critics generally responded positively to *Flight of the Red Balloon* and praised the way a foreign director captured everyday Parisian lives in non-conventional film languages. Jean-Luc Douin (2008) from *Le Monde* considers the use of iconic landmarks and the cityscape – such as the Bastille district, the narrow alleyways, the bourgeois bohemian, and the raised metro line – as an outsider looking at the familiar in unfamiliar ways: 'It is a tourist vision, but we must recognise that it also reflects modification of these symbolic images, in a way that shares the same observation from many contemporary French filmmakers.' Vincent Julé (2008) of Écran Large also says the following:

> I have never seen a film which captures the life of Paris so well, but above all the life of Parisians. It's not cliché, it's not a postcard, no, for me who lives in Paris, it's truly Paris – beautiful, grey, everything – and it's a foreign director who arrives at this. (Translated by Nicholas de Villiers)

In the absence of a Parisian postwar context, the film suggests a radical interrogation of the globalised era, manifested through an awkward clash between

Chinese and French cultures. First, let us consider Je Cheol Park's remarks about the transnational aspects of the film:

> [T]ransnational cultural exchanges between China and France appear in the film in a variety of ways: that a Chinese woman works in a French family, that a French woman translates Chinese puppet shows, that a Chinese woman filmmaker makes a remake of a French film (that reflexively refers to Hou's situation), and so forth. (Park 2013, 104)

The Sino-French exchanges are apparent, but Park conflates Taiwanese and Chinese culture into one 'China' in his observation. Park also fails to recognise the subtle nuances and uncomfortable dynamics between Suzanne and her *au pair*, Song. By uncomfortable, I am referring to the overbearing Suzanne, who is 'crass and often angry' in contrast to the quiet, timid and problem-solving Song, whom Flannery Wilson (2014) describes as 'intelligent, talented and interesting': this reflects their unbalanced relationship and, by extension, an awkward clash between Chinese and French culture (93).

In Taiwan, reviews were often more focused on the puppet theatre rehearsal scenes and how this occasionally reminds viewers of the majestic *Puppetmaster* (Lin 2013). The transcultural exchange is evident in two major scenes: when Suzanne rehearses Chinese puppetry in French and when a Taiwanese puppeteer is invited to Paris to perform and act as a consultant. The scenes are self-reflexive in an offhand way, and when juxtaposed with Binoche's eccentric vocalisations for the puppet theatre, this mirrors her character's chaotic domestic life. Incorporating Chinese puppetry – an ostensibly self-conscious meditation on Hou's earlier work – alternatively poses the question of who is the outsider here: is this a film about seeing Parisian life through the eyes of a Taiwanese director, or it is about revisiting and rendering Chinese theatricality through a middle-aged Parisian woman? Aside from recognition of *The Puppetmaster* as emblematic of Taiwanese culture, the French song at the end of the film, 'Tchin Tchin' (sung by Camille Dalmais), is in fact a remastered version of 'The Forgotten Time', a hit folk song by the famous Taiwanese singer Tsai Chin (who starred in two of Edward Yang's films: *Taipei Story*, 1985, and *A Brighter Summer Day*, 1991). Such a cover, along with the intertextual reference to Hou's own film and the inclusion of Song, the Chinese film student, is the director's way of introducing and projecting a Taiwanese/Chinese perspective into the seemingly 'French' film (Lin 2008).

The cultural exchange here is not just about a French woman appropriating Taiwanese puppet shows; it is also about a Chinese woman remaking a French film. In the movie, Song is seen videotaping graffiti stencils in Paris as part of her film project about red balloons (Figure 3.5). The making of

Song's film-within-the-film and her fascination with red balloons are not just narrative devices; they provide viewers with a *mise en abyme* and a reflexive glimpse into an already convoluted world. To speak of reflexivity in film – the awareness of film as a process and not merely as a finished product – allows viewers to imagine the film as a representation of a kind of transnational community characterised by homogeny and otherness. Reflexivity is the inversion of narrative schemas, which allows audiences to reroute their comprehension skills to the visual senses. It forces viewers to utilise their senses

Figure 3.5 *A mural stencil of a red balloon in* Flight of the Red Balloon (2007). *Still frame.* © *Les Films du Lendemain.*

Figure 3.6 *Song Fang showing her video work to Suzanne on a laptop in* Flight of the Red Balloon. *Still frame.* © *Les Films du Lendemain.*

Figure 3.7 *A close-up shot of Song Fang's video work, or the film-within-the-film moment in* Flight of the Red Balloon. *Still frame. © Les Films du Lendemain.*

and memories to understand events, as opposed to narrative interpretation. Reflexivity highlights the cognitive process in an almost untraceable and uninterruptable way, which may include internal awareness of how the shots and sequences are constructed via camera angles, lighting, editing, and so on.

By virtue of the textual elements in *Flight of the Red Balloon*, the sense of alienation and estrangement is amplified by the world we see through Song's lens. Song's videotaping (or documenting) of random images or abandoned red balloons she finds on the street is reflexive not only of the diegetic space but also of the moments of interruption – the disruption of continuity (Figure 3.6). Up to this point, the reflexivity has several complicated layers. The separation between the actor's temporal and spatial relationship with the audience prescribes the differences between onscreen and offscreen action. When Song videotapes Simon and the balloon, or when she stops for a red-balloon stencil on the streets, she is simultaneously scouting locations for the *actual* film outside her diegetic world, and real audiences are watching *in sync* with the filmmaking process (Figure 3.7). The act was never an improvisation; it was premeditated and pre-recorded. It also fuses different viewpoints: are viewers to perceive *Flight of the Red Balloon* through the lens of Song's video camera or through Hou's rendering of a film student's outsider perspective? Michelle Bloom (2016) calls Song Fang's character 'Hou's alter ego' as she is seen remaking *Le Ballon rouge* with her digital camcorder, thereby creating a rich *mise en abyme*. But is it possible that Song is more complicated than a simple stand-in because she is, instead, the embodiment of the objective, mechanical eye? The imagery she captured presents a Paris cityscape, which is an ironic play of the familiar and the strange moments that transcend the diegetic and non-diegetic world. This allows the audience to imagine a kind of transnational community, which is simultaneously local and global, homogenous and heterogeneous.

Flight of the Red Balloon not only reinterprets French culture but also intersects with a variety of self-reflective work, ranging from an internal remake of *Le Ballon rouge* to a visit to the Musée d'Orsay to see the Impressionist painting *Le Ballon* (*The Ball*). During Hou's trip to the Paris museum, the director recalled that the museum was generous when it came to touring its vast collections. At one point, the museum curator demonstrated to Hou and his crew how to hang or take down paintings properly in art galleries. Hou was completely fascinated by the exhibition space: the rooftop, the attic, the transformation from a railway station to a contemporary museum, and the gigantic gold clock in the hallway. But nothing stood out as much as Swiss painter Félix Vallotton's 1899 oil painting *Le Ballon*. This painting, with its pastel colour palette and bird's-eye view of a park, features a child with a yellow hat and white summer shirt running across a broad stretch of ground, contrasted with the mixed shades of the trees, and chasing a dot-like red ball (Figure 3.8). As it happens, Hou did not discover the painting by himself. Since the Musée d'Orsay required that participating directors (then including Assayas and others) shoot at least one scene in the museum grounds, Hou handled the task without hesitation and asked the museum staff 'if they had any Impressionist paintings with red objects, preferably balloons' (Lin 2008).

The painting is the centrepiece of the final moment of the film: a group of schoolchildren gather around it and a teacher is discussing it when one of the children exclaims that the little boy in the painting is 'looking for something … a red balloon!' This scene is reflexive of both the narrative and the technical level; it is a doubling of a boy chasing a red balloon (Figure 3.9), which echoes the literary criticism term *mise en abyme* – the mirror effects of an image within an image. As Lucien Dallenbach (1989) explains, *mise en abyme* is an artistic definition akin to placing a mirror and its reflection in a painting. By exploiting its reflective properties, the use of a mirror is to compensate for the limits of the spectator's vision and to show viewers what usually lies beyond it. If this internal reflection is to be applied to film studies, *mise en abyme* expresses not only a film within a film but also a film being made within a film and the narrative of a film within the film, which does not reduce either aspect to one simplistic view of duplication alone. Given these threefold recognitions, the term is best described in Dallenbach's (1989) words as the manifestation of 'any internal mirror that reflects the whole of the narrative by simple, repeated or "specious" (or paradoxical) duplication' (36).

Figure 3.8 The Balloon *or* Corner of a Park with a Child Playing with a Balloon, *1899. Oil on cardboard on wood, 48 × 61 cm. Artist: Félix Vallotton (1865-1925). Photo: Hervé Lewandowski. © RMN-Grand Palais/Art Resource, NY.*

Figure 3.9 *A scene from* Flight of the Red Balloon, *in which the glass in the picture frame blurs Félix Vallotton's oil painting, causing glare and reflection. Still frame. © Les Films du Lendemain.*

Thirty years later, the term *mise en abyme* resurfaced in the writings of Taiwanese film critics. The original Chinese translation of *mise en abyme* means 'layers in film', but Isabelle Wu (2007) has translated it as the 'complexities' in cinematic expression in order to give it a full-bodied expression – an attempt to avoid the simplistic view of repeated duplication. Adapting the newer translation, Wenchi Lin (2008) agrees that Wu's translation is much more suitable, as it moves away from its original heritage in literary studies, which limits the idea of a mirror image effect to the *nouveau roman*, a type of 1950s French novel that diverged from classical literary genres. Lin further suggests that when applied to film studies in conjunction with the notion of intertextuality, *mise en abyme* enables spectators to recognise and consider the relationship between one visual text and another, assuming the meaning of the visual is not transparent unless mediated in a larger, comparable framework. In *Flight of the Red Balloon*, the protective glass on the painting literally echoes *mise en abyme*. In utilising these visual features, images are often reflected in mirrors or windows, creating doubles of people or objects. In the scene from *Le Ballon*, the glass of the painting reflects images of art patrons passing by that appear to be superimposed on Vallotton's painting. This recognition is in accordance with the characteristics of the fictional *mise en abyme*:

> A combination of the usual properties of iteration and of second-degree utterances, namely the capacity to give the work a strong structure, to underpin its meaning, to provide a kind of internal dialogue and a means whereby the work can interpret itself. (Dallenbach 1989, 55)

When asked about the scene with the Vallotton painting, the director again justified his cinematic techniques in the most pragmatic terms:

> When I decided I wanted to use Vallotton's *Le Ballon* in my picture, I was told that this painting was already wrapped up, ready to be shipped to Japan for an exhibition in Tokyo, because the Japanese loved this painting. After several negotiations, the museum took the painting out to hang it temporarily just for my film shoot. The framing protection had to stay, so the glass reflection was inevitable. People often asked me why I like to use glass and reflection in my films; my answer is that it was simply a result of trying to overcome technical difficulties in a situation like this. (Hou 2008; my translation)

The result is rather artistic and picturesque, with glare and reflection coming from the glass in the picture frame, rendering a poetic overlay of the museum's surroundings. What appear to be duplications in cinematic expression stem from a desire to overcome technical difficulties in the space. And during the process, it becomes an extension of Hou's becalmed visual style. This visual style is simultaneously deliberate and accidental – a unique complexity that communicates a sense of otherness. In this way, what appears to be reflexive of spectral techniques potentially allows viewers to be more aware of film as a process and not merely a finished product encompassing a narrative for viewers to decode.

Conclusion

In mobilising a multifaceted portrayal of life, Hou's filmmaking provides a refreshing perspective that enables spectators to imagine transnational communities to come. Throughout this chapter, I have illustrated that *Flight of the Red Balloon* and *Café Lumière* are rich in intertextuality – from layers of remaking *Le Ballon rouge* to Ozu's cinematic shadow, and from postcolonial history to their reflexive moments. The gaze of these transnational homages at the city would not have been possible without the female *flâneurs*, where a woman's freedom to move about in the city, observing and being observed, is demonstrated in quite literal ways. As I have suggested, the aesthetics of the urban walking experience and the tactics of 'making do' (Song Fong's videotaping and Hou's pragmatic filmmaking) epitomise the complex cultural geometry between Taiwan, Japan, and China. Hou's transnational ventures also effectively call attention to the predicament of art house directors today – that is, it is not so much a director's preference for foreign capital and making films abroad but the lack of funding at home that propels them to find resources elsewhere to sustain their work. Nonetheless, through international co-production and museum funding, Hou's filmmaking style creates a certain transnational imagining and remapping of borders and nations: these films partially escape from their respective textual spaces and intervene on a cross-cultural level, with an ontological time-space for viewers to negotiate between formal, cultural, and thematic similarities and differences. By undertaking a thorough analysis of the films' intertextuality, the relationship between the film and its reflexive layers reveals the cinematic revisiting and reimagining of cultures, fostering an essential transnational viewing experience. As signs of institutional and aesthetic change, the cinematic gaze can begin to consider how films highlight new modes of connection and imagination across the world.

CHAPTER 4

Going West: Tsai Ming-liang at the Louvre and Cinema in the Gallery

Tsai Ming-liang's unique filmmaking has garnered both cinematic and curatorial acclaim. As one of Taiwan cinema's noted art house directors, his work in the last decade has extended from that of feature length to short art films and installations, such as *Your Face* (2018), *Days* (2020),[1] and the *Walker* series (2012–).[2] Prior to his crossing over to the art gallery, Tsai highlights in his films the cinematic echoing and intertextual citation of French New Wave and New German Cinema, particularly that of François Truffaut and Rainer Werner Fassbinder.[3] The connection between French cinema and Tsai's work

---

[1] *Days* (2020) marks Tsai's poignant return to feature filmmaking after his retirement speech in 2013, when he announced at the Venice Film Festival that the film he had in competition, *Stray Dogs*, would be his last. He has since then pivoted to a series of realist short films that fully embodies and embraces the concept of Slow Walk cinema (see following note). The 127-minute running time of *Days* would qualify the film as feature-length, considering where it has been shown (competing for the Golden Bear at the 70th Berlin International Film Festival, winning the jury's Teddy Award for films dealing with LGBTQI+ topics, and having its North America première at the 2020 New York Film Festival online). The meditative quality of *Days*, demonstrating much fewer cuts than the director's previous work and a deliberate choice to offer a subtitle-free dialogue experience, makes it hard to place it into the standard narrative film category, not to mention that it was initially slated to première at the Museum of Modern Art in April 2020 but this was postponed due to the COVID-19 pandemic.

[2] To date, Tsai has made a total of eight experimental short films known as the 'Slow Walk, Long March' series. In this series Lee Kang-sheng is seen walking extremely slowly as the character of Xuanzang, a Buddhist monk known for his pilgrimage from China to India in the seventh century. These films can be best described as featuring no acting, no performance, no emotions, no plotline; one simply observes bodily movement across the screen.

[3] Tsai stated time and again in many interviews his fascination with Truffaut's films. For one example, see Tsai (2011), 'On the Uses and Misuses of Cinema', *Senses of Cinema*, no. 58 (March), n.p.

Figure 4.1 *Lee Kang-sheng falling asleep with the TV on in* What Time Is It There? *(2001). Still frame. © Homegreen Films.*

can be traced back to *What Time Is It There?* (2001, hereafter *What Time*), a film that is said to be haunted by the ghosts of European art films (Martin 2003). In *What Time*, the protagonist, Hsiao-kang (Lee Kang-sheng, Tsai's signature actor), is seen falling asleep (Figure 4.1), in front of a TV playing Truffaut's *Les Quatre Cents Coups* (1959); later, the iconic French New Wave figure Jean-Pierre Léaud – best known for playing Antoine Doinel in Truffaut's films – has a cameo scene at the end of the film. On the festival scene, *What Time* competed for the Palme d'Or at Cannes Film Festival and went on to win twelve awards, including those for best director, best picture, and best cinematography, at festivals worldwide.

Tsai's later films are seen as the ultimate exploration of pure cinematic form, a departure from his early focus on postcolonial Taipei and its social critique.[4] Such is the hallmark status of *Visage* (2009), part of the Louvre's

---

[4] I am suggesting a shift of focus but do not necessarily mean that there is an absence of social critique in his later works, such as *Stray Dogs* (2013). This observation is made in relation to Tsai's trajectory of filmmaking. For instance, both his first film, *Rebels of the Neon God* (1992), and the documentary he made four years later reflect

first collection of the moving image. The all-star cast of *Visage* includes Jean-Pierre Léaud, Fanny Ardant, Jeanne Moreau, and Laetitia Casta, and the film certainly epitomises the highest form of recognition Tsai received in France. When asked by Henri Loyrette, Louvre director at the time, 'What are you planning to film?', Tsai's initial response was: 'I wanted the film to feature Jean-Pierre Léaud and Lee Kang-sheng, and they will meet in the museum's grounds' (Tsai 2010a). Tsai has never shied away from his obsession with Lee as his muse, nor from his admiration for Truffaut's films. For Tsai, shooting a project like *Visage* was not only an opportunity to pay tribute to Truffaut, but also an attempt to reverse the fading interest in the aging Jean-Pierre Léaud. Léaud, known as the poster boy for the French New Wave that began with *Les Quatre Cents Coups*, went on to reprise similar roles in six of Truffaut's films that span a period of twenty years, illustrating the great rapport that developed between director and actor. Tsai did not choose Léaud because of his stature; he chose him because he wanted to show his aging side, and by extension the perpetuity of the French New Wave, in a highly reflexive and referential film.

If *Visage* illustrates a move to bring filmmaking practices and the museum space closer, the importance of approaching Tsai Ming-liang as a transnational auteur hinges on the possibility of a critique of the intricacies between exhibition practices and the question of '*Qu'est-ce que le cinéma?*' in today's ever-changing multimedia environments. Additionally, for a film to be commissioned by the Louvre represents film festivals' consequential influence on fostering international cinephilia because of the role they play in helping a film transition from local production to the global art market. Tsai's making of *Visage* is not coincidental; nor is it an occasional exploration of alternative viewing conditions in art galleries and the museum space. Instead, *Visage* should be viewed as a continual exploration of the many themes from Tsai's body of work, particularly his love for the movie theatre. Chiang Ling-ching (2012) argues that Tsai is to date the only film director in Taiwan who has translated his work into installations that were exclusive to art galleries, while continuing to produce feature films for traditional theatrical release. The reason that Tsai stands out from other media artists is because he enters the art gallery as a film auteur, which allows the director to transplant his signature

---

an immediate concern with AIDS in Taiwan. Gradually, Tsai's films have moved toward an elaborate treatment of disintegrated times, spaces, and human relationships; as Wen Tian-Xiang (2002) suggests, the films '[dig] deeply into modern subjectivity almost without any sense of historicity' (9). See Wen Tian-Xiang (2002), Guangying dingge: Tsai Ming-liang de xinling changyu [Freeze-frame in Light and Shadow: The Spiritual Site of Tsai Ming-liang] (Taipei: Hengxing).

slow style – long shots and long takes – to a new exhibition space (Chiang 2012, 55). Tiago de Luca (2016) also points out that 'it is striking that many filmmakers who have crossed over to art galleries in recent years are often placed under the slow cinema umbrella, and that they often recycle their own cinematic works' (35). Specifically, Tsai's slow style – among other filmmakers in this group such as Tarr, Kiarostami, Lav Diaz, and Weerasethakul – allows a 'remarkably smooth transition to the art gallery and the museum as more and more directors associated with the trend make films and installations for these spaces', when the 'international film festival has been over the past two decades the institutional and culture home of slow cinema' (de Luca 2016, 24–35).

Tsai Ming-liang's ventures into new exhibition spaces might be more fruitfully understood as a metareflection on the triangular relationship between his theatre experience, French cinephilia, and cinema in the gallery. If we look at his earlier film and video installation work, such as *It's a Dream* (2007), Tsai's cinematic creations are better understood if situated in the intersection between moving images and alternative viewing experiences, and between the global and regional film cultures present at this specific theatre-within-a-gallery site. While Tsai's slow film aesthetics can be traced in relation to his prior theatre practice, his installations and films in the gallery are grounded in his belief that cinema needs to be resurrected in the museum. The interrelations between Tsai's video installation and feature films show that they originate from, and are still part of, a love for cinema. Susan Sontag (1996) has put it poetically: 'If cinephilia is dead, then movies are dead too . . . If cinema can be resurrected, it will only be through the birth of a new kind of cine-love.' As film viewing today becomes more and more dispersed and individualised, with the traditional movie-going experience interrupted by digital streaming, Tsai's move to the museum space exemplifies a possibility for the future of cinema: it may lose its exclusivity of the collective experience in the movie theatre, yet still privileges a certain architectural set-up there.

The intention here is to conduct a broader enquiry into the relationship between Tsai's fascination with cinema and his mourning for the movie-going experience as he moves into the realm of film and video installation. In what follows, a start is made by tracing the key events that have pushed Tsai toward crossing over to art galleries and by situating them in a transnational context. The chapter then explores the ways that French cinephiles advocated for his film styles and helped to situate him in the global art market. Through Roland Barthes's critique of the pre-hypnotic cinematic experience, the chapter proceeds to demonstrate how the experimental conditions of *It's a Dream* and *Visage* are Tsai's attempt to enter into a dialogue with the gallery space, and the possibilities of alternative exhibition. To conclude, I explore how these exhibitions are not simply about introducing cinema into the gallery. Rather, they constitute a process of thinking about how an alternative exhibition space can challenge our habitual viewing of cinema.

JOURNEY TO THE MUSEUM

If we were to trace the key moments of Tsai Ming-liang's filmmaking career, the 22-minute short *The Skywalk Is Gone* (2002) stands as a prelude to the filmmaker's subsequent explorations between art cinema and gallery space. This is the director's first attempt at a non-documentary short-length film and is also his first French-commissioned work. As an epilogue to *What Time*, the film presents two parallel worlds: a young woman wandering around in Taipei, the modern, bustling capital of Taiwan, in search of a skywalk over a busy intersection that she once walked on; and at a casting session, a young man is being asked to strip all his clothes off for a role in a pornographic film. The young man's story is a prelude to one of the most controversial (and yet most commercially successful) films Tsai has ever shot in his career to date – *The Wayward Cloud* (2005). *The Skywalk Is Gone* stems from a real-life event when a skywalk was torn down – a long-term landmark bridging the iconic Shin Kong Mitsukoshi department store and Taipei's central station. If the skywalk in *What Time* was a place of memory, the short film documented the disappearance of landmarks as the city plans to modernise existing sites. This film, like many of Tsai's subsequent ones after *The Hole* (1998), was assisted by foreign funding. Commissioned by Le Fresnoy, a public centre for the arts in northern France that had exhibited many important contemporary art and experimental films, including works by Bill Viola and Michael Snow, *The Skywalk Is Gone* advanced Tsai to join the ranks of other global filmmakers creating gallery or installation versions of their cinematic works.

Tsai's first hands-on experience with and crossover to art installation came around 2007, when the Cannes Film Festival was wanting to commemorate its sixtieth anniversary. Gilles Jacob, festival president until 2014, commissioned a group of thirty-three well-known international directors to make a 3-minute film each about their experiences with the movie theatre. Each approached the interpretation of this assignment very differently, but most pieces reflected the emotional and cognitive effects in film viewing conditions. Many include a film-within-a film or question the death of cinema (de Villiers 2007), while others, like Tsai, draw on their own childhood memories of grand movie theatres. This resulted in Tsai's *It's a Dream*; shot in an abandoned theatre in Kuala Lumpur, this 3-minute short invokes the filmmaker's own fascination with and fetishisation of the theatre, the auditorium chairs, and the floating dust in the cone of light from the projector. One of the most memorable scenes is when a family is sharing and eating durian fruit, an East Asian tropical delicacy, and a woman offers pears on a skewer to the man sitting in the row behind her, all in a silent moment of contact, typical of Tsai's oeuvre.

Shortly after *It's a Dream* premièred in Cannes, the film travelled to Italy's Venice Biennale, where Tsai participated in a group exhibition organised by Taipei Fine Arts Museum of Taiwan at the regional pavilion. This work featured the extended 22-minute version (as well as the Cannes 3-minute short), and the original seats that were torn from the abandoned theatre were shipped to Venice as part of the installation. The red leather theatre chairs play a major role rather than being merely backdrop 'seating': audiences were able to (re)create their own unique viewing experience in the pavilion. Tsai cannot hide his fondness for these seats when he describes them as not just any normal seats, but distinctive in style; they are reusable and, as the spectator sits on one of them to watch the footage he has made, 'you are *in* my work,' as he says to the audience (Tsai 2011).

The significance of *It's a Dream* is that it mobilises Tsai's status as both a filmmaker and an artist who is making considerable inroads into the gallery scene while continuing to produce films for traditional theatrical release. When this work was later acquired by Taipei Fine Arts Museum as the first

Figure 4.2 *Installation view of Tsai Ming-liang's* It's a Dream, *2007, colour, sound; 21 min 54 sec. The suite shown here is part of the exhibition* Intersecting Vectors – Experimental Projects *at Taipei Fine Arts Museum, 2013. © TFAM Collection, Taipei.*

film to be part of its permanent collection (Figure 4.2), Tsai said in an interview with Noah Buchan from the *Taipei Times*,

> It's the first time that I sold a video installation to a museum and this is the first time for a Taiwanese museum to buy a film as part of its collection. The Louvre was the first in the world to collect film. These events signal that we are now looking at film as a form of art. (Tsai 2010b)

He goes on to say that 'gradually, my movies find a home, and that is the museum' (Tsai 2010b). For Tsai, there is evidently a move toward the gallery space, as an attempt to bridge the gap between artists and filmmakers. In 2011, Tsai turned a boiler room in a former factory in Taipei into an exhibition space for a video work titled 'The Theatre in the Boiler Room: Art Installation'. In this exhibition, the filmmaker recycled auditorium seats and a large clock (a recurring motif in his films) that had been abandoned by the historical Taipei City Hall. There is always an agenda behind Tsai's works, whether they are cinematic or video art; he admits they are all 'a conscious act of rebellion against the way cinema is perceived in today's society' (Vagenas 2013). One of his concerns is that historic movie theatres are gradually disappearing and becoming largely forgotten, and he is very much invested in the idea of using cinematic means to preserve time, history, and the artefacts and experience of movie-going. But the question remains: what are some of the implications of his shift in practice?

Tsai Ming-liang's turn to the gallery does not necessarily mean leaving the studio; rather, it should be seen as a creative move toward expanding the format of cinema. In a talk Tsai delivered at National Central University in Taiwan, the filmmaker argued that, although auteur cinema had existed in Taiwan for about twenty-five years, 'The Taiwan New Wave did not really succeed in creating a large cinephilic audience with a distinguished taste and artistic sense' (Tsai 2011). What he is really implying is that there is always a need to be fully committed to creating films that challenge mainstream audiences and spectators. While film is essentially a visual art, audiences do not usually expect to have to go to a museum or gallery to see it – it has been situated in a theatrical setting since the nickelodeon era. Cinema, since its invention, has been placed in a darkened space, in which audiences are seated according to a fixed spatial arrangement of screen, chairs, and projector. Commercial or artistic, mainstream or experimental, film screenings are likely to be equipped with a projector, even for visual artists such as painters, sculptors, and photographers who work outside the film industry. When the German-born sculptor Isa Genzken made a short film, *Two Women in Combat* (Zwei Frauen im Gefecht), in 1972, for example, she insisted that it had to be shown in a standard cinema and not in a museum space. In fact, there has never been a shortage of pioneers who experimented with moving images in the gallery space – Andy Warhol, Nam

June Paik, Jonas Mekas, Valie Export, Martha Rosler, Barbara Hammer, and Stan Douglas, to name but a few. And not to be forgotten, Alexander Sokurov's *Russian Ark* (2001) is one of the most memorable feature-length films to be commissioned by a museum. Shot entirely behind the gates of the Hermitage Museum in St Petersburg, this film features what was at one point the longest single, uninterrupted long take ever produced in the history of cinema.[5] While Tsai's move to make films for art galleries may not be ground-breaking, what distinguishes him are the cinematic and theatrical dimensions to his work.

From the Local Theatre to the Global Stage

Tsai Ming-liang's film aesthetics can be traced in relation to his prior theatre practice. In fact, there is a mutual borrowing between the two media. Having moved from a small village in Malaysia to Taiwan in the early 1980s, Tsai spent his early career (1982–7) exercising his creativity in experimental theatre. Tsai's first stage work was very cinematic: *Instant Fried Sauce Noodles* (*sus shi zha jiang mian*, 1981) was about a boy who loves films so much that he spends all of his money on film festival tickets and dreams about cinema at night. On stage, he projected classic movies by refilming them with an 8 mm camera. The filmmaker himself acknowledges the theatrical presence in his films. In an interview with Shelly Kraicer, Tsai says:

> [W]hen I started to make films I found myself pretty much influenced by the stage. It's the long concept of space and time, and the stationary camera. The latter also had something to do with the locations I used. Usually I film in a small room, and as you know there is very limited space for me to move the camera around. On the other hand, if a character is moving outside in a larger space, the camera of course will follow him. So whether the camera moves or does not move has something to do with the characters. In that sense, I feel a kind of freedom. (Kraicer 2000, 583–4)

Tsai's words pinpoint for us his distinct spectatorial positioning in his cinematography, rooted in the legacy of theatre. This dimension of performance can also be credited to the concept of 'living theatre', a style that was later adopted by Tsai for use in his televisual and filmic work. Living theatre refers to a personal attitude in acting that engages the emotions and provokes reactions from the audience. Because this kind of unconventional acting is not grounded in technical competence but rather in personal emotions based on individuals' life experiences, anyone can be an actor playing out his or her

---

[5] This record has been surpassed by Shahram Mokri's *Fish and Cat* (2013), a 134-minute uninterrupted long take.

own everyday life. At the same time, the actor's bodily movement knowingly interacts with and reacts to its surroundings.

Tsai's experience in writing and directing avant-garde theatre plays certainly helped shaped his film aesthetics. *The Hole*, for example, continues the thematic and formal aesthetics of his one-man stage play, *A Wardrobe in the Room (fang jian li de yi gui*, 1983). Produced, directed, and acted by Tsai himself alone, this play is about a character who talks on the phone to his long-distance partner while an invisible man in the wardrobe quietly listens to the phone conversation. Interestingly enough, when Yang Kuei-mei's character in *The Hole* talks on the phone to an imagined lover, this plot device parallels Tsai's one-man theatre; meanwhile, the extreme isolation on stage is also seen in Lee Kang-sheng's solitary existence in the final spotlit scene, created by the hole (Bao 2007, 143). It is worth noting that this kind of acting – non-professional, personal, and monotonous, which is emblematic of Lee's style, was once 'too slow and boring' for Tsai (2011) when they first started working together on *Rebels of the Neon God* (1992). Although Tsai's earlier stage works were often unpolished, his minimalist approach set the tone and predicated the potential for making modernist cinema. The way he managed the tension on stage and off stage affected his future practice in filmmaking. Participating in the modern theatre movement was an integral part of his experience, but his style had not yet been fully explored until he received an opportunity to direct his first feature-length drama, *All the Corners of the World (hai jiao tian ya*, 1989), for public television.

Between 1989 and 1991, or the 'television era' for Tsai, the director was able to engage in making direct-to-TV films after spending some time writing scripts and teaching theatre classes on the side. Tsai's work from this period can be characterised as an intensified social critique, especially when he chose to represent the struggling working class, instead of the nostalgic romanticisation of the image of China for which mainstream directors were grasping at the time. Tsai's sentiments toward teenagers' emotional distress were also incomparable with those of his peers. In 1991, when Tsai was given an assignment to shoot *Boys (xiao hai)*, he met Lee Kang-sheng, then only a teenager, at a video game arcade for the first time. Tsai immediately wrote a screenplay for Lee and proceed to direct his first feature film, even though he was well aware that Lee had never had any professional training or acting experience. This was *Rebels of the Neon God*, a film about teenage rebellion and rivalry, featuring a triangular relationship. The film went on to win a Bronze prize at Tokyo International Film Festival in 1993, and first premièred in Europe at the 43rd Berlin International Film Festival, although it was entered as a film coming from Taiwan, China.

It is not surprising that Tsai Ming-liang burst on to the film scene with a piece whose translated English title alluded to Nicholas Ray's troubled-youth picture *Rebel Without a Cause* (1955). Ray, being one of the central Hollywood figures of the 1950s, was highly influential for young French film critics such as Godard and Truffaut, who sought to revolutionise cinematic languages in their writings and with the French New Wave movement. Consequently, Tsai's authorial voice also benefits from a long cultivation of the unique French cinephilia tradition. The recent discussions on slow cinema provide an opportunity to raise some important but under-explored questions relating to international cinephilia and Tsai Ming-liang's films. I am not suggesting here, however, that slow cinema equates to French cinephilia. My intention is to acknowledge this approach in providing more nuanced insights into the intersections of Tsai's filmmaking style, including questions around slow style and the made-for-festivals films, as well as their imbricated relationship.

Emerging at a moment when technology threatens to obliterate film's materiality, slow cinema is characterised by its minimalism and slow tempo. This cinematic phenomenon is termed 'slow' because it often takes too long for the action to happen, not because of an absence of action. As a resistance to what Deleuze termed 'the movement-image', the viewing process involves 'a trope of waiting that may, for some spectators, become a source of boredom' (Lim 2014, 16). This 'boredom' lies in the technical use of the static long take, open ending, near-absent dialogue, and thematic tropes of the now almost clichéd constituents of the postwar art film: 'alienation, spiritual malaise, social isolation, aimlessness and drift, and failed communication' (Gronstad 2016, 276). In the last decade, slow cinema has emerged as a critical term that is not just connected with a group of artistic directors, but also expanded to programming events such as the AV Festival *As Slow as Possible* in 2012, the very first Slow Short Film Festival in 2017 (both in Britain), and a new video-on-demand platform called Tao Films[6] that is solely dedicated to previously undistributed slow cinema from around the world.

In Taiwan, Tsai's film aesthetics – the unbearably long take, static camera, minimal dialogue, and incomprehensible storylines – have bewildered viewers and received both rave reviews and strong criticism. Because of the lack of action and slow tempo, his works were perceived as 'box office poison' by local audiences. What changed this local perception was the recognition that Tsai's films began to receive at international film festivals in the 1990s, particularly at Cannes, Venice, and Berlin. Domestic film critics, festival-goers, and cineastes[7]

---

[6] Sadly, this service is currently at a hiatus. It ran from 1 January 2017 to 1 January 2020.

[7] Here I refer to a group of domestic film critics who employed literary influences and Western-infused theories to defend Taiwan New Cinema, including Peggy Hsiung-ping Chiao (film scholar and critic), Edmond Wong (director of Taipei Film Archive), Hsiao Yeh (novelist, writer, and producer at Central Motion Picture), and Alphonso Youth Leigh (film critic and journalist).

often find themselves compelled to invoke the names of European auteurs as the lens through which to validate Taiwan New Cinema – Truffaut, Godard, Resnais, and Antonioni, to name just a few. European critics were also quick to claim their approval after Taiwan New Cinema made significant inroads into 'A-list' festivals in Europe. Olivier Assayas (1984) of *Cahiers du Cinéma* even wrote that the French New Wave had been resurrected in Taiwan, thereby designating Europe as the origin of the global new wave phenomenon.

Being associated with *both* the French New Wave and the Taiwan New Wave thus integrated Tsai into the vocabulary of critics and scholars, who subsequently marked him out as and measured him against other New Wave directors. For example, Olivier Nicklaus (1998) was probably one of the first to compare Tsai to Truffaut and to write about his auteur potential after viewing *Rebels of the Neon God*, about which he commented, 'Lee Kang-sheng is to Tsai Ming-liang what Jean-Pierre Léaud was to François Truffaut.'[8] Guillaume Malaurie (1998) in *L'Express* referred to Tsai's pessimistic approach and rich metaphors of homosexuality rendered in long sequences as 'néo-Antonioniesque' (resembling Antonioni).[9] Some compared the performances: in describing the last scene in *Vive l'amour* (1994), Serge Kaganski (1995) wrote: 'At the end [of the film], when the girl can no longer refrain from sobbing, it reminds me of Jeanne Moreau in *La Nuit* (1961).' For Noel Herpe (1995, 25), certain moments in *Vive l'amour* reminded him not only of Robert Bresson's

---

[8] Olivier Nicklaus (1998): 'On retrouve les obsessions du cinéaste : famille sclérosante, appartement vide et inondé. De film en film, on reconnaît les mêmes acteurs, en particulier [Kang-sheng Lee], qui est à Tsai Ming-liang ce que Jean-Pierre Léaud était à François Truffaut. Une référence' [We noticed the filmmaker's obsessions: toxic families and empty and flooded apartments. From film to film, we recognise the same group of actors, particularly Kang-sheng Lee, who is, for your reference, to Tsai Ming-liang what Jean-Pierre Léaud was to François Truffaut]. *La Croix* (France), 25 March; my translation.

[9] Guillaume Malaurie (1998): 'Tsai Ming-liang autopsie, au fil d'ellipses et de hors-champs signifiants, une jeunesse insoumise et pessimiste. Et égrène solitude, incommunicabilité, (homo)sexualité en de longs plans-séquences riches en métaphores (. . .) Parcouru de cercles d'attirances, de répulsions et de sentiments dévastés, le style néo-antonioniesque de Tsai Ming-liang s'imposait déjà en 1992 et en imposait. Il s'est depuis, amplement confirmé' [Tsai Ming-liang dissects, through narrative ellipsis and off-screen significance, rebellious and pessimistic youths. Each long take is rich in metaphors that shed light on solitude, uncommunicativeness and (homo)sexuality. Weaved in the movement of attraction, repulsion and devastating feelings, Tsai Ming-liang's neo-Antonioni style was already imposing itself since his 1992 debut film and continued to be impressive in his subsequent filmmaking]. *L'Express* (France), 26 March; my translation.

films, but also of novels by Julien Green (an American novelist who wrote primarily in French).[10] French critics also liked to discuss some of the recurring themes and philosophical concerns in Tsai's films, such as the Deleuzian *durée* (duration), death, nostalgia, loneliness, emptiness, sleep, meditation, and silence. The most frequent and immediate response to Tsai's *c'est long, très long* take is that it works as a stand-in for the director's pessimistic look at the vanishing future of cinema: it is dark, ghostly, painful, and desperate (Morice 2004).[11] Without the outreach of festivals and the attention to aesthetic qualities and motifs that are articulated and circulated by curators, film reviewers, journalists, and scholars, Tsai's films would not have found a wider international audience.

Tsai Ming-liang is one of the few Taiwanese filmmakers who have continued to achieve international recognition in recent years. (At the time of writing, Tsai had just won the Teddy Award – the official queer prize at the Berlinale, as the Berlin International Film Festival is commonly known – for his latest film *Days*, the third film from Taiwan to win the award after Zero/ Mei Ling Chou for *Spider Lilies* and Huang Hui-chen for her documentary *Small Talk*.) It is impossible to overlook how the international festival circuit has smoothed the growth path to icon status by providing Tsai with the opportunity to receive subsequent endorsements through awards, critical acclaim, and various forms of media exposure. Suffice to say, the international visibility of his films had led to the articulation and discussion of themes and visual styles in his work. These stylistic and thematic traits qualified him for status as an auteur and set up a collection of qualities anticipating his next film. In this respect, film festivals provide films with a set of perceived qualities that are otherwise unavailable outside those networks of exhibition. The beneficial French connection and festival conditions have thus contributed to the evolving and historically unique conceptions of Tsai Ming-liang's films.

Tsai Ming-liang's Movie Theatre

For Tsai, cinema is always nostalgic and works as autobiographical meditation. As he attempts to present a collective memory of the golden age of cinema through his work, the interrelations among the selected set of Tsai's films and video installations, from *What Time* to *It's a Dream*, present an intriguing point of entry into the peculiar dimension of Tsai's artistic practice: that of

---

[10] Noel Herpe, 'Vive l'amour, l'enfer du même', *Positif* no. 410 (April 1995): 25.

[11] Jacques Morice (2004): 'c'est d'un pessimisme glaçant quant à l'avenir du cinéma . . . obscure et fantomatique' [There is a chilling pessimism about the future of cinema . . . obscure and ghostly]. *Télérama* (France), 21 July; my translation.

the cinematic apparatus. In their chronological trajectory, the recurring theme that binds Tsai's films together is his love for the movie theatre. Equally, a reference to silent cinema and the movie theatre marks the postcolonial and modern time lag between East and West. In *What Time*, Hsiao-Kang, who sells watches on the streets of Taipei, wanders into an old movie theatre, steals a clock from the corridor, and sneaks into the auditorium, where he attempts to reset the clock to Paris time – as he has been doing, bizarrely, throughout the film. Hsiao-Kang's scheme is sabotaged by a dumpy man who follows him into the theatre and snatches the clock from him (Figure 4.3); he is lured into the men's toilets, only to find the strange man standing naked in an open stall, with the stolen oversized clock covering his crotch area. Not only is the analogue clock placed in the groin, but its second hand moves up and down, where the man's erect penis should have been, making an obvious pass at Hsiao-Kang. It is humorous, camp, and queer, all at the same time. In another scene, Hsiao-Kang is seen drinking a bottle of red wine (a way of bringing himself closer to French culture) on a rooftop; he climbs on to the clock tower, attempting to adjust the clock hands in his extended grip. Hsiao-Kang is thus performing a very Harold Lloyd-esque stunt, by which I mean it is a postcolonial reference to the famous clock tower scene in *Safety Last!* (1923) when Lloyd grabs the hands of a clock and can barely hang on. Here, this is not merely an intertextual reference to a film from the older silent period, but also, through the reimagining and queering of time, a reflection of a kind of metadialogue between East and West about the modernity gap.

Figure 4.3 *The man who steals Hsiao-Kang's clock in* What Time Is It There? *(2001). Still frame.* © *Homegreen Films.*

The intersection of time and space is further explored in Tsai's next feature film, *Goodbye, Dragon Inn* (hereafter *Goodbye*), a film that consists of shots and long takes of corridors, dark rooms, and toilet stalls in the soon-to-be-demolished Fu-ho Grand Theatre – the same movie theatre seen in *What Time*. The opening scenes of *Goodbye*, like the title, pay homage to a classic Chinese *wuxia*[12] film: King Hu's *Dragon Inn* (1967). This is done by intercutting and juxtaposing the illuminated screen in front with the darkened theatre, red auditorium chairs, and a crowd of spectators' heads, in reflexivity of the conditions of cinematic viewing. Anyone who is an aficionado of Tsai's works would immediately spot his cameo appearance (along with critic Alphonso Youth Leigh) as their heads are seen among the audience watching *Dragon Inn*. Alternating between screen and spectator, the projection of King Hu's film runs through the entire length of *Goodbye*, with the offscreen characters drifting around the theatre like ghosts. By using converging and colliding martial arts films from the glory days of Taiwan cinema, *Goodbye* is really saying goodbye to the golden age of Chinese film.

If the example of *Goodbye* highlights both the conditions of film projection and the film itself as a text, then the reuse of theatre chairs in *It's a Dream* demonstrates the traces and extension of 'haunted cinema'. The particularity of this installation is not just the memory of cinema but the space the seats inhabit. The way the seats are set up bears little resemblance to typical theatre seating. Instead, the red cloth chairs are placed diagonally, with no rows lined up parallel to the screen or to each other; the seats are intentionally arranged to intersect with each other, disrupting the customary sense of viewing. As the director declared, the audience is participating in his work. When this film is placed in the white gallery space rather than the black movie theatre, the viewing experience is transformed from the darkness of the cinema that Barthes (1986) proposed in 'Leaving a Movie Theatre' to art appreciation in a white cube. Notably, when watching a film in a theatre, one is less able to move about or leave in the middle of the screening, contrary to the flexibility one would have in an art gallery because it is situated in a (seemingly) open space. In addition, the constant looping of the film in a gallery removes the exclusive regulated relationship a theatre screening would have with time and space.

---

[12] *Wuxia pian*, or swordplay films, are Chinese martial arts films (but different from *kung fu*), and were especially popular in the 1970s and the 1980s in Taiwan, Singapore, Malaysia and Thailand. Influenced by Western and Japanese samurai films, they often feature chivalrous heroes and women warriors cruising in the fictional world called *jiang hu* (literally translated as rivers and lakes): the wild and bohemian underworld of assassins, thieves, gangs and fighters where courts of laws are either dysfunctional or almost non-existent.

Art patrons enjoy the non-exclusiveness of the screening in that they may enter, leave, and re-enter the viewing at their convenience. In this respect, while *Goodbye* proclaims the death (or memory) of cinema, the installation of the theatre seats announces the resurrection of cinema. As Andrew V. Uroskie (2011) notes, in thinking about the postwar emergence of cinema in the gallery space as expanded cinema,

> It is not a question of simply introducing cinema into the gallery situation. Rather, it was a process of thinking how the temporality and kineticism of the moving image might be divorced from its habitual situation within [the] commercial theatrical project. (35)

This is not to say that all work placed in the gallery space is not theatrical, or that any work placed in a movie theatre should not be considered art. The point here is the emergence of a new institutional situation for moving images, one divorced from the theatrical viewing of cinema, providing an opportunity to reapproach cinema in this conflict situation.

While the spectatorial experience of *It's a Dream* takes place in a mock theatre space, the deliberate disorientation of cinema viewing implies a more precise construction of the spectator as a conscious dreamer. The installation is composed of two elements that cannot be separated: the film on the screen and the chairs taken from a 'dead' cinema. Similarly, the cinematic apparatus is a totality of what constitutes the viewing situations by way of: first, the film itself; second, the way moving images are constructed (cinematic language and editing techniques); third, the conditions of film projection; and fourth, the conscious as well as unconscious perceptual process of spectatorship (Stam et al. 1992, 145). Tsai Ming-liang is deploying the concept of interpellation when he asserts that you, as the spectator, are *in* his work because, by sitting on chairs that are both in the work and outside of it, on screen as an imprint and off screen as actuality, the spectator is in a space watching a space that no longer exists, mutually reinforcing the spectator as always already the subject. When one sits on the chair watching the same chairs on screen, not only does it provide a ruptured time-space, but also, because of the particular way the chairs are placed, one can spend time observing one's neighbours and let other art patrons block or disturb one's view. Without the blackness of the movie theatre and the self-regulating courtesy to others that make the spectator's entry into a dream state a smoother transition, Tsai purposefully situates the spectator to be fully aware of themselves, of the viewing experience, and of the existence of neighbours interfering with that experience. While the original spatio-temporality of the Malaysian movie theatre has entered into the cinematic space, the spectators' active making use of the *real* space is also a reconstruction and resurrection of the cinema. 'It sounds like a contradiction,' Tsai says, 'but movies need to leave today's theatres in order to be resurrected' (Tsai 2010b, 13).

AT HOME AT THE MUSEUM

When the spectator sits on the chair that is 'borrowed' from the past, stripped from a foreign theatre, and stretched out away from the onscreen space, the totality of this viewing experience conjures rich possibilities for viewers to explore their own memories of cinema. Similarly, *Visage* is also about leaving the movie theatre and engages in a 'metacinematic cruising' of memory and nostalgia (de Villiers 2008). *Visage* is Tsai Ming-liang's ninth feature film and is not his first transnational production between Taiwan and France. His fourth feature, *The Hole*, was commissioned by French production company Haut et Court and the European television channel La Sept-Arte as part of their *fin de millénaire* series *2000 Vu Par* (as a result, the film exists in two cuts: a 95-minute feature film and a 60-minute television version). Tsai's eighth film, *I Don't Want to Sleep Alone* (2006), was financed as part of the New Crowned Hope project, established by American theatre director Peter Sellars to celebrate the 250th anniversary of Mozart's birth, and was loosely based on the story of *The Magic Flute* (*Die Zauberflöte*). If these cross-cultural productions predicated Tsai's working with the Louvre, it is also worth noting that instead of presenting the glamorous side of the museum, Tsai has his eyes set on its secret chambers, dusty shafts, and grimy underground tunnels. The film centres on a Taiwanese director, Hsiao-Kang, attempting to shoot a film in the Louvre's grounds. The film-within-a-film is based on the story of Salome, the stepdaughter of Herod, who demanded the head of John the Baptist. Like many of Tsai's previous films, *Visage* deals with alienated people wandering around in an empty museum. The film also paints a vague, puzzling, but aesthetically pleasing picture that bears the least sense of narrative of all of Tsai's films.[13]

---

[13] Michelle Bloom has already provided a detailed intertextual reading of *Visage* and Sino-French culture, invoking Truffaut's films, Oscar Wilde's *Salomé*, 1940s Shanghai music, and Leonardo da Vinci's painting of *St John the Baptist*. Because of limited space in this chapter I will not repeat the arguments here. My attention, however, is attracted by the façade of space within the film and by the exhibition practice. See Michelle Bloom (2011), 'The Intertextuality of Tsai Ming-liang's Sinofrench Film, Face', *Journal of Chinese Cinemas* 5, no. 2: 103-21. For an extended reading of *Visage*, also see my (2022) article, '*Visage* (2009): That Obscure Face of the Muses', in the anthology *32 New Takes on Taiwan Cinema*, edited by Emilie Yueh-yu Yeh, Darrell William Davis, and Wenchi Lin 346–59 (Ann Arbor: University of Michigan Press).

While Tsai attempts to portray many faces with cinema, the Louvre is the most important façade the director tries to visualise. Like the characters who wander in this labyrinth, struggling to find an exit, the film invites its onlooker to shuttle between narrow corridors, prowl in goods lifts, and check out a web of underground tunnels. While the film title literally translates as *face*, audiences are not really looking at the appearance of things but rather exploring the façade of the museum buildings that operate like organisms. Interestingly enough, among the vast collections and galleries, Tsai opted to show only the most famous Grand Gallery at the end, where Léaud climbed out of a hole in the Louvre wall below a Leonardo da Vinci painting of *St John the Baptist*. *Visage* makes sense between what is shown and the gaps between the scenes, trying to break through the isolation and parallel worlds. In other words, the film's rich symbolism is rendered in the physical space and in the actors' reactions to the unseen fears and urges surrounding them. *Visage* in some ways echoes *Goodbye*, which is filled with metaphors of ghosts and living people. There is one scene with Jeanne Moreau and Fanny Ardant, who appear out of nowhere and occupy the famous, luxurious oval dinner table in a room in Napoleon III's apartments, while later the same composition is repeated but with the chairs empty, as if their occupants had simply vanished like ghosts. *Visage* is also a very referential film, containing nods to other filmmakers as if trying to recover its past lives. At one point in the story Lee Kang-sheng is outside with Léaud and a little bird, and Léaud says about the bird: 'Titi is a great director.' The conversation is followed by exchanges of directors' names: Pasolini, Fellini, Antonioni, Orson Welles, Keaton, F. W. Murnau, Truffaut, Carl Theodor Dreyer, Andrei Tarkovsky, and Kenji Mizoguchi. In *Visage*'s final segment, ghosts and fantasies manifest for a moment as the characters perceive each other: Salome comes to kill Lee in a silent, seductive dance; Ardant comforts Léaud as they look into the mirror and tells him he will be okay; the model shuts off the apartment light as she says to her boyfriend, 'Just look at me and you'll love me.' As characters begin to reconcile, these three relationships symbolise people reaching for what they cannot see or even do.

Whether the characters are real or illusory hardly matters. Unlike Keaton in *Sherlock Jr.* (1924), who climbs into the movie screen and lingers between different frames and landscapes, *Visage* is literally displaced in terms of the actual screening venues. When the film premièred in Taiwan, screening took place, for the first time, at the National Theatre Concert Hall in Taipei. Built in 1987, this hall is the most prestigious venue in the capital of Taiwan to host world-class musical, dance, and theatre performances, but never in its history had it been used for cinema. To show a film in such an unusual space encourages a different kind of movie-going experience, which brings the mechanism and architecture of cinema to light. Typically, the spectator is perpetually fixed to the mirror-screen, temporarily gluing the cinephile's gaze to the screen. Barthes describes this situation as pre-hypnotic and prefigured by the darkness of the theatre: 'Not only is the dark the very substance of reverie; it is also the "colour" of a diffused eroticism ... it is in this urban dark that the body's freedom is generated' (Barthes 1986, 346). Most importantly, it is just not the naturalness of darkness, but the space where our bodies are situated: 'Whenever I hear the word *cinema*, I can't help thinking *hall*, rather than *film*' (Barthes 1986, 346). Barthes asks us to accept the hypnotic effects of cinema largely because of the darkness of the theatre and the architecture of the cinema experience (sound, the space of projection, the mass), making possible a bliss of discretion (anonymous, populated, numerous) and bodily pleasure (gay cruising). The fascination of the cinema requires us to divorce our minds from our bodies, and the spectator is both conscious of and unconscious of the dream state they enter, facilitated by the darkness of the movie theatre. So what happens when modernist filmmakers attempt to move beyond the dichotomy of being transfixed by the mirror images or disruption to the mechanisms of projection?

'This is not the most appropriate site to show movies,' said Tsai on stage, as he gleefully introduced *Visage* at its première at the National Theatre Concert Hall on 22 September 2009. Tsai went on to remark apologetically to the audience that they might notice a few scratchy noises caused by the running film reel (because the projector was not set up in a separate room), or worse – when the sound failed to synchronise during projection. Tsai's concerns may be too trivial for anyone growing up watching films with a running projector (instead of digital projection) or who has hands-on experience with celluloid film, but it is precisely the working of the cinematic apparatus that makes most audiences forget their surroundings when watching a movie. Audiences are 'stitched' (Silverman 1984) into the diegetic world by a chain of cinematic techniques; in other words, spectators perceive the narrative from images and their symbolic meanings, and these registers do not require an exploration of events happening outside the frame. So when a director like Tsai urged his audiences not to pay attention to what was happening in the actual *space* where his film was to première, he inadvertently primed their senses to look out for any extradiegetic incidents or technical mistakes, turning this ordinary viewing experience into an unordinary one. If going to the cinema evokes a site-specific pilgrim-like experience for cinephiles that is akin to going to an art gallery or museum to view the original paintings there, *Visage*'s non-traditional exhibition venue and the exclusive practice highlight the space as the protagonist, and in such a concept the configuration of space is the main driver for the viewers' sensory experience of image operations. In short, this exhibition practice decants the aura of the movie theatres.

CONCLUSION

Situating moving images in art galleries, museums, or music halls shows how Tsai Ming-liang crosses the boundaries between cinema and theatre. These exhibitions do not just represent Tsai's move to recycle abandoned objects and places; he is also criticising the modern lifestyle with its fast speeds, over-consumption, and waste in which objects, along with the memories of using them, are simply disregarded. In *What Time*, the movie theatre is only one part of the larger intersecting dislocation of time and space (Paris and Taipei, the traveller and the local merchant), and this temporal relationship of simultaneity is extended with *Goodbye* as it returns to a vanished movie theatre. *It's a Dream* displaces patrons and spectators alike in between the darkened theatre and the white gallery. While the original spatio-temporality of the cinematic apparatus is preserved in Tsai's feature-length films, *It's a Dream* and *Visage* represent a spatial practice that marks the transition from movie theatres to new exhibition sites – a move to prompt audiences to rethink the meaning of cinema. In the long run, what Tsai Ming-liang is doing is not just about embracing new ways of resurrecting the cinema, but about providing an alternative home for cinema (as opposed to the digital platform). Given the transnational nature of their content and production, Tsai's films offer a critique of the intricacies between exhibition practices and how audiences consume a plural understanding of cultural flow and the moving image.

CHAPTER 5

A Southbound Turn: Dreaming Taiwan in Midi Z's Realist Films

When the Ministry of Culture of Taiwan announced that it had chosen director Midi Z's *Ice Poison* (2014) to compete for Best International Feature Film at the 2014 Academy Awards, the director said he was stunned by the decision. This was not just a matter of showing humbleness: Midi Z admitted he was surprised because the film does not appear to be a quintessential representation of Taiwanese society. *Ice Poison* mostly centres on a couple trying to survive in the ghettoised parts of Myanmar and the experience of drug dealing and addiction. The total production budget was under NT$10 million (approximately US$30,000), and the storytelling is far from entertaining. Its slow pace is configured by extensive long takes, occasional shaky hand-held cameras, and an absence of major movie stars.

Midi Z declared the film's official recognition to be a sign that Taiwan 'respects diversity and sees possibility in the film' (Zhao 2015), but not everyone on the Taiwanese film scene agreed with the decision. Some critics thought a lack of word-of-mouth marketing would hurt the film's chances at an Oscar. Other industry professionals pointed to the other strong contenders in the selection pool, including Tsai Ming-liang's *Stray Dogs* (2013) and the well-liked, top-grossing, baseball-themed *Kano* (2014, dir. Umin Boya), and wondered why these films lost out to *Ice Poison*. There were a few raised eyebrows at the opaque selection process and demands that the government release a list of the names on the juror committee (Xu 2014). Implicit in all these critiques is an underlying bias against a non-mainstream film by an immigrant director, particularly one from Southeast Asia. They also underscore the industry's narrow-mindedness: its inability to fathom a film's potential when it is not a genre piece set in contemporary Taiwanese society.

Midi Z (Zhao Deyin)[1] was born in Lashio in northern Burma/Myanmar[2] and is of Chinese descent. Employing a guerrilla style of digital filmmaking and relying in part on the Taiwanese government's *fudaojin* subsidy policy, he makes films that deal with the harsh economic and social circumstances in his home country of Myanmar and with issues relating to neighbouring territories, such as Laos and Thailand. Midi, who arrived in Taiwan as a teenager to pursue what Southeast Asians perceive as the 'Taiwan Dream' (*Taiwan meng*), represents the sentiments of displacement and negotiated identity generated by a forced migration experience akin to that of an exile. Like many new immigrants working in Taiwan, Midi Z – through his very nature as a Southeast Asian migrant and member of an ethnic minority – calls attention to a certain implicit racial and social class hierarchy among what and who is considered 'Taiwanese'. If Taiwan's film industry has been slow to accept him as one of their own, his fellow Burmese have been just as reluctant, criticising his films for not being 'Myanmar enough' due to subtle nuances of Sino-Burmese intersubjectivity juxtaposed against a translingual audioscape (Bernards 2021).

Expanding upon what Luke Robinson (2020) calls 'network aesthetics from below', this chapter uses Midi Z's films to explore how the aesthetic style of Taiwan New Cinema has been reconstituted in Southeast Asia. The particular interest is in how Midi Z was able to translate the problems of the Chinese diaspora in Southeast Asia and the Burmese diaspora in Taiwan into what Lúcia Nagib (2020) refers to as 'realist cinema'. The chapter culminates

---

[1] Midi Z's full name in Mandarin is spelled (or pronounced) as Zhao Deyin, in which Zhao is the family name and by convention is listed first. Outside of Sinophone communities, Zhao goes by his English name, Midi Z, which combines his nickname 'Midi' with 'Z', abbreviated from his family name. Midi means 'the youngest brother' in Southwestern Mandarin (*xianan guanhua*), also known as Upper Yangtze Mandarin. This accent is spoken mostly in southwest China, including in Sichuan, Yunnan, Chongqing, Guizhou, and some parts of Hubei, Hunan, and Guangxi. The language is also commonly spoken in northern Myanmar and is used in Vietnam by its ethnic minorities.

[2] For generations, the country was called Burma after the dominant ethnic group. In 1989, the ruling military government changed the country's name from Burma to Myanmar. Many residents of Myanmar still use 'Burma' today to refer to their country, as does Midi Z during many of his interviews. In this chapter, 'Burma' and its adjective 'Burmese' are used interchangeably with Myanmar to describe the country and its people or to refer to their language and culture.

in a discussion of Midi Z's long-time collaboration with muse and actress Wu Ke-Xi, and on the way his film *Nina Wu* (2019), in which Wu stars, complicates the notion of authorship. *Nina Wu*'s storyline is associated with the global #MeToo movement, and it is often considered the first Taiwanese film to stir conversations around #MeToo. The film, which premièred in the 'Un Certain Regard' section at the 2019 Cannes Film Festival, is regarded by critics as a high point in Midi's career. It also marks a clear departure for him and an elevating of women's voices: Wu drafted the original screenplay independently of Midi, and the film (more of a fable inspired by Wu Ke-Xi's work-induced trauma than a factual disclosure of sexual assault) is also Midi's highest-budget and most genre-driven film to date.

From *Fudaojin* to the World Cinema Fund

When Midi first arrived in Taiwan in 1998, he was only sixteen years old. He studied graphics and printing at a vocational school before obtaining a master's degree from the National Taiwan University of Technology and Science. His first short film, *Paloma Blanca* – also his 2006 graduation thesis, was invited to international film festivals in Busan, Lyon, Copenhagen, Australia, and Spain. In 2009, he was one of only a few prospective filmmakers selected to participate in the first Golden Horse Film Academy (an initiative by the film festival of the same name), an intensive directing workshop led by veteran Taiwanese art house filmmakers Hou Hsiao-hsien and Ang Lee. Under Hou's tutelage, Midi completed *Huasin Incident* (2009), a short film that follows a group of young Sino-Burmese migrants and their street life in Taipei. This workshop experience marked the first official filmmaking training Midi received. He has often recalled how Hou and Lee's guidance has affected his subsequent work, especially when Hou recommended that he use long shots and long takes to allow non-professional talents to perform more naturally. By comparison, Lee's advice to Midi was that a film director's job is to be empathetic toward the subject rather than being too concerned about how audiences are going to react to the story (Zhao 2015, 224). Through the Golden Horse Film Academy training, Midi realised he could transition to the filmmaking world, seizing the opportunity to tell stories about poverty-riven life in his birth country and the unspeakable abuses from the Burmese military dictatorship he repeatedly witnessed in childhood.

From 2011 to 2014, Midi made three features, together known as his Homecoming Trilogy: *Return to Burma* (2011), *Poor Folk* (2012), and *Ice Poison* (2014). All were shot in less than fifteen days with a budget of under US$10,000 each. He completed the shooting for his first feature with a bare-minimum film crew: himself, a principal actor, and a location sound recordist.³ This is not to say that the precarity of the shooting conditions was by choice. In retrospect, Midi remarked that he missed having access to a big budget and a 40–50-member crew, as he did in training. Fortunately, Midi's persistence paid off: *Return to Burma* was nominated for the Busan New Currents Competition and the Rotterdam Tiger Competition. Both are known for their prestige and their tendency to uplift up-and-coming international film talent. The trilogy's third instalment, *Ice Poison*, was devised and completed with only seven crew members while Midi was producing a segment for *Letters from the South* (2013), a collective film project (in which Tsai Ming-liang also took part) sponsored by the Chinese broadcasting company Phoenix Media. *Ice Poison* won Best International Film at the Edinburgh Film Festival, Best Director at the Love and Peace Film Festival in Sweden, and Best Director at the Taipei Film Festival. Midi was nominated for Best Director at the Golden Horse Awards and the film was subsequently named as Taiwan's official entry for the Oscars' foreign language competition in 2015.

Midi's Homecoming Trilogy (which was labelled as such by the distribution company as a marketing strategy, rather than being indicative of an intentional, pre-planned arc on the part of the director; Zhou 2015, 30) opened many doors for him. It established the director as a recognisable auteur whose art house sensibilities share the aesthetics of slow cinema with his mentor Hou Hsiao-hsien and with Tsai Ming-liang. And, crucially, the success of the Homecoming Trilogy meant that Midi and his production team were able to receive grants from the Taiwanese government for his next feature-length film, *The Road to Mandalay* (2016).

The official mission of the Taiwanese government funding scheme for films – known as *fudaojin* in Mandarin – is to assist 'domestic production of feature-length films', so long as the sponsored work 'cannot be filmed entirely overseas', meaning that much of it must be shot in Taiwan but portions can be set in another country (Ministry of Culture 2007). This production assistance grant has advanced many successful Taiwanese directors' careers, from Hou Hsiao-hsien and Ang Lee, to Tsai Ming-liang. As Midi mainly films in Myanmar and Thailand, he had not been a successful grant recipient in the past. Midi's film editor, Lin Sheng-wen, has attested to this limiting condition: in a roundtable session promoting *Ice Poison*, Lin mentioned that the team had

---

³ Midi describes this project as having only a three-person film crew: himself, his principal actor Wang Shin-Hong (also his childhood best friend and line producer), and sound recordist/sound designer Lin Sheng-wen. The film credits from Seashore Image Productions, though, add Wu Ke-Xi (the principal actress in the film) to this list, crediting her as assistant director.

applied for *fudaojin* as they did for all previous projects, but said that they had never made it past the first round of interviews. The reason for their unsuccessful attempts was obvious: 'If you take a closer look at the requirements to compete for *fudaojin*, you will know that if much of the shooting location is set abroad, this film project will not be eligible for further consideration for the grant' (Sun 2016). The fact that *The Road to Mandalay* successfully obtained a grant from the Taiwanese government (albeit for distribution rather than production) despite much of the film being set in Thailand points to a gradual shift in state policy and new possibilities for Midi.

In addition to receiving the coveted *fudaojin* grant from Taiwan, *The Road to Mandalay* secured prestigious external funding from the West: the World Cinema Fund of the German Federal Cultural Foundation and the Berlinale. With its mission to support the production and distribution of feature-length films and documentaries, the World Cinema Fund focuses exclusively on projects from the Global South: Latin America, Central America, the Caribbean, Africa, the Middle East, Central Asia, and Southeast Asia. The receipt of funding from this fund – the same one that has helped advance world-renowned directors such as Thai independent Apichatpong Weerasethakul – places Midi among the exclusive networks of world cinema auteurs.

But it is not just the funding that places Midi Z alongside fellow slow cinema auteurs like Apichatpong. Writing for *Variety*, Richard Kuipers raved about *The Road to Mandalay* as the director's best work yet, stating that its observational tactics place Midi 'in the top rank of Asian social realists' and are reminiscent of the aesthetics of filmmaker Jia Zhangke, an underground Chinese director who is censored in China (Kuipers 2016). The aesthetic commonalities among the two directors may have to do with their 'sharing' a production team: Matthieu Laclau for editing and Taiwanese composer Lim Giong for expressive sound design (Lim is also the composer on Hou Hsiao-hsien's 2001 film *Millennium Mambo*). After *The Road to Mandalay*, Midi would continue to receive *fudaojin*, gaining funding from the Taiwanese government for his fifth feature, *Nina Wu*, described by news media in Taiwan as his 'first film outside of Myanmar' (Chen 2019).

Beneath the Film Subsidies and the Southbound Policy

It would appear that Midi's flourishing career illustrates the quintessential immigrant success story, or what the director himself calls the 'Taiwan dream'. From Taiwan's standpoint, Midi is the typical and desired *qiao sheng* (Chinese diaspora student), targeted by government policies to study abroad in Taiwan. These policies were designed to pivot the centre for Chinese studies away from the PRC to Taiwan, as well as to promote the image of the country as an alternative multicultural and Sinocentric hub in East Asia. Such policies targeting students complemented the Southbound Policy (introduced by President Lee Teng-hui in the 1990s and revised in the 2010s under the name New Southbound Policy by the Tsai Ing-wen administration), which sells Taiwan as the promised land to Southeast Asian migrant workers. These were especially appealing to overseas Chinese living in the Southeast region (in Singapore, Malaysia, Vietnam, and Myanmar), and many Vietnamese and Burmese Chinese now live and work on the outskirts of Taipei: for example, in Zhonghe and the municipal borough of New Taipei City. The educational and economic policies certainly attracted Midi and his family, who considered themselves to be Yunnanese of Chinese descent. They saw emigrating to a developed country like Taiwan as an alternative 'American dream' because of the geographical proximity of Myanmar and Taiwan, and the linguistic similarity between Mandarin and Yunnanese. Cultural studies scholars and sociologists Kuei-fen Chiu and Yu-yueh Tsai (2014) remark that Taiwan is now a destination country for immigrants from many Asian countries, who 'migrate with the hope of improving the economic situation of their families back home' (112). Taiwan has repositioned itself as a new cultural imperialistic centre in Southeast Asia.

As soon as these Southeast Asian immigrants and migrant workers arrived in Taiwan, however, they faced a harsh reality: not the 'Taiwan dream' of their fantasies but arduous living and working conditions. And the higher their expectations, the more bitter the experience that the migrants would face upon realising that they were again marginalised because of their race, cultural background, and socioeconomic status (Lu 2008). Of course, migrant workers can be pragmatic, more willing to accept disappointments and adjust their expectations. Midi, for example, has disclosed in interviews that he did not come to Taiwan because he needed a better education or dared dream of becoming a film director. He simply wanted to take advantage of the government-sponsored study abroad opportunity to escape his birth nation for a higher-income country, where he could work part-time and provide for his family remotely.

Midi Z lays out the 'Taiwan dream' in his film narratives from a bottom-up perspective. This pattern is most obvious in the first instalment of his original trilogy, *Return to Burma*. In a scene from the film, the main character's younger brother, played by the real-life brother of Wang Shin-Hong (the leading actor in the trilogy), sits around with his friends on the floor of someone's house, smoking and noodling away at a guitar (Figure 5.1). Shin-Hong's brother starts to play a Taiwanese pop song, another friend smokes, and the rest hum along. One comments that they should all go to Malaysia and pursue careers as singers. The small talk then turns to how to leave the country, which involves a

Figure 5.1 *Shin-Hong's friends wonder where the country of 'Taipei' is in* Return to Burma *(2011). Still frame.* © *Seashore Image Productions.*

long wait and the difficult process of obtaining a passport. In Midi's autobiography, he mentions that not only is it considerably more expensive to pay for a visa or a passport in the Global South, but too much can be at stake to obtain one (Zhao 2015, 53–4). Apart from facing great expense and a long wait, applicants must often bribe the authorities to ensure their passports will not be seized by corrupt officials. Midi's family had to scrounge together about 57,000 Myanmar Kyat (approximately US$2,500 at the time) for bribes. The hush money was enough to feed his entire family for almost five years!

Taiwan enjoys 'a privileged position in the ideoscape of the film's protagonists', as Robinson (2020) explains, but for most these desires remain limited to *dreaming* about Taiwan – 'a desire to achieve the good life through overseas labour that can never practically be realised' (106). In fact, in *Return to Burma*, the characters do not even seem to process where (or what) Taiwan is. In an earlier scene, Shin-Hong's friends are under the impression that Taipei (the capital) and Taiwan are two different countries, even though the protagonist has just returned from Taipei. One asks: 'Taipei? Or Taiwan? Where is this nation called Taipei?' Shin-Hong's brother interrupts and says confidently: 'Taipei is close to China; Taiwan is close to Japan.' This confusion is driven in part by the ambiguities of the moniker 'Chinese Taipei', which Taiwan has been forced to adopt at such international venues as the Olympic Games, meetings of the World Health Organization, and even Miss Universe pageants.[4] In contrast to this name, which seemingly suggests an affiliation between the city of Taipei and the PRC, Taiwan is known as having enthusiastic, friendly feelings towards Japan. The geographical disorientation and incorrect mapping of the region by the characters are both a humorous narrative device and an emblematic moment, revealing a glass ceiling over those who might seek to enter global labour networks.

Like many developed countries pushing for a multicultural agenda, Taiwan is still fraught with racial bias and structural economic inequalities on so many levels. Obscured by Taiwan's Southbound Policy, which aims to integrate regional development in cultural, technological, agricultural, and educational resources, is the country's overwhelming reliance on exported labour from the Global South. The drive to strengthen Taiwan's trade and economic ties with Southeast Asia comes at a clear cost. While cheap labour gives Taiwan the leverage to privilege itself as the centre, the domestic Taiwanese public is usually ignorant, uninformed, or simply unaware of the high costs and structural inequities that feed their nation's economic gains.

POVERTY, THE GAZE AND THE MODE OF PRODUCTION

There is no doubt that Midi's distinctive filmmaking style and unmatched quality stem from his migrant background and the emigrant experience. This, in turn, opens up his film texts to readings beyond the usual calibre of film and media studies, moving between anthropology, sociology, cultural studies, and political science. One of the most prevalent connections discussed is the onscreen representation of poverty culture and precarious labour. Although Kun Xian Shen (2018, 45–7) considers this type of literal reading to be limiting and unproductive, placing too much emphasis on the indexicality of the medium itself, it is understandable that realism is audiences' first impression of these films. Few films – let alone feature-length narratives circulating at international film festivals – have covered or documented the ethnic Chinese community from Myanmar. My goal here is not to discount the ways in which these films lend themselves as an aperture into the living conditions in Myanmar. Rather than focusing on the reality effect for the viewer (privileging

---

[4] Beverly Chen of Miss Taiwan reported that she was not allowed to compete for Miss Universe at the contest in Panama City in 2003 because the pageant organisers had succumbed to pressure from China. She was barred from appearing unless she dropped the Miss Taiwan title and wore the 'Chinese Taipei' sash instead (Chen 2003).

representation as a real experience), I acknowledge Midi's efforts to *produce* reality, echoing what Nagib (2020) terms 'realist cinema'. This is defined by the film's mode of production, beyond its raw aesthetics. But first, we need to survey the general discussion on poverty culture as realism.

In 2015, the Asia Society Museum in New York organised a film retrospective for Midi Z. Curator La Frances Hui (2015) characterised Midi's films as presenting individuals' lives 'stripped of drama and sentimentality', and the realism portrayed by the director as 'honest, non-judgmental, and filled with compassion'. Further, she used phrases such as 'poor', 'displaced', and 'illegal' work 'in drug and human trafficking' to describe the onscreen characters and their activities. Midi responded to this characterisation by explaining that these stories drew inspiration from ordinary people he knew who were involved in the drug trade. Unfortunately, many people living in Myanmar must turn to such activities in the face of harsh living conditions. The coping mechanisms can be explained through American anthropologist Oscar Lewis's definition of the culture of poverty, as 'both an adaptation and a reaction of the poor to their marginal position in a class-stratified, highly individuated, capitalistic society' (Lewis 1996, xliv). Lewis might argue that poverty is largely inescapable and self-perpetuating – something to be coped with rather than to be solved – but transnational migration opens up new possibilities. Wen-Chin Chang (2016, 51) argues:

> For people of the underdeveloped world, migration to wealthy countries has been a primary means to improve their lives. Their mobility through various countries and experiences in multiple life situations have strengthened their awareness of the discrepancy and inequality among people of and within different societies

– thus effecting change not just for themselves but for their families back home. As Chang (2016, 54) explains, 'going to Taiwan for education is an enviable choice for many ethnic Chinese students in Burma (especially Yunnanese Chinese) and is considered an upward move'.

In interviews, Midi frequently recalls his childhood to illustrate how tough it was to live and grow up in Myanmar. He shares his ambivalence about shuffling between Chinese language school and ordinary Myanmar education. But his most horrifying experience comes from having to witness the abuse and racial discrimination exercised by Myanmar's military dictatorship on an almost daily basis: soldiers would arbitrarily arrest, detain, and search the homes of civilians. Worse, there was little repercussion if soldiers sexually harassed (or abducted!) household members during such searches (Zhao 2015, 99–101). Further, like most Yunnanese migrants, Midi's parents and family were refugees who fled from Yunnan to Myanmar after the Chinese Communist Party took over in China (Chang 2016, 52). Bearing the identity of Yunnanese exiles and Yunnanese descendants living in Myanmar while being discriminated against for their Chinese cultural background moves Midi from marginalised (in his home country) to double marginalised (in the host country).

The double-marginalised status does not necessarily hinder creative freedom. Rather, it can be empowering. Focusing primarily on the use of popular music as both a narrative device and an identification with the Chinese diaspora under globalisation, Wan-jui Wang (2017) points out that the use of language in Midi's films is part of the realistic polyphonic soundscape. In the Homecoming Trilogy, dialogues indiscriminately shift between Thai, Burmese, Mandarin, and Yunnanese. The multilingualism in Midi's films corresponds to what Michel Chion highlights as 'polyphonic cinema' or what Hamid Naficy calls 'accented cinema' in diasporic filmmaking (Wang 2017, 157). Additionally, the digital realism in Midi's filmmaking reflects a certain 'transnational aesthetics' (Wang 2017, 159), in which migrant subjects are aware of their own predicament and surrounding socioeconomic inequalities.

Melissa Chan (2017) draws on the concept of panoptic coercion to argue that the digital realism in Midi's films invites a consideration of the filmmaker's 'surveillance aesthetics', or his resistance to state censorship. Loosely evoking the French philosopher Michel Foucault's theory of Panopticism – a kind of internal surveillance and thus discipline – Chan argues that Burmese state censorship mobilises Midi to resist. In so doing, however, Chan seems to confuse realist cinema's observational quality with surveillance, prompting her to conflate everything from resistance to inverse surveillance. We should turn our attention, instead, to the question of authorship: who is the intended audience? What roles does poverty inflict on the ethics of filmmaking? And what are the ethics of filmmaking between modes of production, circulation, exhibition, and reception?

As can be seen, the common thread across these views is the interconnection between poverty as reality and realism as a form of agency. If Midi's films present an important 'realistic and polyphonic soundscape' (Wang 2017) – or what Kun Xian Shen (2018) prefers to call a 'cinema of distance', in which the films maintain a critical observation of the subject but narrate the fictional story of migration with cinematic (or documentary-like) realism – then what motives Midi's practices is not the Burmese government's censorship and control. Nor are his practices a form of resistance falling back on inverse surveillance/observational tactics. They might be better characterised as the broadly construed notion of the return of the gaze, given that his films were made after Midi, now a Taiwanese citizen, finally returned to Myanmar from Taiwan.[5]

In a way, when Midi returned, he was both Taiwanese émigré and Myanmar expatriate, but ultimately an exile. As an expatriate, Midi shares a sense of solitude and the alienation of an exile: isolation, displacement, estrangement. But he also recognises his flexible identity, and he sees himself as thinking and acting like a Taiwanese. He is largely ambivalent toward his birth country (Zhao 2015, 20). As Edward Said (2002) explains the different types of exile, from political refugees to displaced self-exiles, he notes that expatriates and émigrés may share comparable feelings of solitude and estrangement. Still, they do not suffer the same degree of rigid state policies and banishment. For Said, émigrés 'enjoy an ambiguous status'; anyone who decides to live in another country with the possibility of reversing their decision and returning to their home country epitomises a freedom of choice (Said 2002, 144). Essentially, exiles do not leave their home country by choice but expatriates can always return. Another difference between exiles and émigrés is how they approach their new surroundings and their willingness to assimilate in new environments. Said characterises exiles as bitter and resentful. The exile tends to make a fetish out of their state of exile, which is used to justify their continued distance from all connections and commitments to their host country. Literary work produced by exile writers tends to romanticise, glorify, or fetishise their home country and feelings of nostalgia toward the past due to 'the sheer fact of isolation and displacement, which produced the kind of narcissistic masochism that resists all efforts at amelioration, acculturation', and commitment to local community (Said 2002, 146). This self-prescribed not-belonging mentality is an enabler for exiles continuing to define themselves as outsiders and not one of the local community.

What separates Midi's experience from that of an exile is his willingness to be flexible, his refusal to anchor his identity to either home or host country.

---

[5] Midi Z was unable to return to Myanmar until 2008 due to the Myanmar government restricting its nationals from visiting Taiwan to appease China. It was perhaps not a coincidence that he began shooting his first feature film, *Return to Burma* (2011), after he obtained Republic of China/Taiwan citizenship. Midi mentions in his autobiography that one reason to return to and shoot a film in Myanmar was that he wanted to witness the May 2008 Constitutional Referendum, which was happening at the time. He thought the new constitution would usher his home country into a new era of genuine democracy in a meaningful way, including economic reform, respect for human rights, guarantees of freedom of expression, and more.

In her book *Independent Filmmaking Across Borders in Contemporary Asia*, Ran Ma (2020) contends that independent filmmaking in Myanmar is less about a filmmaker's aspirations to create specific kinds of cinema that speak to global art house audiences, and more a mode of production on the filmmaker's part. By this, Ma means that the low-budget, understated aesthetics are a reflection of Southeast Asian filmmakers' precarity. On the one hand, the filmmaker is struggling to find a way out of the impoverished community; on the other, to be able to return the exilic gaze, one must circumvent 'the bureaucratic procedure of applying for the government's filming permit and going through the censorship check' (Ma 2020, 209), especially when the constraints and conditions of location shooting affect the modes of production (for example, Midi's long takes).

Song Hwee Lim (2018b) aptly proposes that Midi's films exhibit a 'poor cinema aesthetics', in which poverty becomes a paradoxical premise for the mode of filmmaking. Or, more curiously, poverty exerts itself as a method for film production, especially when Midi and his camera crew have had to circumvent local censorship by resorting to shooting guerrilla-style. To avoid the suspicious authorities during his filming in Burma, Midi's cast and crew sometimes had to pretend to be tourists, simply snapping pictures of the scenery, which gives the film an observational documentary quality (Bernards 2021). Often, the camera occupies a concealed position. Still, if it could not be hidden (whenever there is a tracking shot of the characters on a motorbike, for example), Midi confessed to using his survival instincts and resorting to little white lies, telling anyone who asked that they were shooting for a local TV station (Zhao 2015).

In recognising the ethnographic impulses codified with filmic conventions in Midi Z's films, it is equally important to note that realism does not necessarily have to be defined by the filmic (re)presentation of reality. Nagib (2020) argues that the emphasis of realism should be placed on '*how* these images and sounds are manufactured and captured, and the tremendous effort a number of film crews and casts from all over the world put into *producing* as well as reproducing reality' (22). Realism can thus be processed as the film's relation to the real, moving beyond the semiotic reading of a reality effect that occurs only at the point of reception. For instance, Midi's Homecoming Trilogy can be considered intentional 'covert videography' (Bernards 2021, 355). Each project had to be completed in a single trip in Myanmar due to an insufficient budget. Not only did Midi and his crew need to make sure that they did not miss a single frame shot while shooting on location, but it was unlikely they would be able to return to exactly the same spot and reshoot a desirable take once they left the area controlled by the authoritarian regime.

Additionally, shooting a film without obtaining a permit (whether due to lack of funds, reluctance as a means of protest, or avoidance of corrupt officials) means that Midi and his crew have had to navigate dangerous waters and stay under the radar in order to avoid the attentions of the local police or military sympathisers. An early scene in *Ice Poison* offers a good example (Figure 5.2). In the scene, Sanmei (played by Wu Ke-Xi) has just arrived at the central bus station in Lashio, and is meeting the other main character, A-Hong, for the first time. A 'government intrusion' happened on the seventh day of the shooting, when Midi wanted a retake of the scene at the busy bus station. They set up their camera on the rooftop of a three-storey restaurant they rented, using a long framing shot to capture the planned performance. Midi was fully aware of the great risk he was taking, potentially drawing the attention of the police or military, not to mention undercover police, drug cartel members, thugs, or nosy onlookers. And that is just what happened on this day: someone noticed their filming activity and called the police. During the subsequent interrogation, Midi, thinking on his feet, quickly explained that they were journalists visiting from Taiwan, shooting an assignment on tourism in Myanmar. Midi also 'bribed' the police authority with Taiwanese cigarettes and 30,000 Myanmar Kyat (approximately US$16) to ensure that his crew would not be taken into custody.

On another occasion, the crew was intercepted by a low-ranking soldier. Midi secretly instructed the cinematographer to take a few scenic pictures on their digital single-lens reflex (DSLR) camera, pretending to be a tourist,

Figure 5.2 *The scooter taxi scene in* Return to Burma *(2011). Still frame.* © *Seashore Image Productions.*

a ruse that seems to have worked. (One advantage of shooting a low-budget film with a DSLR in a country like Myanmar is that the digital camera can achieve filmlike cinematography while still passing as equipment for still photography to an undiscerning eye; Zhao 2015, 101–6; 187–8). In retelling such stories, whether in his autobiography or during interviews, Midi remains unruffled, even as he confesses to feeling so horrified at the time that he could not stop sweating, just like when he first stepped on the tarmac at Yangon Airport to board the plane to Taiwan (Zhao 2015, 106). Somehow, his calm and collected manner in describing these troubling events leaves a reader like me feeling shattered and distressed. It is hard for someone who has never experienced anything like this at first hand to imagine how unsettling and traumatic it could be in the unfolding.

Into the Soundscape and the Film Industry's Exploitation of Women

Midi was able to work just as skilfully through similar unwelcome trauma in the thriller *Nina Wu* to convey his screenwriter Wu Ke-Xi's suppressed memories – concerning the bartering system of sex and power in the film industry – even though it was not directly his own experience. *Nina Wu* uses surrealist storytelling conventions to portray the experiences of the titular character, an aspiring actress hoping to receive her big break from a formidable and abusive producer of the likes of Harvey Weinstein. Utilising a film-within-a-film framework, the movie blurs the boundaries between dream and reality, crouched between scenes of the protagonist experiencing sexual harassment and workspace abuse in flashbacks, dream sequences, imagination, and fantasy. Through it all, the film uses incidental (non-dialogic, non-lyrical) sound effects and sound design by musician Lim Giong, a well-known figure on the Taiwanese experimental electronic music scene. The film begins with a tunnel scene through a point-of-view shot, presumably travelling on an underground train in Taipei. The ambient sound of train noises is met with station buzz in the next scene. We are shown the commuter crowds exiting carriages at a Taipei Mass Rapid Transport (MRT) station. Among the crowd is Nina. As we follow Nina ascending to street level, a digitally composed music score overpowers the scene, pushing street ambience and a faint ambulance sound into the background and creating suspense. We are in Nina's apartment in the next frame, moving around in several rooms characterised by different audio cues. First, the sound of soup boiling is heard while Nina is making dumplings; as the sound of boiling water increases in volume, the soundtrack is suddenly interrupted by an iPhone alarm. Nina reluctantly turns the alarm off, heads over to her clothes rack, and fumbles through the hangers, producing metal clanking chimes. The first word the audience hears is when Nina sits on the bed – five minutes into the film – and speaks to her propped-up iPhone on a stand. The protagonist, we learn, is an influencer live-streaming her daily routine to her followers.

Throughout the entire opening sequence of *Nina Wu*, there is no conversational exchange or voice-over, only crafted sound design and effects that either bridge between shots or emanate into the foreground. The ambient noise effects do more than set the story's tone; they are placed in lieu of voice-over narration to convey effectively what has transpired and why. In the same live-streaming scene, a sudden change in Nina's voice and tone provides viewers with a sharp contrast between the social and the actual self. The Nina that was first introduced to the audience is a disguised one. This influencer seems excessively sweet in an insincere way – clearly a performative act she puts on alongside an app-filtered appearance. The illusion of her cuteness is soon disrupted by a phone call from Mark (her agent, as we quickly learn), informing her of a casting call. Nina's cold, detached, and almost slightly annoyed tone – presumably the real Nina – surfaces when she speaks to Mark off camera.

At this point, it is impossible to ignore the naming resonances of Nina and an earlier film protagonist, Mima, from Satoshi Kon's animated thriller *Perfect Blue* (1997). *Perfect Blue* is a psychological horror that depicts the dark side of celebrity fandom and a possibly schizophrenic protagonist, traversing between her mind and the diegetic world and blurring the line between what is real and what is not. The phonic similarity – whether coincidental or deliberate – in naming foreshadows what will come in the film, as the plot later reveals in the third act that Nina's story unfolds from a deconstructed perspective, suggesting to viewers that the scenes showing the abusive treatment Nina receives from the film industry may or may not have happened in a chronological way. Through Nina's suppressed memories and hysteria, and things left untold (as revealed through flashbacks, imagination, and a feeling of unsettledness), the film blurs the line between reality and surrealism.

Nina Wu is easily labelled as a film of the #MeToo era, and it was marketed as such by the production company and the actress/writer Wu Ke-Xi herself. While promoting the film, Wu voiced how much the work was inspired by the Harvey Weinstein scandal and drew heavily on her personal experience when she was drafting the screenplay. After the film debuted at the Cannes Film Festival in the 'Un Certain Regard' section, reviews were mixed. A common sentiment from film critics was that their high expectations had met with some disappointment. While they anticipated a female revenge story of a young actress working in the film and television industry and falling prey to powerful movie moguls, the film is, in fact, a surrealist metacommentary on the post-traumatic stress disorder (PTSD) suffered by the victim. Beatrice

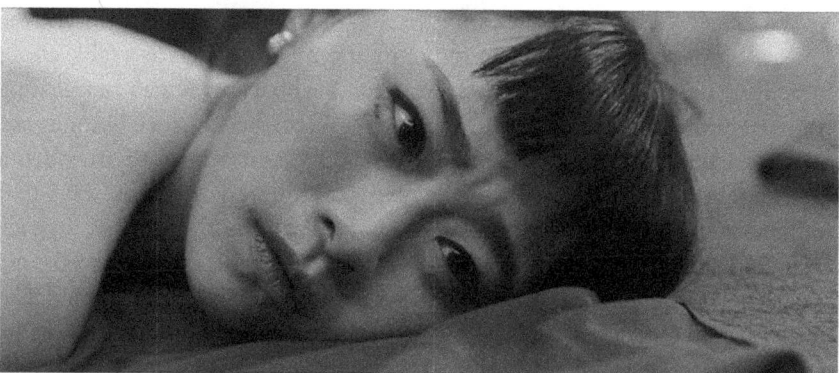

Figure 5.3 *The final moment from* Nina Wu *(2019), showing the titular character (played by Wu Ke-Xi) in despair. Still frame. © Seashore Image Productions.*

Loayza (2021) of *The New York Times* observes that the film is not interested in didacticism or justice served, as might be expected of a #MeToo movie. To Ela Bittencourt (2021), the film is 'a mesmerising yet frustrating portrayal of film industry exploitation', which, out of a desire to avoid stereotypes, 'skips over the more complex fallout of sexual trauma'. Nicholas Yap (2021) recognises the unusually broad attention this film received. 'Hailed as Taiwan's answer to the #MeToo movement', he writes, the film is supposed to centre on 'accountability, exploitation, and women's autonomy'. And yet, in his view, the film merely co-opts trauma as an embellishment instead of offering a sensitive study of the victim's perspective. Even with the best of intentions, the final scene of *Nina Wu* (Figure 5.3) – as Nina lies on the carpeted floor in tears while the movie producer lies on top of her, raping her (although some viewers argue this to be a quid pro quo instead of rape) – does not 'correspond to an incisive, empathetic voice' (Yap 2021). Even so, Yap (2021) recognises that the fragmented, embellished qualities of the film's narrative structure (which he criticises) potentially embody an abused subject's perspective and are 'conditionally true to how victims process and recollect information'.

These reviews pinpoint wishful thinking on the part of the writers: to them, it is not enough for a film to provide a frank depiction of sexual abuse in the film industry. *Nina Wu* should have demonstrated women's resistance or well-deserved social justice. Even in terms of its scorching indictment of systemic exploitation in the industry, the film falls short (according to these critics) of acknowledging the system and the collective complacency that enables the abuse in the first place (Bittencourt 2021). Worse, the film takes the idea of sexualisation and exploitation of women to its most literal conclusion (Ehrlich 2021).

But in its evocative and disturbing visuals, the film is trying to articulate the irreversible experience of trauma rather than presenting itself as a fable about assaults against women. With each repeated flashback to Nina's humiliating audition in the hotel room, flashes that manipulate the audience like a jigsaw puzzle, each suppressed recollection shows a different version of truth from the sequence. All paths point to the abstract exploration of the ways that trauma alters one's perspective, identity, and mental health. As Nina repeats, again and again, 'They don't just want to take my body, they want to take my soul.' This film is very much about patriarchy gaslighting the feeble mind. Or, in *Variety* film critic Jessica Kiang's (2019) words, it is about 'how the taking of a body can cue the taking of a soul', and how the abused victim 'can be subconsciously convinced of her own complicity in it'. Kiang recognises the very fabric of trauma that a sexually assaulted victim would experience, and the way that such misconduct in the film industry might affect and trigger young women subjected to its humiliations. More precisely, this fabric of trauma is embodied in the spatial and hollowing ambient sounds that represent the character's psychosis and are foregrounded as a narrative device to carry the story forward.

The two most humiliating moments Nina experiences are when the diegetic film director overcorrects her while she is on set shooting for the film-within-the-film (a wartime melodrama called *Spy Love*) and when the same man violently slaps Nina's face to unlock her emotions in front of the camera. In the first such moment, Nina is on the film set sitting at a round table with commanders and generals ready for the cue for action. Nina is the movie's double agent, and she finds a folded note hidden in the dumpling she is served. While acknowledging the secret note, she needs to pretend her

Figure 5.4 *The film director (played by Shih Ming-Shuai) keeps over-correcting Nina. Still frame from* Nina Wu *(2019). © Seashore Image Productions.*

allegiance to the general next to her. Yet the director constantly interrupts Nina's performance in the utmost of condescending ways, criticising and correcting her every move, and refusing to listen to her when she tries to explain her delivery style (Figure 5.4). In dealing with an over-correcting director, a mortified Nina pulls through with resilience and silence, bitterly biting the third, the fourth, and the fifth dumpling in take after take (in great contrast to the exuberance she displays at the beginning of the film when she is eating the homemade dumplings). As the production camera slowly pulls away from the focus, the almost-too-quiet room is layered with uncomfortable clicking sounds from officers picking up and setting down chopsticks and ceramic bowls on the table.

Because of their stature and the hierarchy in the movie industry, film directors are often in a position of power over people in weaker positions, compared to television production, where writers and showrunners have more influence on set. In Wu Ke-Xi's case, many Taiwanese film critics suspect that *Nina Wu* is more than an instance of art imitating life. It is insinuated that the screenplay she wrote is a parody of her working experience with the award-winning filmmaker Yang Ya-che while she was shooting *The Bold, the Corrupt and the Beautiful* (2017), just two years prior. Several eyewitnesses and journalists (Ong 2017; Gao 2017; *ETtoday* 2017) reported constant frictions on set between the director and Wu during the shooting of the film, a crime drama about a family's ruthless scheming and revenge. At one point, a frustrated Wu was heard yelling at Yang, 'I don't think you know how to direct [a film]' – coincidently, the same line that a humiliated Nina angrily snaps back at the director after he slaps her for the second or third time (Figures 5.5 and 5.6). Other tabloids reported that Yang hurled all imaginable expletives at Wu when shooting on location near the sea, leaving the stunned actress dissolving into tears. The production company later denied these accusations. Indeed, it is easy to draw parallels between *The Bold, the Corrupt and the Beautiful* and *Nina Wu*. Aside from the obvious involvement of Wu Ke-Xi as leading actress, they both feature a threesome love scene (in *Nina Wu* this is presented as an emotionless blocking rehearsal[6]), and both films blow up a fishing boat

---

[6] Blocking means the precise staging of actors in terms of their position (in relation to the camera), and how they are going to move around physically in a scene and where they need to be when delivering certain lines of dialogue. Blocking a scene also lets the cinematographer and lighting crew know where their equipment needs to be to keep the shots consistent. Blocking, in essence, is to choreograph movement. When nude and simulated sex scenes are being filmed, the seemly effortless and lustful eroticism on screen often involves a great deal of planning, technicality and coordination beforehand.

at one point in the story. In *Nina Wu*, the film-within-the-film director repeatedly demands that Nina search for different 'layers' of emotions; it is perhaps not a coincidence that the word 'layer' (*tseng tsz*) happens to be director Yang Ya-che's personal catchphrase, as is known to film crew.

Leaving aside the question of the film's relation to Yang (my point here is not to convict Yang based on gossip headlines, in the absence of a direct

Figure 5.5 *The director (played by Shih Ming-Shuai) forcefully attempts to unlock the emotions of Nina (played by Wu Ke-Xi) in front of the camera. Still frame from* Nina Wu *(2019). © Seashore Image Productions.*

Figure 5.6 *In a* Nina Wu *behind-the-scenes featurette, actor Shih Ming-Shuai describes the challenge of shooting a slap scene, expressing his commitment to perfecting the act (and ambivalence to the physical process). Wu Ke-Xi is seen photobombing the interview by making a grudging face in the background to tease Shih. Still frame. © 2019 Seashore Image Productions.*

sexual abuse accusation by the victim), I find most interesting the ways that a surrealist reading can be applied to *Nina Wu* and its dream logic. Whether the story reflects actual, traceable events that befell its creator is secondary to the discussion. Actress-cum-screenwriter Wu Ke-Xi, as is well known, claims that some scenes reflect her experience from her early career. But in any work based on a true story, the creators will omit, exaggerate, simplify, and interpret certain events in accordance with artistic licence. If we turn to Roland Barthes's meditation on the formation of meaning from 'The Death of the Author', textual qualities can outweigh the intentions and biographical context of the creator. In advocating for more agency during interpretation and fluidity in the text's predetermined meanings, Barthes (1977, 143) questions the author-as-god status and asks why it is that 'the *explanation* of a work is always sought in the man or woman who produced it, as if it were always in the end, through the more or less transparent allegory of the fiction, the voice of a single person, the *author* "confiding" in us'. The radical reversal provided by surrealism, in contrast, helps divest the author of their sacred status by constantly disrupting meanings (with the surrealist 'shock'), by entrusting the hand with automatic writing (subliminal associations), and by embracing the principle and the experiment of collective writing (Barthes 1977, 144).

To return to the narrative structure of *Nina Wu*: as the flashback becomes more frequent and lingers in duration, viewers might wonder whether this is all a fantasy or dream of the titular character. Who is the dreamer, the source, or the observer if this is just a dream? Might the whole film be seen as a series of dreams narrated in flashback? A sharp observer may have noticed that early in the film, when the first audition scene is introduced, the director crosses off Nina's CV with a red X on her headshot, signalling a rejection. The scene then cuts to an exterior shot, tracking the disappointed, tearful Nina as she walks mindlessly down an arched passageway between the street and the building, in the same red dress she wore for the audition. Audiences are likely to assume at this moment that Nina did not get the job, but this assumption is suddenly disrupted by an offscreen voice yelling 'cut'. As it turns out, not only did Nina get the part, but what viewers are seeing is Nina shooting a scene on the film set. The boundaries in the film (diegesis/movie set, nightmare/reality, flashback/present time) are not only blurred but constantly punctured and transgressed by urban noises (tunnel and train sounds, dogs barking, heels clicking) or heavy echoes, especially with the leitmotif of the increasingly loud bubbling sound of boiling water.

The use of sound effects in *Nina Wu*, especially during the moments when loud noises disrupt parts of the dialogue and drown out the conversation, brings other filmic examples to mind, such as the opening scene in Dennis Hopper's *Easy Rider* (1969), or works from contemporary filmmakers like Wes Anderson and Steven Soderbergh. But none of these directors has played with the subversion of sonic codes as extensively as did the quintessential Spanish–Mexican surrealist Luis Buñuel. Agustín Sánchez-Vidal (1991, 99, qtd in Mora-Catlett 1999, 44) describes how Buñuel's *The Discreet Charm of the Bourgeoisie* (*Le Charme discret de la bourgeoisie*, 1972) – better known as the film of interrupted dinners – 'shows us as its *theme* a series of frustrations' while at the same time using its cinematic form to frustrates viewers' consumption of the story. *Nina Wu* contains many surrealist elements that generate frustration in viewers by subverting the expectations of a conventional story from/about a sexual violence survivor. This film operates on the subliminal: the dream effects, together with sonic intervention, create a non-linear narrative structure that plays with time, memory, confusion, suspension, and repetition. These elements can be understood as taking cues from the often involuntary, temporary paralysis a sexual assault survivor experiences during a brutal attack or traumatic event. Mainstream media have led the public to believe that active resistance among victims is possible when, in fact, the survivors are much more likely to experience tonic immobility during the attack and to develop PTSD and severe depression afterwards (Möller et al. 2017).

What does it mean for Midi Z, then, to make a film like *Nina Wu*, which departs from his primary thematic concern with the consequence of globalisation and capitalism for Myanmar's citizens? *Nina Wu* signifies a transition from risky, illicit, secret videography to elaborate images and multinational co-productions.[7] The film demonstrates a narrative and spatial shift from Midi's previous filmmaking style: it moves from commodity narratives (transnational movements of people and the grey economy) to an inversive Taiwan dream (the search for a successful career in the entertainment business). Or, more accurately, it is a film that explores a woman's search for identity and self-affirmation in the wake of workplace trauma. Despite the spatial and authorial shifts, the film's takeaway has much in common with that of his earlier films. The bleak ending of *Nina Wu* ultimately conveys hopelessness and the character's inability to improve her situation, much like what Midi's other characters experience in the Homecoming Trilogy.

Conclusion

The question of how Midi Z's *Ice Poison* came to represent Taiwan's national cinema in the 2015 Academy Awards is ultimately best considered not just

---

[7] Excluding Taiwan-based and Midi Z's own film production companies, *Nina Wu* is co-produced by two other foreign ventures: Malaysia-based Jazzy Pictures and Myanmar Montage Pictures (which also co-produced the 2016 *The Road to Mandalay*).

in the context of that one film but in light of his full body of work. Perhaps most productive is Ran Ma's (2020, 210) proposal of a 'translocal authorship' framework. She argues:

> Whereas Midi Z has been wildly/widely celebrated as *the* Burmese auteur, it is equally important to look at how his auteurship dialogues with the discursive construction of a 'national cinema' of Taiwan, especially when such correlations cannot be neatly explained by merely turning to Midi's passport identity as a Taiwanese citizen.

Midi might not have been part of the initial Taiwan New Cinema movement, but neither does his emergence correspond to the later revival of genre films. His work should, instead, be regarded as a continuation of the New Cinema direction. In response to the widespread criticism of the Ministry of Culture's choice of *Ice Poison* to represent Taiwan, Ang Lee explained: 'the film has inherited the aesthetic style of Taiwan New Wave yet uses the linear narrative structure of mainstream cinema' (Li 2014). This observation is true of much of Midi's oeuvre, not just of this film. Brian Bernards (2021, 354–5) details the technical aspects of New Wave's modest influence on Midi, describing how the director uses 'frequent medium-shot long takes in which action unfolds both in front of and off camera', and observing that 'the camera eye is not dictated by action', creating a sense of disorientation among audiences. And yet, as Song Hwee Lim (2018b, 9) observes, even as the use of extensive long takes in Midi's films 'places him in the tradition of Taiwan New Cinema auteurs Hou Hsiao-hsien and Tsai Ming-liang', those long takes 'tend to have slightly more action and also more sonic elements'. His work represents an evolution in Taiwan New Cinema, not more of the same.

Ultimately, Myanmar-born director Midi Z challenges the concept of 'Taiwaneseness' through his films, which incorporate a hybrid style of realist cinema and a 'bottom-up perspective' of globalisation (Robinson 2020) to challenge the narrative norms about the global economy in the so-called developed world. Midi's films adapt elements of Taiwan New Cinema style and slow cinema, but they refashion this style by way of the soundscape and inject ambiguity into the narrative form as well as the sonic space. Ultimately, however, hopelessness reigns. From economic exploitation to sexual exploitation, and despite the characters' unrelenting efforts, hopeless resolution is a commonality throughout Midi's filmography. Configured by the 'disjunctive' and 'chaotic' consequence of global flows (Appadurai 1990), Midi's filmic subjects are fundamentally impeded by the larger political and capitalist forces obstructing their every move and every decision, whether it is migratory, economic, or gendered.

CHAPTER 6

To the Future: Film Festivals as Producers and Sleeping in the Cinema

A man with a shaved head wearing a Buddhist monk's robe is seen slowly leaving a building. His slow steps contrast with the open door behind him, which shows the world moving in real time. The film redirects audience attention to the urban commotion on the other side of the door: a cyclist, a bus, a man in a purple jacket. This is the first scene in *Walker* (2012), a 25-minute short film that is a philosophical reminder to slow down in the fast-paced city of Hong Kong. The 2-minute opening shot lasts long enough for the viewer's gaze and mind to wander to the background, at which point it is no longer possible to tell whether the monk is really moving or has been standing still the entire time.

Walker is one of the instalments in a larger project with the same title by Tsai Ming-liang, also known as the 'Slow Walk, Long March' series. This collection includes other experimental short films such as *Walking on Water* (2013), which is Tsai's contribution to the anthology film *Letters from the South* (2013), produced by a Malaysian woman director, Tan Chui Mui. The anthology comprises vignettes from a total of six Chinese diaspora filmmakers from Southeast Asia, including Myanmar-born director Midi Z. (Midi Z's contribution, *Burial Clothes*, was later extended into the feature-length version *Ice Poison* (2014), discussed in Chapter 5.) The films of the Slow Walk series feature Tsai's long-time muse Lee Kang-sheng walking unbelievably slowly as the character of Xuanzang – a real Buddhist monk known for his pilgrimage from China to India in the seventh century – through the streets of international cities and countries such as Tokyo, Hong Kong, Malaysia, and France. Throughout his career as a film director and auteur, Tsai Ming-liang has specialised in making films that emphasise duration and the passage of time. The *Walker* series, on the other hand, has no action, no story, no performance, no emotions; the viewer is simply invited to observe bodily movement across the screen. These works are almost entirely constituted by repetition, making this more a staging of the labour of walking (Lim 2017, 180–96) than a linear narrative experience. At the same time, before the film begins, audiences sit through the opening credits and view what is typically accepted as nominal and customary: multiple logos listing various film funds and sponsorships which the filmmaker received to develop, produce, and distribute his film (Figure 6.1). *Walker*, and the subsequent work *No No Sleep* (2015), were commissioned by the Hong Kong International Film Festival and Youku, a video hosting service based in Beijing, China. First released on Youku's website, *Walker* is a segment of the collection 'Beautiful 2012: Four Masters' Micromovie produced by Youku', which had already been seen by over 4 million viewers by the time of the festival.

This type of collaboration to make a festival-funded film is nothing new. For example, since its infancy, the Pusan Promotion Plan, based in South Korea, has funded many Asian film projects. Many of the completed films that received funding from the Pusan Promotion Plan went on to win festival awards, garnering greater global recognition and jumpstarting the then lesser-known or unknown directors' careers and their sustainable future. Films such as *Platform* (Jia Zhangke, 1998), *The Circle* (Jafar Panahi, 2000), *Beijing Bicycle* (Wang Xiaoshuai, 2001), *Address Unknown* (Kim Ki-duk, 2001), *Oasis* (Lee Chang-dong, 2002), and *Woman Is the Future of Man* (Hong Sang-soo, 2004) are a few examples of completed projects funded. Similarly, many now celebrated, highly conceptual independent films from East and Southeast Asia (such as those of Apichatpong Weerasethakul, Midi Z, and Song Fang) benefited from this type of production and distribution support, from entities such

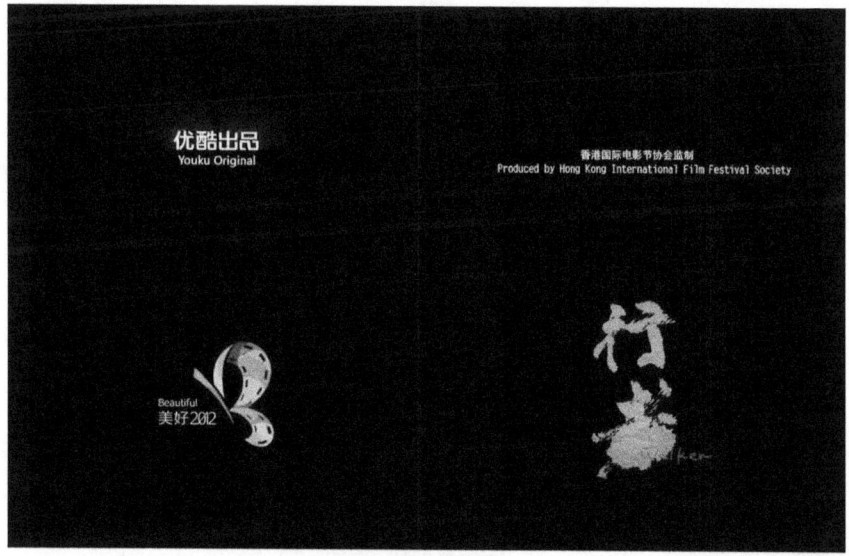

Figure 6.1 *The opening credits of Tsai Ming-liang's* Walker *(2012). Film stills.*

as the Berlinale's World Cinema Fund and the Hubert Bals Fund of the International Film Festival Rotterdam. Both funds provide financial support – especially to filmmakers from under-served regions and countries – at every stage of the filmmaking process, from script development to post-production and distribution.

Scholars have previously focused attention on 'the festival film', and particularly on how festival funding tends to support a filmmaker's artistic vision over a film's marketability (Falicov 2016, 209–29; Ostrowska 2010, 145–50; Ross 2011, 261–7). As Tamara L. Falicov (2016) points out, film festivals are now more than ever acting as 'brokers' between international producers and seasoned directors, and between new directors and film festival curators (210). The existence of these funds raises questions about the ways in which film festivals shape contemporary art cinema at large and how the projects became part of the global film festival establishment. In this chapter, I want to trace filmmakers' crossover to an alternative exhibition fostered by such opportunities, using Tsai Ming-liang as a case study. As we have seen, what is unique about Tsai and his work is that he moves back and forth between museums and movie theatres; while making considerable inroads in the gallery, Tsai continues to produce films for traditional theatrical release. In Roger Beebe's (2014) view, artists' cinema and moving-image art are not mutually inclusive. The museum installation format may work well for some films and videos created by feature-film directors; at the same time, it may defeat experimental film's purpose of rejecting the art world. In Tsai's films and cine-installations, it is not just about the significance of relocating films in the art gallery space; it is also about a conceptual form of alternative 'distribution' at these gallery sites, where the filmmaker is somewhat conscious of and actively involved in the museum's ticket sales for his exhibition (Tsai 2019). And vice versa, the deliberate choice to insist on providing a traditional cinema experience for one of his recent works, *Your Face* (2018) – a work reminiscent of Andy Warhol's *Screen Tests* (1964–6) that has been criticised for being better suited to a separate gallery installation – is an inversion of what Tsai describes as 'an attempt to transform a movie theatre into an art museum' (Your Face & Light, n.d.).

This chapter surveys the recent development of film festival funding, examines the role it takes in positioning film festivals in the global economy of the film industry, and assesses how a transmedia project like Tsai's series of *Walker* films contributes new meaning to the label 'festival film'. While I focus on one specific auteur here, my intention is to conduct a broader enquiry into the relationship between affects, exhaustion, duration, funding projects, and the production of spectatorship. Does a kind of transnational co-production infuse the works' form, style, and content? What does it mean when viewers are encouraged by the film director to sleep amongst moving images in front of the silver screen or in the gallery space, or invited to 'camp out' in the museum grounds? How do we think about the experience of film-viewing and sleeping in the cinema at these new exhibition sites where film no longer has 'an exclusive presence' but becomes 'something that seems to "take place" from time to time' (Casetti 2015, 12)? I argue that Tsai Ming-liang's shift in practice (from the movie theatre to the art gallery) benefits from the global economy and hierarchy of curatorial practices lifted from film festivals to expand a global vocabulary of slow aesthetics. The act of relocating the films and repurposed cine-installations is a rebellion against the unforeseen consequences of an accelerating world.

Festival Co-production and Financing

In the last two decades or so, film festivals have increasingly taken on the role of managing producers. Film festivals are no longer simply exhibitors and disseminators of films and emerging media (for example, virtual reality and augmented reality). They are also nodes for film markets and industry events, a meeting place for financiers, investors, potential international co-productions, and transnational flows of personnel and labour. Aside from catering to audiences, critics, filmmakers, sales agents, and so on, major festivals have developed promotion programmes, since 1989, to fund promising directors and producers directly – classified as recognising and supporting new talents, often from under-served parts of the world – and to claim the work produced by recipients and its future success by association through an 'exclusive' or 'new discovery'. Each festival's funding programme mission varies in degree: in large part, they favour filmmakers who come from developing countries (Rotterdam's Hubert Bals Fund, Tribeca's Latin American Media Fund) or transitioning countries (Berlinale's World Cinema Fund, Sundance Labs), promote regional identity (Asian Project Market, formerly the Pusan Promotion Plan), or champion those who are 'the next generation of international filmmakers' (Cannes's Cinéfondation) (Ostrowska 2010, 145–50).

While notable festival funds have been around since the 1990s, this 'deeply interwoven tapestry of transnational funding modules' intensified when the global economy shifted to a neoliberal model in the new millennium (Falicov 2016, 211). The film funds serve two primary functions: one, to assist directors from places where funding is limited, or places that lack a viable film industry and culture, in the filmmaking process at every stage from early script development to post-production and distribution. Second, while each grant has different requirements, finished projects gain better access to exhibition venues and distribution opportunities, if not a guaranteed place or even the spotlight at its funding festival. The funding modules benefit both sides. According to Julian Stringer (2001), many European film festivals benefit from being able to 'claim' their part in 'discovering' the potential of the projects they fund that support Global South filmmakers (134–44). While film funds' policy can vary year by year, many of them focus their support on the production and distribution of feature films and documentaries from the Global South exclusively, referring to projects from or about Latin and Central America, the Caribbean, Africa, the Middle East, and Central and Southeast Asia. Recognising projects coming from the 'Global South' – a term that has gained much cultural currency in recent years, and has replaced the antiquated and politically charged 'developing countries' or 'Third World' from the First/Second/Third World divide – accentuates the framework of the centre (Western Europe and wealthy North America) versus the periphery in capitalist and labour markets. The term Global South also highlights countries, typically former colonies (some experiencing brisk economic growth – not all are low-income), that are still 'wrestling with the legacies of colonialism' (Falicov 2016, 210).

At the same time, between the rivalry and mutual imitation of port-city festivals (Hong Kong, Shanghai, Tokyo, and Busan), film festivals in Asia have been growing at a rapid speed since the 1990s (Iordanova 2011, 1–33; Davis and Yeh 2008; Stringer 2012, 239–61). These festivals not only are major players in the region, but also appear to be a one-stop destination for film markets, especially trade events on the global stage. While film festivals are inherently transnational, even when a festival is launched with a nationalist agenda in mind (Iordanova 2016, xi–xvii), it is nearly impossible to divorce the concept of film festivals from the city or land that the physical events occupy. Issues concerning where a film festival is located (geography) and when it was conceived and developed through time (history) are vital to understanding power relations on the international film festival circuit. To quote Stringer (2016) again: 'it is necessary... [to] consider where film festivals have (or have not) been set up and where they have (or have not) flourished' (34). The significance of the Pusan Promotion Plan (PPP) to the Busan International Film Festival, then, is that it makes it the first festival in Asia to be modelled on these funding initiatives, which enabled it to compete on circuits dominated by Western European and North American festivals (Ahn 2012, 105). It speaks to the ways in which, in order to be considered viable in the regional and global contexts, film festivals need to find a way to position themselves strategically in the industry by leveraging their role in a global economy. This is particularly so when the aura of prestige – traditionally linked to theatrical premières at select sites such as Cannes, Venice, Berlin, and Toronto – reflects the A-list film festivals' gatekeeping practices in the film eco-system (Elsaesser 2005; de Valck 2016, 100–16). Most importantly, to create a sustainable future, film festivals have much to gain from being involved in the production stage rather than being co-dependent on the accessibility and availability of films. The PPP model, through financing, developing, co-producing, and marketing film projects specifically from Asia, counterbalances Western domination in its ambition to create a greater output of festival-funded productions. Servicing its neighbouring Asian countries, PPP aims to act as a co-producer to Asian cinema it deems both cutting-edge and commercially viable, as well as a one-stop hub for the distribution of European art cinema for Asian audiences.

The impact of PPP directly contributed to the rising status of the Busan International Film Festival (BIFF) as a new power player in the global film market. SooJeong Ahn (2012) noted that it was at an open forum in 1997, a year after the BIFF went live, that critical questions raised during discussions prompted the organisers of the festival to reflect on their conditions of operation. These questions mainly concerned issues related to distribution: for example, an attempt to identify key marketing and pre-sale companies for Asian cinema. They asked: how are Asian cinemas introduced and presented to the European public? Why was it challenging to market Asian cinemas in North America (in the late 1990s)? These questions were central and urgent because, as Ahn (2012, 104) has observed, while Asian cinemas (particularly Chinese) were seen as a 'new discovery' in the West and have been favourably received by international festival audiences, the same films tend to fall short on marketing for theatrical releases and instead thrive using less desirable venues of circulation such as video-on-demand and home-viewing options. These questions thus compel the BIFF to recognise the power a film festival can have over investment and distribution arrangements by creating a marketing event that departs from the existing ones seen at Cannes (Marché du Film) or the Berlinale (European Film Market). Aside from providing exclusive support for Asian cinema, the biggest differences from other film markets at the time, between the late 1990s and early 2000s, had to do with the PPP starting off as a meeting place – rather than offering direct funding – for financiers to buy project ideas that are still at the conceptual or pre-production stage. Once a project is finalised, PPP recipients receive a guaranteed distribution deal in South Korea. This new model further strengthens the connection between film festivals as a producer and as a 'brand', when a festival's funding plan, such as the PPP, capitalises on the part it plays in arranging and providing financial resources. The finished projects are labelled as made in Busan: the product (film) was 'chosen' and 'created' by Busan (Ahn 2012, 106). Under these branding tactics, the BIFF, arguably, has been fostering its own kind of entrepreneurship to increase visibility in the crowded global marketplace, and successfully utilises the tools of marketing to create its own competitive national identity for South Korea.

The success of the PPP and the recognition it received on the global stage have attracted other funding institutions; for example, since 1998, the International Film Festival Rotterdam has been partnering with the PPP and has become a primary driving force in financing East Asian films at its co-production market, CineMart. Similarly, European Film Promotion, an organisation that works across the board with thirty-eight countries from Europe to offer a broad range of sales and promotional strategies for the European film industry, chose the BIFF as a key festival partner in Asia over Hong Kong or Tokyo. The PPP, now renamed the Asian Film Market, is 'the must-attend Asian event in the autumn for Europe's sales agents' (Davis 2019). The cooperation between European Film Promotion and the PPP not only gestures toward expanding ties and networks between Europe and Asia, but also signals a stamp of approval from Europe in recognising Busan as an important, central nodal point in market-oriented festivals anchored in East Asia. The success story of PPP also inspired neighbouring festivals to launch their own funding plans and project markets: for example, the Tokyo Film Creators' Forum at the Tokyo International Film Festival, and the Hong Kong Asia Film Financing Forum at the Hong Kong International Film Festival, discussed below.

Festival Film

The Hong Kong Asia Film Financing Forum (using the acronym HAF) has been the financing platform of the Hong Kong International Film Festival since 2000, although it had to skip a few years in the beginning due to the severe acute respiratory syndrome (SARS) epidemic around 2003 and has been operating at full speed only since 2005. The HAF was created as a part of an initiative to achieve a greater international presence for the festival since, at the time, government funding provided few incentives for programmers to network. Currently, the HAF is co-organised by the Hong Kong Trade Development Council, and financially supported by the CreateHK and Film Development Council; both public bodies operate under the Commerce and Economic Development Bureau of the Government of the Hong Kong Special Administrative Region. The initiative was to bring Asian filmmakers with upcoming film projects to Hong Kong for co-production ventures with financiers, producers, bankers, distributors, and buyers. The HAF has since collaborated with a range of film festivals throughout the world: ACE (France), Busan (South Korea), Copenhagen International Documentary Film Festival, Taipei Golden Horse, and festivals in Moscow, Rome, and

Shanghai. Each year the HAF selects around 25-30 projects among 1,000 submissions and from at least thirty-five countries and regions (Asia Film Financing Forum, n.d.).

In listing its selection criteria, the HAF emphasises that its preferences are for films that 'display a high market potential for Asian and/or international markets' and 'exhibit both artistic and commercial qualities' (Asia Film Financing Forum, n.d.). The funds tend to be distributed to directors whom it considers to be the next generation of international filmmakers. At the beginning, the funds mainly went to East Asian and Southeast Asian countries, and (not surprisingly) projects from Hong Kong received the lion's share. This funding, however, was reduced significantly in 2007, when filmmakers from the PRC outnumbered film professionals from Hong Kong. From 2007 onward, the HAF decided to expand the range of countries selected, shifting from filmmakers predominantly based in East Asia to ones from Australia, Israel, Lebanon, and others (Asia Film Financing Forum, n.d.). The number of transnational projects significantly increased around 2010 when almost half of the selections (11 out of 25) were co-productions. Often these were regional collaborations (Hong Kong/China/Macao or Singapore/Malaysia); others reflect a larger globalised, cross-cultural production and reception. In 2012, the HAF partnered with Fox Networks Group and introduced the HAF/FOX Project Award, which aims to encourage the development of Chinese-language cinema to secure the representation of the Chinese-language community.

For the HAF to fund films from the Asian region proportionally not only is a strategy to use these films' subsequent box office success or festival awards to promote the festival's image better, but also extends the economic infrastructure within the Asian film festivals' eco-system. Predominant among the long list of notable past participants and award recipients at the HAF are art house veterans: for example, Tsai Ming-liang, Jia Zhangke, Park Chan-wook, and Apichatpong Weerasethakul. In tying the festival to their names, the endorsed funding bodies help shape the distinctive look of the event. While funding bodies have claimed to have given to a variety of genres, Falicov (2016) asserts that the narratives of the films produced by festivals in general are still 'of the "art house" variety, which we might define as a film with a particular aesthetic and set of narrative conventions made for an educated audience and from a higher socioeconomic class stratum' (213). In his definition of festival films, Rick Altman (1999) considers the films circulated at festival sites to be 'defined by their exhibition rather than by their textual characteristics' (91). Building on the notion of the exhibition, Julian Stringer (2003) argues that festival films not only are 'exhibited *at* festivals', but are frequently 'produced *for* festivals' (143). In thinking about the role that film festivals play in terms of influencing taste, Marijke de Valck (2007) adds that festival films are 'not only predominantly produced for the festival circuit, but also partially by (and with the cultural approval of) the festival circuit' (181). One should acknowledge that as far as commissioning and producing the work of selected filmmakers go, festival organisations do not directly intervene, but they may have an indirect effect on the stylistic choices filmmakers make because the image of a festival extends not just to the curatorial work but to the local audiences that attend the physical screenings. This echoes Stringer's (2003) observation that an examination of the festival film phenomenon 'reveals much about the production of cultural hierarchies of taste on an institutional and international scale' (143).

The film *Walker* by Tsai Ming-liang, mentioned earlier, a slow cinema piece commissioned by the Hong Kong International Film Festival (HKIFF), occupies, in this context, a unique position as it was neither produced through the funding competition (it was directly commissioned) nor screened exclusively at the film festival that funded it (the film premièred on the Youku website on 12 April 2012, about a month earlier than its Cannes release). While the HKIFF is responsible for commissioning only two films (the other one being *No No Sleep*) out of the entire *Walker* series, the experience inspired Tsai to continue building and expanding this example of framed slowness. The rest of the instalments were commissioned by and initially distributed across the following platforms: *No Form* was a commercial for a Chinese mobile phone.[1] *Diamond Sutra* and *Sleepwalk* were part of the Taiwan Pavilion exhibition (Architect/Geographer-Le Foyer de Taiwan) at the Venice Biennale in 2012. *Walking on Water* was another Hong Kong production with Phoenix Satellite Television, while *Journey to the West* was supported by the Marseille International Film Festival. The latest addition is *Sand*, a 79-minute film co-produced by a Taiwanese Scenic Area Administration off the island's northeast coast. The entire *Walker* series was later exhibited at a visitor centre-cum-art gallery in Taiwan called the Dune, where Tsai hosted several sleepover events at which registered campers enjoyed a series of outdoor activities with the director and slept amongst these films, which were projected on gallery walls.

The *Walker* series is an interesting departure from the director's previous body of work. First, the films embody the 'materiality of the location' (Lim 2017, 182), referring to the shooting location typically being where the

---

[1] The production of *No Form* actually proceeded *Walker*, but because *No Form* was intended as a mobile phone commercial and was slated for local release in the PRC, *Walker* was the first of the instalments to have been publicly released at international film festivals (in 2012).

funding institution is situated, providing a trans-spatial experience for the viewers. Second, while most of Tsai's feature films offer a variety of narrative schemes, these works are almost entirely constituted by a repetition of the same procedure – a slow-moving body presented as near stillness, the long duration. Third, the *Walker* series not only challenges the viewing experience of time and space on screen, as it involves a considerable amount of patience and waiting (or exhaustion and boredom), but also prompts Tsai to expand the extreme slowness off screen back to the black box theatre, amplifying the notion of what Song Hwee Lim (2017) calls 'staging slow walking as a spectacle … where Lee's appearance becomes an attraction' (181). Lim's written characterisation of the *Walker* series resounds throughout the 2014 live performance Tsai conducted, entitled the 'Monk from Tang Dynasty', a real-life extension of Lee Kang-sheng's slow walk, staged in the abandoned space of the Cinéma Marivaux, at the invitation of the Kunstenfestivaldesarts (festival of the arts) and Cinéma Galeries in Brussels, Belgium. The emphasis on slow aesthetics is typical of the director's attempt to subvert an increasingly globalised commercial film industry, particularly in the East Asian region, as Tsai (2016) has said many times during interviews (16). Tsai considers 'film as art' a concept that needs to be defended and challenged constantly, especially in the face of the mainstream audiences in Taiwan who expect to be entertained with movie stars and big-budget effects. For an expanded-cinema type of work manifested at film festivals and later moved into the gallery space, Tsai's efforts spotlight a desire to follow the self-made, self-produced, self-distributed mode of collective bargaining often associated with experimental filmmaking. Likewise, the embodied slowness on screen is a laboured protest from Tsai against an industry driven by money and a location that marginalises non-mainstream aesthetics and local identities.

If the objective of festival co-production and financing is to facilitate the creation of new works by filmmakers or new talents from the Global South that would, in turn, help raise the event's profile and consolidate cultural hierarchies of taste, then this support also signifies the co-dependency that film festivals have with filmmakers. Filmmakers needed the festival platform for exposure, to brand their style, to reassert their authorial presence, and to help them enter the global film industry. Likewise, film festivals needed to cultivate new ways to ensure a continuous supply of fresh material: preferably films that are exclusive to them or have some type of niche market value. The type of short films and exhibitions that Tsai Ming-liang is now making with his *Walker* series, examined more closely below, operates on aesthetics and styles that channel globally interconnected systems under the reception of slow cinema and cinematic sleep.

THE SLEEPY SPECTATOR

> 'When I watch a film by Hou Hsiao-hsien, Edward Yang, Tsai Ming-liang, I always fall asleep. I think maybe there's a special power to these films that take viewers to a different world, a different state of relaxation, where we can leave ourselves behind.'
>
> Apichatpong Weerasethakul, *Flowers of Taipei*

Writing in 2016, Justin Remes (2016) discloses that Abbas Kiarostami is the only director he has discovered who directly encourages his viewers to sleep. In describing Kiarostami's fondness for 'cinematic sleep', Remes claims the director's films are a statement, allowing viewers to surrender the rigorous ritual which a cinephile often upholds around film viewing ('I've got to see a picture exactly from the start to the finish'), to let go of the restraints and allow themselves to watch a film however they want (232). As one of Iran's most influential directors, Kiarostami emerged as a part of a generation of filmmakers who launched the Iranian New Wave movement. He is often linked with other contemporary slow cinema directors such as Tsai Ming-liang, Béla Tarr, Alexander Sokurov, and Kelly Reichardt, among others. Building from Kiarostami's *Five* (2003), Remes attempts to work through several important questions concerning film's relation to spectatorship in a reflective and contemplative mode. He asks: what does it mean when one dozes off and sleeps in the cinema? How do you characterise this kind of experience when spectators are free to go into a meditative state or withdraw from attentiveness, and break away from the consciousness of subjectivity? In posing these questions, Remes interestingly proposes that all of this 'moves us towards a radically non-anthropocentric cinema' (236). It is not because human appearances in these types of films are very sparse, but because the film is self-sufficient, able to prevail 'without a single conscious observer' (236).

Naturally, Kiarostami was not the only director who staged a provocative invitation to sleep during his films. Weerasethakul, known for his dreamy, personal, and slow aesthetics, has famously said that he does not mind people falling asleep in the cinema when watching his movies. He even built a *sleepy* motel – a one-off, pop-up exhibition site called Sleepcinemahotel – at the 2018 International Film Festival Rotterdam: a fully functioning, open-spaced lodging with beds, showers, and moving images projected on to a large, round screen that hung from the ceiling at the end of the hall. Similarly, Tsai Ming-liang not only has suggested in multiple interviews (sometimes in an ironic tone) that he tolerates sleepy spectators, but also has hosted several sleepovers and camp-out events with his cinema: most recently, at a public gallery space that exhibited all of the experimental short films from his *Walker* series to date – eight, to be exact. This gallery space is the Dune, a visitor centre in the town of Zhuangwei, Taiwan. Located just thirty miles southeast of Taipei, this visitor centre-cum-gallery space was designed by the famed architect Huang Sheng-yuan, who was greatly inspired by the area's natural sand-dune landscape. The interior of the visitor complex is created to look like a labyrinth, with winding tunnels and cave lighting, every turn lost in quiet appreciation of the dune. With a mission to serve local artists from a wide range of backgrounds, the exhibition hall (built in 2018) features a rotating schedule of artists. The gallery space was committed to film installations from Tsai's *Walker* series from the years 2018 to 2022.

Tsai, who curated his own exhibition, wrote this introduction in the pamphlet describing the space:

> Shapeless, like sand in the wind,
> As if it had emerged from a primordial land,
> the flow of the air,
> with lines on walls that resemble dunes of sand,
> and wavy, uneven floor.
> Anyone who enters
> will naturally slow down
>
> (Tsai 2018)

Note the way Tsai sets the mood for his patrons and how he suggests they interact or immerse themselves in the space in this stanza. He adds: 'You can enter barefoot, sit or lie down,' which is possible because the entire exhibition floor is covered with slopes of dark, grey sand (Tsai 2018). This dark labyrinth where windows were supposed to go is covered with wrinkled paper, with drawings of tree branches repurposed from a stage play Tsai created for the National Theatre back in 2011, a performance that is credited with being the origin of the *Walker* series. Each half-enclosed, dome-shaped room, named Dust, Wind, Sea, Rain, Tide, and Moonlight, showcases the *Walker* series, which was initially commissioned by different film festivals and funding bodies. Each space varies in size and shape; not all rooms provide the traditional red theatre chairs so often seen in Tsai's feature-length films, and even if there are chairs, they are often positioned in odd places that are not necessarily facing the screen (Figures 6.2 and 6.3).

In the park adjacent to the gallery, Tsai has hosted several sleepover events where registered campers enjoyed a series of outdoor activities with the director (who sang and cooked) before sleeping amongst his moving-image art. At the first event, during the summer of 2018, patrons toured the park, conversed with the director, and listened to him perform an impromptu concert. At night, the crowd watched Taiwanese filmmaker Lee Hsing's *Beautiful Duckling* (1965) before they were herded back to the visitor centre. Inside, everyone was free to sit, lie down, stare at their own leisure, and go to 'bed',

Figure 6.2 *Installation view of* Sand *at the Dune Gallery in Zhuangwei, Taiwan, 2020.* © *Homegreen Films. Photograph by the author.*

Figure 6.3 *Installation view of the exhibition* Walker, *at the Dune Gallery in Zhuangwei, Taiwan, 2020.* © *Homegreen Films. Photograph by the author.*

figuratively, in a sleeping bag in the company of Tsai's films, perhaps to travel to the streets of Taipei, Hong Kong, Tokyo, and Marseille in their dreams. In the morning, Lee Kang-sheng, who plays the 'monk' in *Walker*, woke everyone up. Together, they strolled to the Zhuangwei seaside to have breakfast and enjoy the sunrise over the Pacific Ocean. For patrons, the event was an odd one: a *tête-à-tête* with the famous director while simultaneously enjoying a night of camping. As mentioned above, the films exhibited in this space can be best described as having no acting, no performance, no emotions, no plotline. While the *Walker* series marks a departure in Tsai's films – from visualising cramped apartments and unequal city lives to a Buddhist meditation on body and movement – for viewers, the immersive experience is of an opposite kind: it is a shift from temporarily forgetting their suspended state in a dark theatre to becoming aware of themselves and keenly observing the surroundings. To be able to have the time and patience to sit in front of a work that is equally about the duration of time and labour allows everyone to be more attentive to the passage of time. On the projected screen, Lee Kang-sheng moves so slowly that nothing seems to be happening; but the long take is stretched long enough for something to happen, for a situation to develop, as long as one patiently observes it.

Figure 6.4 *Installation view of* No No Sleep *at the Dune Gallery in Zhuangwei, Taiwan, 2020. © Homegreen Films. Photograph by the author.*

Figure 6.5 *Image showing the Japanese actor Masanobu Ando from* No No Sleep. *Installation view of the exhibition at the Dune Gallery in Zhuangwei, Taiwan, 2020. © Homegreen Films. Photograph by the author.*

Of all the eight works exhibited at the Dune, *No No Sleep* is the most curious. Beyond the apparent lack of the red-robed monk who appears in all the previous instalments, what really stands out is the set-up for this installation at this site-specific exhibition. In an oval space that sunlight penetrates from a hole in the ceiling, a small plated sign on the wall before the entry reads, 'Caution, due to nudity presented in this work, parental supervision is advised'. But there is no door, no staff guard the entrance, and the sign is so small it is nearly impossible to see and one could easily overlook it. Once you step inside, a large, shallow pond sits between the standing area and the projector screen, with two shop stools placed in the middle of the water, both welcoming and uninviting at the same time (if a viewer wants to sit on a stool they will have to traverse the water and get their feet wet; Figure 6.4). Aside from the colourful, abstract, fleeting, and sometimes kaleidoscopic water reflections that change alongside the moving images, the viewing condition of this space is an exquisite one. It brings to mind the unconstrained condition in early cinema – before institutionalised censorship and before the rating system was enforced. I am referring to the early years of cinema when the exhibition space was not hemmed in by safety regulations relating to hygiene, lighting, safety, and the broader question of whether children should be exposed to content that was deemed immoral and mature.² This comparison is not to liken the exhibiting room of *No No Sleep* at the Dune to the same kind of viewing habitat specific to the historical context of early cinema, especially that of silent cinema, but to point out the unmonitored or even permissive space which allows viewers temporarily to lose the inhibitions that one often associates with controlled viewing conditions in the contemporary cineplex. It also speaks to the paradoxical attitude that society holds regarding nude art; it is permissible and celebrated in museum and art gallery spaces, following tradition since the days of ancient Greek art, but sexual content in cinema needs to be evaluated for age appropriateness due to the indexical quality of 'likeness'. In reality, of course, the warning sign to *No No Sleep* is perhaps more of a sidestepping of a required parental acknowledgement, for there is only one scene of nudity (the non-sexual, full-frontal male nudity of Masanobu Ando, the Japanese actor) in this 34-minute short (Figure 6.5).

This cine-installation and sleepover experiment calls into question the purpose of cinema and its function as aesthetic meditation. Two sets of questions emerged out of this practice. First, what is the significance of a filmmaker encouraging their viewers to sleep? Is the 'sleepiness' of a sleepy spectator conditioned by the surroundings, a hypnagogic environment fostered by the darkened movie theatre? Or is it induced by the aesthetics of slowness in the film itself? To speak of aesthetics, I am referring to the slow tendency often seen in the contemporary festival film, yet it might be more productive to expand this beyond the metrics of duration and narrative uneventfulness. Most importantly, how do we characterise the spectator's experience at these sites? To Buñuel (1958), 'film audiences are *lazy* and they are always *half asleep* during the movie' (478; my emphasis). Are film audiences inherently 'lazy', as the Spanish–Mexican surrealist filmmaker jokes? Or is dozing off ultimately part of a performance, as Francesco Casetti (2015) has suggested when he says 'to watch a movie has become a *performance*' (13)? Consider the concept of spectatorship, which encompasses one's perception not only of the film or the screening room, but of oneself. Is this practice not always rooted in a body, a situation, and affective emotions instigated by diegesis? Second, does

---

² For more discussion on the conditions of early cinema, spectatorship, and the historical transformation of the public sphere, see Miriam Hansen (1994), *Babel and Babylon: Spectatorship in American Silent Film* (Cambridge, MA: Harvard University Press). Hansen argues that what made Hollywood cinema so successful was not necessarily the 'classical editing style', but more the newness, the shocking sensation that came with exhibition, or the 'situations over plot' as she calls it.

this kind of 'cinematic sleep' really move away from anthropocentric cinema because of the lack or temporary suspension of spectator agency, as Remes characterises it? Or, by way of Tsai Ming-liang's unique cine-installation at the Dune, does 'cinematic sleep' seek a closer equilibrium between cinema and the Anthropocene?

To unpack the complexities of these questions, it might be helpful to start with the second set of enquiries: that is, looking at how Tsai's cine-installation mediates the relations between cinema and the environment when he relocates his work and transcribes the dimensionalities of the gallery space into an artificial natural world. The Anthropocene, an unofficial new geological epoch first described by earth scientists and stratigraphers, points to the substantial impact that humans have on the planet. As scientists suggest, excessive carbon use and dramatic climate change are so entrenched in today's world that it appears we are now living in the Anthropocene era. In Jennifer Fay's book *Inhospitable World: Cinema in the Time of the Anthropocene* (2018), she asserts that the Anthropocene 'is to natural science what cinema, especially early cinema, has been to human culture' (3). If human world-building activities are a new nature – perhaps it is not so much that the artificial has replaced nature, but that nature has, instead, become lost in the mix – then cinema 'helps us to see and experience the Anthropocene as an aesthetic practice' (3). In particular, what the Anthropocene aesthetic does to cinema is to make 'the familiar world strange to us', transforming and temporally transporting humans and the natural world into a new cinematic experience (3). To return to Tsai Ming-liang's cinematic sleep, it is worth mentioning that the idea of 'camping out' with his moving images came before the installation at the Dune. It was first introduced when the filmmaker brought his feature film *Stray Dogs* (2013) to the Museum of National Taipei University of Education (MoNTUE) for an interactive, solo exhibition, shortly after he announced that he planned to retire after his tenth feature film (and, of course, broke his 'promise'). '*Stray Dogs* at the Museum' is more complicated than simply screening the film at the museum. Besides the museum being turned into a darkened space akin to a movie theatre, patrons were encouraged to sit on the floor, sleep, eat, and even spend the night in the museum grounds. Over the ten weeks of the exhibition, not only was the feature film *Stray Dogs*, along with a conversation piece of his, *Afternoon* (2015), projected on what appeared to be crumpled, recycled drawing paper, but also Tsai brought actual tree branches that had been blown off in a typhoon not long before into the exhibition space to accompany the screening, turning it into a half-forest, half-tunnel environment surrounded by nature.

To be clear, I am not suggesting that what Tsai did with his cine-installation was radically new. It may be unusual for Taiwanese patrons to stroll into a museum at 2 am and watch Lee Kang-sheng eating a crispy-fried chicken leg on the big screen while they devour their own chicken bento box (Figure 6.6). Here, the close-up shot of the chicken leg shows more than just a savoury victual. It is a symbol of the economic ladder in Taiwan, a popular local staple reminding citizens how the country has transitioned from poverty and agriculture to a linchpin of the global economy. The fact of patrons eating their chicken bento box also implies that viewers could perform a number of activities in the white cube space where social conventions and museum policies would normally prohibit them from doing so. At the same time, there has been a long history of artists combining natural and artificial objects in museum exhibitions: for example, Brazilian visual artist and sculptor Helio Oiticica, whose environmental art called *Tropicalia* (1966–7) offered an interactive, embodied experience that could be seen as a precursor to *Stray Dogs* at the museum.

Emerging in the 1950s, Oiticica is recognised as a distinguished artist whose work, particularly in the 1970s and the early 1980s, redefined what constitutes a proper art object, foregrounding 'the engagement between the object and the individual' (de Salvo, n.d.). In *Tropicalia*, the viewer walks into a space covered with sand and gravel that provides both a path to walk on and a playground in a space surrounded by tropical plants. In this space, we see simple wood-framed booths made of colourful fabrics and tinted plastic sheets, partitioning the room for patrons to step through. Sounds from Amazonian

Figure 6.6 *Lee Kang-sheng devouring a chicken leg in real time. Film still from* Stray Dogs *(2013).*
© *JBA Production.*

parrots deepen the sensory surroundings for people who walk into the structure. In Oiticica's work, the artist places the spectator *inside* the work of art; it is not just the textiles or walking on sand that bring the viewer closer to the art, but the viewer becomes *part of* the artwork while participating in the work of art itself. The significance of Oiticica's work is about constructing the structure and embodied architecture. In comparison, Tsai's work is about moving or relocating his cinema in a gesture I call *resiting*, to amplify the associated sensory experience. *Resiting* plays on the word site/cite, or more precisely, builds on what Jean Ma (2010) refers to as the auto-citational tendency of Tsai's entire filmography. Citation, or to cite, is a form of intertextual reference to other films, whether it features a series of visual textures, codes, thematic tropes, or motifs. Tsai's feature films are certainly not short of intertextuality: most notably, *What Time Is It There?* (2001) and *Visage* (2009) feature a series of references to French cinema and Renaissance paintings, as discussed in Chapter 4. And auto-citation, referring to borrowing, extending, expanding, or repeating visuals, motifs, and codes from earlier work, is not specific to Tsai, but common in films by filmmakers who are recognised as auteurs, which analogises filmmaking to authorship in order to draw on the long history and cultural cache of literature and pop culture.

And yet, this resiting, as I point to the materially complex work of citation with the Dune or *Stray Dogs* at the museum, is also a consideration of space. Resiting a filmmaker's own cinematic work is a form of effective recycling; by emphasising the connection between cinema and the deliberately transported natural surroundings, Tsai's cine-installation furthers a contemplation of the Anthropocene. In her work, Fay (2018) also looks to the Chinese Sixth Generation filmmaker Jia Zhangke's *Still Life* (2006) as an example of Anthropocentric cinema, illustrating how Jia uses film to capture a place or to record the disappearing landscape 'at the moment of its undoing, a place that is changing too fast' (19). If we compare Tsai to Jia – for both filmmakers express a substantial amount of nostalgia in their cinema and have a tendency to reminisce about the past in their authorial present – then the connection between cinema and objects from the natural world (sand, water, fallen tree branches) in reaction to the disappearing wilderness further reinforces the significance of resiting: to relocate.

Casetti's *Seven Key Words for the Cinema to Come* offers a practical theoretical framework that may be used to answer my earlier set of questions relating to spectatorship (namely, what is the significance here, and how do we characterise the sleepy spectator at these site-specific events?). In Casetti's (2015) key word approach, the writer unpacks the term *relocation*, where he states that though digitisation has changed and reshaped what we used to think of as films (if removed from the projector–film theatre complex, they are just digital files now), we still identify all viewing experiences as 'cinematic' because of habit, because of memory association, because we are building on what we are used to (the institutionalised cinematic apparatus) as we continue to imagine, or decide that *this is* cinematic experience (20–2). In other words, these experimentations enrich and regenerate the cinematic experience, on the one hand, and contest it, on the other.

At these site-specific events, the *Walker* series' exhibition site becomes a space for spectators to have a conversation with the sleeping mind. If we turn to the films themselves, whether it is *Walker* or *No No Sleep*, Elena Gorfinkel's (2012) 'affects of exhaustion' provides a valuable lens to think through why there is a strong connection between slow aesthetics and sleep (311–47). Slow cinema has too often been linked with boredom, and this boredom lies in the stillness of the long static take, open-ended, the near absence of dialogue, and thematic tropes that are the now almost clichéd constituents of the postwar art film. In Gorfinkel's work, however, she prescribes two major elements beyond the concept of boredom that spotlight spectatorial agency: endurance and duration. To endure the slowness, as she sees it, emphasises the temporality of cinema's corporeal aesthetics (such as seeing a 'sleeping body' on screen). While exhaustion is related to time and labour, on screen and off screen, the tropes of waiting and tiredness do not necessarily imply inactivity, but a reflexive consciousness: 'the body waiting for itself to recharge, re-energise … waiting for an approaching relation to the world' (Gorfinkel 2012, 342). The process of waiting is a practice of drifting. To wait, or to drift, locates us in relation to the world, to everything that has already happened and everything about to happen. Drifting can also be described as a form of auto-cruising: adapting Nicholas de Villiers's (2021) term 'cruisy' both in the queer context and as a general type of experience, a spectator engages with the agency of feeling 'sleepy'.

Thus, the power of sleep also goes beyond a conduit to dreams. Surrealists like André Breton (1924) believe that the dreams produced by sleep are not inferior to moments of reality or being awake, but a hybrid state of sleep and waking consciousness, imagining the possibility for 'sleeping logicians' and 'sleeping philosophers' (Harrison and Wood 1992, 87). If *Walker*'s slow aesthetics invite spectators to fall asleep (as everything sinks below the surface in a waking state described by the surrealists), they are validating the vulnerable act of sleeping too. Sleeping is essential to any spectator in terms of building their waking life in a world where the pace of life, driven by corporate culture and capitalism, only continues to accelerate rather than slow down. Instead, we should be asking: 'is stillness an extreme form of slowness?' Here, stillness, linked to inactivity or sleep, is very much about meditating on the passage of time. Sleeping in/with the cinema is not exclusively tied to boredom, tiredness, or resignation to the content; it is about acceptance, a time to refresh your memory, to reset the consciousness, to connect. There is an agency to sleeping in the cinema, particularly when spectators drift in and out of sleep, though the goal is not to sleep through the entire screening. Sleeping is not absent, nor does it create an absent spectator; it anchors in a different kind of cognitive state. To sleep in cinema means to be intimate with cinema because it requires retreating (both consciously and physically), often into a private space. For an audience to sleep, they must let their guard down and be comfortable enough to suspend their minds and senses temporarily. It is an uncanny, strategic practice of intimacy.

Approaching Tsai's cine-installation and camp-out events as a kind of anthropocentric cinema allows us to explore the exhibition hall and engage with the question of slowness and sleepiness. These site-specific events are very much about remediating and restructuring the apparatus, where the event is a materially complex work of citing (the director's own work), resiting (situating moving images in a new space), and recycling (the sustainability of the Anthropocene). The exhibition, along with the moving images projected, is a spatialised duration where people sleeping are part of the exhibition, not solely the spectators. An invitation to sleep at these events points to a desire for the filmmaker to invest in a deeper connection with the audience as a way to respond to and navigate the chaos we currently inhabit. At the same moment, to be able to transition, or 'distribute' the *Walker* series at a gallery space, highlights the intrinsic quality of the works themselves by way of slow aesthetics, as well as the transportability of the surroundings through resiting and recycling, which ultimately brings a hybrid consciousness to spectatorship: between stasis and movement; between awake and asleep.

Postscript: An American Girl in Taiwan

This book reflects a lifelong quest for me, the writer, introspectively trying to understand better and search for the meaning of 'hyphenated people'. My immigration and repatriation experience instigated a continuing academic interest in the past and fraught future of Taiwan's unique status as a country, as well as national identity. Having been forced to uproot from a comfortable life in the liberal US and transplanted into the collectivistic society in Taiwan, as a young teenager, I was relentlessly rebellious to my parents and teachers at school while constantly being taunted and rejected as an outsider by my peers, labelled as the obnoxious 'American girl'; worse, scorned for not being able to follow the 'unspoken rules' in Taiwanese society and double-marginalised for not being 'American' enough. My darker brown skin tone often drew a discriminatory racial question based on the premise of whiteness in America: 'if you say you came from the US, why is your skin colour so dark?'

To my amusement, with the recent release of new director Feng-I Fiona Roan's debut film *American Girl* (2021), I thought I was watching an autobiography of myself, except that I did not have to deal with a family member who is bedridden with a terminal illness. *American Girl* is a coming-of-age story of a Taiwanese girl who feels her world has been unplugged, after years of living in Los Angeles, when she is suddenly forced to move back to Taiwan with her family. Although the protagonist, Fang-yi, still speaks Mandarin, she has fully adapted to American culture and American English, and feels disorientated in the strange environment. She struggles to accept her new reality 'back home', and her frustration with the living situation is reflected in the tensions in her unhappy home life, especially with her mother, who has been diagnosed with cancer. Her reverse culture shock is exacerbated by the young teen's growing dissension with Taiwan's militaristic education system, most evidently with the school's enforced hairstyle regulations and uniform-wearing, not to mention the public shaming and caning practices the teenage girl experiences in classrooms that were considered typical of the time. The film is semi-autobiographical for director Feng-I Fiona Roan, particularly in the backdrop to the story: it is set in 2003, when the deadly 'flu', SARS, struck in China and Taiwan (I also share the same structure of feelings about it); the infection had a similar sweeping effect to what we are presently witnessing as COVID-19 tears through our lives. *American Girl*, a family drama set during the SARS outbreak, was ironically shot during the COVID-19 pandemic.

American Girl could give us a glimpse into the future to see where Taiwan New Cinema could go from here. It has been hailed as the 'must-see' Chinese-language film of the year and received five award wins and seven nominations at the Golden Horse Film Festival and Tokyo International Film Festival in 2021. It was an across-the-board nomination and resulted in wins for Best New Director (Feng-I Fiona Roan), Best Cinematography (Giorgos Valsamis), and Best New Performer for young actresses Caitlin Fang, who made her acting debut at only fifteen years old. The film was a hit in Taiwan, as reflected in domestic box office sales, encouraged through word-of-mouth marketing (it ranked second on its opening weekend). It was indeed a rarity in the history of Taiwan cinema in terms of it narrating a girl's coming-of-age story told by a woman director (most Taiwan films centre on a boy, such as *A Summer at Grandpa's*, 1984), and is an embodiment of the New Cinema style that is reminiscent of the poetic quietude and subdued acting found in the works of the New Cinema cohort – Hou Hsiao-hsien, Edward Yang, and Ang Lee – as observed by film critics and general audiences.[1] *American Girl*'s premise is loosely shared with Yang's *Taipei Story* (1985) in the way that both main characters return from Los Angeles to find themselves in a strange city, dealing with a certain longing to escape back to the US, which is seen as a solution to all the problems. Both films' open endings leave viewers wondering what is next for the characters. Will they ever find a way out of the impasse?

Other Taiwanese viewers confessed that they do not see the relevance of the story to their everyday life experience in Taiwan – they find the very concept of the 'American dream' outdated and share no empathy with the protagonist's desperation to return to the US – or that they are less interested in the 'slow cinema' style often associated with festival films. Yet, despite the general audiences' hesitation and perplexity, their comments showed how decisively Taiwan New Cinema has influenced subsequent filmmaking,

---

[1] See, for example, the film review by Zen Da (2021), 'A Review of *American Girl*: Family Drama Through Everyday Life'. *Zen Da's New Life in Dunnan*. Blog, 3 December. Available at <https://zen1976.com/american-girl/> (last accessed 16 August 2022). See also Wen Wen Kai (2021), '2021 Golden Horse Awards *American Girl* Film Review'. *The News Lens*, 28 October. Available at <https://www.thenewslens.com/article/158153/> (last accessed 16 August 2022).

whether consciously or unconsciously; it is not a matter of whether contemporary filmmaking and audiences can ever abandon the New Cinema framework, but instead it becomes crucial to recognise the spirit of New Cinema filmmaking that has been imprinted on the younger generation.

The story of *American Girl* may be modelled after the director's repatriation experience, but the resulting work is a product of different inputs from and collaboration of a small but cosmopolitan film crew. The screenplay was co-written with Bing Li, of the Chinese diaspora, who previously served as a script consultant on the director's graduation thesis, *Jie Jie*, while Roan was studying at the American Film Institute in 2016. At the pre-production stage of *American Girl*, Roan's insistence on using Greek cinematographer Giorgos Valsamis, rather than hiring a veteran Taiwanese cinematographer, raised questions from the *fudaojin* jury when the project was under consideration for a domestic production subsidy (Chen 2021). Roan's justification was that she wanted to create an outsider's look at the old Taipei to maintain an objective distance without being overly attached to actual memories of the locations. The executive producer for this film, Tom Shu-Yu Lin, fully supported Roan's decision. As an acclaimed director, screenwriter, and recipient of major festival funds, not least from the Asian Cinema Fund of the BIFF, Tom Lin's name being attached to the project helped convince the *fudaojin* jury to back the production. The subdued storytelling reminiscent of the Taiwan New Cinema's makeshift style is probably the result and combination of using non-actors and shooting mostly in enclosed spaces (such as the apartment, schools, restaurants, Internet cafés, and so on) because the film crew had to work under many restrictions during the COVID-19 pandemic. The film's connection to the New Cinema is also built on one obvious factor: during interviews, Roan (2021) frequently discussed the filmmakers that inspired her, not least the pioneers of Taiwan New Cinema alongside other world cinema auteurs such as Yasujiro Ozu (Japan), Hirokazu Kore-eda (Japan), the Dardenne brothers (Belgium), Asghar Farhadi (Iran), and Andrea Arnold (UK). Her international mindfulness speaks to her understanding of a set of narrative and aesthetic expectations associated with the type of films that made it to the final festival selection.

If the future of filmmaking belongs to the transnational film crew making 'accented cinema' (Naficy 2001), what would the future of film festivals be like, considering not just format changes in the post-pandemic context but the interventions they may produce for world cinema, especially the production of cinema from a small nation? Myanmar-born Taiwanese filmmaker Midi Z's continued spotlight at the Cannes Film Festival in 2022 is a telling sign of how filmmakers and festival platforms rely on each other to capitalise on copious cultural exchanges and unity in diversity. After *Nina Wu* was screened as part of the 'Un Certain Regard' section at the Cannes Film Festival in 2019, Midi was invited back to Cannes to host the two-week 'La Fabrique Cinéma', a workshop that prioritises assistance for young directors from Africa, South America, Asia, Eastern Europe, and the Middle East, and was created in 2009 by the Institut Français, the French government agency for cultural development. Midi too benefited from his participation in the workshop and from the accreditation of the Cannes co-production platform L'Atelier. Both network opportunities opened the doors for Midi to receive production funding from the Berlinale's World Cinema Fund for his 2016 film *The Road to Mandalay*.

It has also been announced that Midi Z's long-standing muse, Wu Ke-Xi, will star in *The Perfumed Hill*, the upcoming project of award-winning Mauritanian-born Malian director Abderrahmane Sissako (known for his Mauritanian–French drama *Timbuktu*, 2014); the film was due to begin shooting in Taiwan in the summer of 2022. This goes to show that none of these links or the success in achieving international film festival funding was a one-way street or an isolated moment; again and again, they accentuate the hyphenated identity and the inherent transnational qualities of Taiwan art house cinema that can be recognised by tracing how these films are situated in and produced by the international film festival circuit. The increasing role of film festivals as key producers, along with their funding schemes, continues to highlight the transnational connections of Taiwan New Cinema as multidirectional, complex, interactive conjunctures that are temporally and spatially bounded. These practices simultaneously underscore the uphill battle that many filmmakers face due to political or social instability and lack of infrastructure and insufficient funding support on either the private or the state level in some parts of the world. If we need to imagine the future of cinema, we hope to see that film festivals are at a critical moment not only in transforming the cinema landscape and advancing under-represented minorities to take centre stage, but also in restructuring the platform to allow the Global South to become a significant player in production incentives and expand as significant regional production hubs.

Bibliography

53rd Golden Horse Awards. 2016. *United Daily News*. Taipei: udnSTAR, 26 November.
AlloCiné. n.d. 'Le Voyage du ballon rouge: les secrets du tournage'. Available at: <https://www.allocine.fr/film/fichefilm-112179/secrets-tournage/> (last accessed 11 August 2022).
Ahn, SooJeong, 2012. *The Pusan International Film Festival, South Korean Cinema and Globalization*. Hong Kong: Hong Kong University Press.
Altman, Rick. 1999. *Film/Genre*. London: BFI.
Anderson, John. 2005. *Edward Yang*. Champaign: University of Illinois Press.
Appadurai, Arjun. 1990. 'Disjuncture and Difference in the Global Cultural Economy'. *Theory, Culture & Society* 7: 295-310.
Asia Film Financing Forum. n.d. Available at: <https://www.haf.org.hk/> (last accessed 12 April 2021).
Assayas, Olivier. 1984. 'Notre reporter en République de Chine'. *Cahiers du Cinéma* 366: 57-66.
Assayas, Olivier. 1997. 'Cinémas d'Asie: Par Hou Hsiao-hsien' [Asian Cinema: Films by Hou Hsiao-hsien]. *Cahiers du Cinéma* 512 (April): 22–8.
Bao, Weihong. 2007. 'Biomechanics of Love: Reinventing the Avant-garde in Tsai Ming-liang's Wayward "Pornographic Musical"'. *Journal of Chinese Cinemas* 1, no. 2: 139-60.
Barthes, Roland. 1977. *Image, Music, Text*. Translated by Stephen Heath. London: Fontana.
Barthes, Roland. 1986. 'Leaving the Movie Theatre'. In *The Rustle of Language*, 345-9. Translated by Richard Howard. Oxford: Blackwell.
Baudelaire, Charles. 1995. *The Painter of Modern Life and Other Essays*. Translated by Jonathan Mayne. New York: Phaidon Press.
Beebe, Roger. 2014. 'On "Artists' Cinema" and "Moving-Image Art"'. *The Brooklyn Rail*, July–August. Available at: <https://brooklynrail.org/2014/07/criticspage/on-artists-cinema-and-moving-image-art> (last accessed 12 April 2021).
Benjamin, Walter. 1973. *Charles Baudelaire: A Lyric Poet in the Era of High Capitalism*. London: New Left Books.
Bernards, Brian. 2021. 'Sinophone Meets Siamophone: Audio-visual Intersubjectivity and Pirated Ethnicity in Midi Z's *Poor Folk* and *The Road to Mandalay*'. *Inter-Asia Cultural Studies* 22, no. 3: 352-72.
Berry, Chris. 2020. 'An Alternative Cinema of Poverty: Understanding the Taiwanese-language Film Industry'. *Journal of Chinese Cinemas* 14, no. 2: 140–9.
Berry, Chris. 2021. 'What is Transnational Chinese Cinema Today? Or, Welcome to the Sinosphere'. *Transnational Screens* 12, no. 3: 183–98.
Berry, Chris and Mary Farquhar. 2006. *China on Screen: Cinema and Nation*. New York: Columbia University Press.

Berry, Michael. 2005. *Speaking in Images: Interviews with Contemporary Chinese Filmmakers*. New York: Columbia University Press.

Bittencourt, Ela. 2021. 'A Mesmerising Yet Frustrating Portrayal of Film Industry Exploitation'. *Hyperallergic*, 1 April.

Bloom, Michelle. 2011. 'The Intertextuality of Tsai Ming-liang's Sinofrench Film, Face'. *Journal of Chinese Cinemas* 5, no. 2: 103-21.

Bloom, Michelle E. 2016. *Contemporary Sino-French Cinemas: Absent Fathers, Banned Books, and Red Balloons*. Honolulu: University of Hawai'i Press.

Breton, André. 1924. 'First Manifesto of Surrealism'. In *Art in Theory 1900-1990: An Anthology of Changing Ideas*, edited by Charles Harrison and Paul Wood, 87-8. Oxford: Blackwell, 1992.

Brody, Richard. 2014. 'An Auteur is Not a Brand'. *The New Yorker*, 10 July. Available at: <https://www.newyorker.com/culture/richard-brody/an-auteur-is-not-a-brand> (last accessed 2 August 2022).

Buñuel, Luis. 1958. Interview by Fausto Carrillo in *México en la Cultura* (11 May), 478. Quoted in Juan Roberto Mora Catlett, 'Buñuel, the Realist: Variations of a Dream', in *Luis Buñuel's The Discreet Charm of the Bourgeoisie*, edited by Marsha Kinder, 41-59. Cambridge: Cambridge University Press, 1999.

Canby, Vincent. 1988. 'Rootless in Americanised Taiwan'. *The New York Times*, 30 September.

Casetti, Francesco. 2015 *Seven Key Words for the Cinema to Come*. New York: Columbia University Press.

Central Daily News. 1989. 'Shen cha bei qing cheng shi, xin wen ju fou ren "dong guo jian dao"' [Censoring *A City of Sadness*: Government Information Office denied 'Editing'], 28 September.

Certeau, Michel de. 1984. *The Practice of Everyday Life*. Translated by Steven Rendall. Berkeley: University of California Press.

Chai, Ling-ling. 1989. 'Theoretical Myths Around *A City of Sadness*: Semi-critique of the Problems with Modern-day Film Criticism in this Country'. *Independent Morning Post*, 10 October.

Chan, Melissa Mei-Lin. 2017. 'Mail-order Brides and Methamphetamines: Sinophone Burmeseness in Midi Z's Burma Trilogy'. *Concentric: Literary and Cultural Studies* 43, no. 2 (September): 11-31.

Chang, Shih-Lun. 2002. 'Taiwanese New Cinema and the International Film Festival Approach'. *20th Anniversary of Taiwanese New Cinema*, edited by Ya-Mei Li, 21–39. Taipei: Taipei Golden Horse Film Festival.

Chang, Wen-Chin. 2016. 'Poverty and Migration from Burma: Within and Without Midi Z's Films'. *Independent Journal of Burmese Scholarship* 1, no. 1: 43-85.

Chen, De-lun. 2021. 'Things You Only Realise After You Grow Old'. *The Reporter*, 18 November.

Chen, Liya. 2019. 'Zhao Deyin's *Nina Wu* is His First Non-Burmese Film'. *Initium Media*, 25 July.

Chen, Melody. 2003. 'Miss Taiwan in Beauty Pageant Shocker'. *Taipei Times*, 11 July.

Chiang, Ling-ching. 2012. 'Architecture as the Key to Connect Film Installations and Film Aesthetics: Using Tsai Ming-liang's Works as Example'. *Journal of Taipei Fine Arts Museum* 23: 51-79.

Chiao, Peggy Hsiung-ping. 1984. 'Yu lian fu bian zhe dui tan: xin dian ying de chu jian yu wei ji' [Conversation with the Managing Editor: New Cinema's Current Situation and Crisis]. *United Daily News*, 3 January.

Chiao, Peggy Hsiung-ping. 1985. 'These and Those People: Foreigners who Study Chinese Cinema'. *Sibaiji* [400 Blows] 1: 19–23.

Chiao, Peggy Hsiung-ping. 1987. 'You qing tian di: lian lian feng chen' [Sentient World: Dust in the Wind]. *Central Daily News*, 27 January.

Chiao, Peggy Hsiung-ping, ed. 1988. *Taiwan Xindianying* [New Taiwan Cinema]. Taipei: China Times Publishing Co.

Chiao, Peggy Hsiung-ping. 1989. 'Shi fu Taiwan shi shi: Beiqing chengshi' [Poetic Exposition in Epic Poetry: A City of Sadness]. *China Times Express*, 16-17 December.

Chiao, Peggy Hsiung-ping. 1993. 'A Case Study of Taiwan New Cinema: Hou Hsiao-hsien'. In *Passionate Detachment: Critical Essays on Hou Hsiao-hsien*, edited by Wenchi Lin, Shiao-ying Shen, and Chen-ya Li, 21–8. Taipei: Mi-tien.

Chiao, Peggy Hsiung-ping. 1994. 'Post Nostalgia and Escapism Confusion: An Overview of Taiwan Cinema in the 1950s and the 1960s'. *Unitas*, May.

Chiao, Peggy Hsiung-ping. 1999. 'Taiwanese Films Ranked Third Worldwide by the West in the 1990s'. *Liberty Times*. 28 December.

Chiao, Peggy Hsiung-ping. 2018. *Ying xiang Taiwan* [Film Taiwan]. Taipei: Gaea Books.

China Times Express. 1989. 'Xiu jian? Fang xing? Jin yan? Chu jian beiqing chengshi yin lai zhen zhen cai yi' [Edit, Release, or Ban the Film? The First Examination of *A City of Sadness* Attracted a Wave of Suspicion]. 11 September.

Ching, Leo T. S. 2001. *Becoming 'Japanese': Colonial Taiwan and the Politics of Identity Formation*. Los Angeles: University of California Press.

Chion, Michel. 1994. *Audio-visual: Sound on the Screen*. New York: Columbia University Press.

Chiu, Kuei-fen and Yu-yueh Tsai. 2014. 'Two Migration Documentaries from Taiwan'. In *Migration to and from Taiwan*, edited by Kuei-fen Chiu, Dafydd Fell, and Lin Ping, 112-24. London: Routledge.

Chiu, Kuei-fen, Ming-yeh T. Rawnsley, and Gary D. Rawnsley, eds. 2017. *Taiwan Cinema: International Reception and Social Change*. Abingdon: Routledge.

Chow, Rey. 1993. *Writing Diaspora: Tactics of Intervention in Contemporary Cultural Studies*. Bloomington: Indiana University Press.

Chu, T'ien-wen. 1989. 'Thirteen Questions about *A City of Sadness*'. *Independent Morning Post*. 11–14 July.

Chung, Shu-Yeng. 2012. 'Framing Modern Japanese Domestic Interiors through Cinematic Mapping'. *The Asian Conference on Arts and Humanities Conference Proceedings*: 581-95.

Clifford, James. 1992. 'Traveling Cultures'. In *Cultural Studies*, edited by Lawrence Grossberg, Cary Nelson, and Paula A. Treichler, 96–116. New York and London: Routledge.

Cole, J. Michael. 2020. *Cross-Strait Relations Since 2016: The End of the Illusion*. New York: Routledge.

Cook, David A. 2016. *A History of Narrative Film*. 5th Edition. New York: W. W. Norton.

Dai, Jinhua. 2008. 'Hou Hsiao-Hsien's Films: Pursuing and Escaping History'. Translated by Zhang Jingyuan. *Inter-Asia Cultural Studies* 9, no. 2: 239-50.

Dallenbach, Lucien. 1989. *The Mirror in the Text*. Translated by Jeremy Whiteley and Emma Hughes. Chicago: University of Chicago Press.

Davis, Darrell William and Emilie Yueh-yu Yeh. 2008. *East Asian Screen Industries*. London: British Film Institute.

Davis, Susanne. 2019. Quoted in Jean Noh, 'How BIFF and the Asian Film Market have become Key Events for European Companies'. *Screen Daily*, 5 October.

de Baecque, Antoine. 1990. 'Le Temps suspendu' [Suspended Time]. *Cahiers du Cinéma* 438 (December): 24–8. Translated by Valentina Vitali.

de Luca, Tiago. 2013. *Realism of the Senses in World Cinema: The Experience of Physical Reality*. London: I. B. Tauris.

de Luca, Tiago. 2016. 'Slow Time, Visible Cinema: Duration, Experience, and Spectatorship'. *Cinema Journal* 56, no. 1 (Fall): 23-42.

de Luca, Tiago and Nuno Barradas Jorge. 2016. Introduction. In *Slow Cinema*, edited by Tiago de Luca and Nuno Barradas Jorge, 1-21. Edinburgh: Edinburgh University Press.

de Salvo, Donna. n.d. Whitney Museum of American Art. Available at: <https://whitney.org/exhibitions/helio-oiticica> (last accessed 12 April 2021).

de Valck, Marijke. 2007. *Film Festivals: From European Geopolitics to a Global Cinephilia*. Amsterdam: Amsterdam University Press.

de Valck, Marijke. 2016. 'Fostering Art, Adding Value, Cultivating Taste: Film Festivals as Sites of Cultural Legitimization'. In *Film Festivals: History, Theory, Method, Praxis*, edited by Marijke de Valck, Brendan Kredell, and Skadi Loist, 100-16. New York: Routledge.

de Villiers, Nicholas. 2007. 'We are the World Cinema: *Chacun son cinéma, ou, Ce petit coup au cœur quand la lumière s'éteint et que le film commence*'. *Senses of Cinema*, no. 45 (November).

de Villiers, Nicholas. 2008. 'Leaving the Cinema: Metacinematic Cruising in Tsai Ming-liang's *Goodbye, Dragon Inn*'. *Jump Cut* 50 (Spring). Available at: <https://www.ejumpcut.org/archive/jc50.2008/DragonInn/> (last accessed 4 August 2022).

de Villiers, Nicholas. 2021. 'Sleepy Cinema, Queer Phenomenology, and Tsai Ming-liang's *No No Sleep*'. Presentation, annual conference of the Society for Cinema and Media Studies. Virtual, 17-21 March.

Deleuze, Gilles. 1989. *Cinema 2: The Time-Image*. Minneapolis: University of Minnesota Press.

Doherty, Niina. 2020. 'The Bride Who Has Returned from Hell'. *Eastern Kicks*, 16 September. Available at: <https://www.easternkicks.com/?s=the+bride+who+has+returned+from+hell> (last accessed 1 August 2022).

Douin, Jean-Luc. 2008. 'Le Voyage du ballon rouge: Juliette Binoche fait voltiger le court métrage d'Albert Lamorisse'. *Le Monde*, 29 January.

Du, Yunzhi. 1984. 'Qing buyao [wan wan] guopian!' [Please Don't Play to Kill Our Cinema]. *Ming Shen Bao*, 29 August.

Ehrlich, David. 2021. '"Nina Wu" Review: A Bold and Challenging Thriller Questions an Actress' Role in Her Own Abuse'. *IndieWire*, 26 March.

Elsaesser, Thomas. 2005. 'Film Festivals Networks: The New Topographies of Cinema in Europe'. In *European Cinema: Face to Face with Hollywood*. Amsterdam: Amsterdam University Press.

ETtoday. 2017. 'Film Director Ruthlessly Slaps Wu Ke-Xi's Face with Dollar Bills'. *ETtoday*, 28 March.

Falicov, Tamara L. 2016. 'The "Festival Film": Film Festival Funds as Cultural Intermediaries'. In *Film Festivals: History, Theory, Method, Practice*, edited by Marijke de Valck, Brendan Kredell, and Skadi Loist, 209-29. New York: Routledge.

Fay, Jennifer. 2018. *Inhospitable World: Cinema in the Time of the Anthropocene*. New York: Oxford University Press.

Fisher, Austin and Iain Robert Smith. 2019. 'Second Phase Transnationalism: Reflections on Launching the SCMS Transnational Cinemas Scholarly Interest Group'. *Transnational Screens* 10, no. 2: 114–25.

Gao, Rui-xi. 2017. 'She Was Slapped in the Face with Dollar Bills as a Rookie; Actress Strikes Back Now She is Famous'. *Mirror Media*, 28 March.

Goldsmith, Leo. 2009. 'Best of the Decade #8: *Flight of the Red Balloon*'. *Reverse Shot*, 23 December. Available at: <http://www.reverseshot.org/symposiums/entry/7/8_flight_red_balloon> (last accessed 2 August 2022).

Gorfinkel, Elena. 2012. 'Weariness, Waiting: Enduration and Art Cinema's Tired Bodies'. *Discourse* 34, no. 2-3 (Spring/Fall): 311-47.

Gronstad, Asbjorn. 2016. 'Slow Cinema and the Ethics of Duration'. In *Slow Cinema*, edited by Tiago de Luca and Nuno Barradas Jorge, 273-84. Edinburgh: Edinburgh University Press.

Hansen, Miriam. 1994. *Babel and Babylon: Spectatorship in American Silent Film*. Cambridge, MA: Harvard University Press.

Harrison, Charles and Paul Wood, eds. 1992. *Art in Theory 1900-1990: An Anthology of Changing Ideas*. Oxford: Blackwell.

Herpe, Noel. 1995. 'Vive l'amour, l'enfer du même'. *Positif* no. 410 (April): 25-6.

Higbee, Will and Song Hwee Lim. 2010. 'Concepts of Transnational Cinema: Towards a Critical Transnationalism in Film Studies'. *Transnational Cinemas* 1, no. 1: 7–21.

Hoberman, J. 2008. 'Flight of the Red Balloon Soars'. *Village Voice*, 1 April.

Hong, Guo-Juin. 2011. *Taiwan Cinema: A Contested Nation on Screen*. New York: Palgrave Macmillan.

Hou, Hsiao-Hsien. 1998. *A Complete Screenplay of Flowers of Shanghai*. Taipei: Yuanliu.

Hou, Hsiao-Hsien. 2004. Interview by Harold Manning. *Métro Lumière: Hou Hsiao-Hsien à la rencontre de Yasujiro Ozu*. Northern Line Films. DVD.

Hou, Hsiao-Hsien. 2008. Interview by Wen Tien-Hsian. *Funscreen*, no. 159.

Hsiao, Yeh. 1988. *The White Dove*. Taipei: China Times.

Hu, Brian. 2017. 'Programming Taiwan Cinema: A View from the International Film Festival Circuit'. In *Taiwan Cinema: International Reception and Social Change*, edited by Kuei-fen Chiu, Ming-yeh T. Rawnsley, and Gary D. Rawnsley, 69–79. Abingdon: Routledge.

Huang, Chun-ming. 2001. *The Taste of Apples*. Translated by Howard Goldblatt. New York: Columbia University Press.

Huang, Ren. 1994. *Beiqing Taiyupian* [The Sadness of *Taiyupian*]. Taipei: Wanxing.

Huang, Teresa. 2020. 'The Taiwan Film and Audiovisual Institute's Taiwanese-Language Cinema Restoration Project'. *Journal of Chinese Cinemas* 14, no. 2: 150–5.

Hui, La Frances. 2015. 'Interview: Son of Myanmar Midi Z Returns Home to Tell Its Tales on Screen'. *Asia Society*, 27 February.

Hunt, Leon and Wing-Fai Leung, eds. 2008. Introduction to *East Asian Cinemas: Exploring Transnational Connections on Film*. London: I. B. Tauris.

Iordanova, Dina. 2011. 'East Asia and Film Festivals: Transnational Clusters for Creativity and Commerce'. In *Film Festival Yearbook 3: Film Festivals and East Asia*, edited by Dina Iordanova and Ruby Cheung, 1-33. St Andrews: St Andrews Film Studies.

Iordanova, Dina. 2016. 'Foreword'. In *Film Festivals: History, Theory, Method, Practice*, edited by Marijke de Valck, Brendan Kredell, and Skadi Loist, xi–xvii. New York: Routledge.

Jaffe, Ira. 2014. *Slow Movies: Countering the Cinema of Action*. New York: Wallflower Press.

James, Caryn. 1989. 'Film Festivals: Postwar "Sadness" in Taiwan'. *The New York Times*, 6 October.

Johnston, Ian. 2005. 'Train to Somewhere: Hou Hsiao-hsien Pays Sweet Homage to Ozu in *Café Lumiere*'. *Bright Lights Film Journal*, 30 April.

Julé, Vincent. 2008. 'Le Voyage du ballon rouge: critique'. *Écran Large*, 29 January.

Kaganski, Serge. 1995. *Les Inrockuptibles* (France), 5 April.

Kai, Wen Wen. 2021. '2021 Golden Horse Awards *American Girl* Film Review'. *The News Lens*, 28 October. Available at <https://www.thenewslens.com/article/158153/> (last accessed 16 August 2022).

Kemp, Philip. 1994. 'The Puppetmaster'. *Sight and Sound* (June): 51–2.

Kiang, Jessica. 2019. 'Film Review: "Nina Wu"'. *Variety*, 27 May.
Kraicer, Shelly. 2000. 'Interview with Tsai Ming-liang'. *Positions: East Asia Cultures Critique* 8, no. 2 (Fall): 579–88.
Kuipers, Richard. 2016. 'Film Review: "The Road to Mandalay"'. *Variety*, 8 October.
Lee, Nikki J. Y. and Julian Stringer. 2012. 'Ports of Entry: Mapping Chinese Cinema's Multiple Trajectories at International Film Festivals'. In *A Companion to Chinese Cinema*, edited by Yingjin Zhang, 239–61. Oxford: Wiley-Blackwell.
Lee, Yung-Wei and Hsiao-Fen Peng. 1987. 'Interviews with 17 New Taiwan Cinema Film Professionals'. *Film Appreciation* 26 (March): 5–16.
Leung, Danny. 2017. 'Café Lumière: Modernising Ozu's Tokyo Story'. Video essay, 24 March. Available at: <https://youtu.be/kQDOJaTdzHw> (last accessed 2 August 2022).
Lewis, Oscar. 1996. *La Vida: A Puerto Rican Family in the Culture of Poverty – San Juan and New York*. New York: Random House.
Li, Chenya. 1998. 'From Historical Memory to the Imagination of Space: The Disappearance of Urban Images in Hou Hsiao-hsien's City Films'. *Chung-Wai Literary Monthly* 317: 120–35.
Li, Jinwei. 2014. 'Ang Lee Attends the *Ice Poison* Premiere during the 2014 Tribeca Film Festival'. *Central News Agency*, 19 April.
Liao, Gene-Fon. 1994. 'Towards a Definition of Healthy Realist Films: Memorandum on Taiwan's Film History'. *Film Appreciation* 12, no. 6: 38–47.
Liao, Gene-Fon. 2001. *Vanished Images: Xiaoshi de yingxiang: Taiyupian de dianying zaixian yu wenhua rentong* [Cinematic Representation and Cultural Identity in Taiwanese-Language Films]. Taipei: Yuanliu.
Liao, Gene-Fon. 2020. '*Taiyupian*: A Kaleidoscope of Film Production Flashes Back'. *Journal of Chinese Cinemas* 14, no. 2: 69-71.
Lim, Song Hwee. 2013. 'Taiwan New Cinema: Small Nation with Soft Power'. In *The Oxford Handbook of Chinese Cinemas*, edited by Carlos Rojas and Eileen Cheng-yin Chow, 152–69. New York: Oxford University Press.
Lim, Song Hwee. 2014. *Tsai Ming-Liang and a Cinema of Slowness*. Honolulu: University of Hawaii Press.
Lim, Song Hwee. 2017. 'Walking in the City, Slowly: Spectacular Temporal Practices in Tsai Ming-liang's "Slow Walk, Long March" Series'. *Screen* 58, no. 2 (Summer): 180-96.
Lim, Song Hwee. 2018a. 'Citizen-to-citizen Connectivity and Soft Power: The Appropriation of Subcultures in "Little Freshness" across the Taiwan Strait'. *China Information* 33, no. 3: 294–310.
Lim, Song Hwee. 2018b. 'Towards a Poor Cinema: Ubiquitous Trafficking and Poverty as Problematic in Midi Z's Films'. *Transnational Cinemas* 9, no. 2: 131-46.
Lin, Charlie. 2013. 'Report on the 45th New York Film Festival'. *Funscreen*, no. 129.
Lin, Wenchi. 1995. 'Return, Fatherland, and Two-Two Eight Incident: The History of Taiwan and National Identity in *A City of Sadness*'. *Dang-Dai Monthly* 106: 94–109.
Lin, Wenchi. 2008. 'Missing All the Good Times – Hou Hsiao-hsien's *Flight of the Red Balloon*'. *Funscreen*, no. 161.
Loayza, Beatrice. 2021. '"Nina Wu" Review: Destruction of Body and Soul'. *The New York Times*, 25 March.
Lu, Feiyi. 1998. *Taiwan dianying: Zhengzhi, jingji, meixue, 1949-1994* [Taiwan Cinema: Politics, Economics, Aesthetics, 1949-1994]. Taipei: Yuanliu.
Lu, Hsin-chun Tasaw. 2008. 'Festivalizing Thingyan, Negotiating Ethnicity: Burmese Chinese Migrants in Taiwan'. *Journal of Burma Studies* 12, no. 1: 29-62.

Lu, Sheldon. 2005. '*Crouching Tiger, Hidden Dragon*, Bouncing Angeles: Hollywood, Taiwan, Hong Kong, and Transnational Cinema'. In *Chinese-language Film: Historiography, Poetics, Politics*, edited by Sheldon Lu and Emilie Yueh-yu Yeh, 220–33. Honolulu: University of Hawaii Press.

Lupke, Christopher. 2016. *The Sinophone Cinema of Hou Hsiao-Hsien: Culture, Style, Voice, and Motion*. Amherst, NY: Cambria.

Ma, Jean. 2010. *Melancholy Drift: Marking Time in Chinese Cinema*. Hong Kong: Hong Kong University Press.

Ma, Jean. 2021. 'Sleeping in the Cinema'. *October* 176: 31–52.

Ma, Ran. 2020. *Independent Filmmaking Across Borders in Contemporary Asia*. Amsterdam: Amsterdam University Press.

Malaurie, Guillaume. 1998. *L'Express* (France), 26 March.

Martin, Fran. 2003. 'The European Undead: Tsai Ming-liang's Temporal Dysphoria'. *Senses of Cinema*, no. 27 (July).

Martina, Michael. 2022. 'U.S. Lawmakers Push to Rename Taiwan's de facto Embassy in Washington'. Reuters. 3 February. Available at: <https://www.reuters.com/world/china/us-lawmakers-push-rename-taiwans-de-facto-embassy-washington-2022-02-04/> (last accessed 1 August 2022).

Maslin, Janet. 1986. '"Time to Live" Recounts Story of Taiwan Family'. *The New York Times*, 23 September.

Mazabrard, Colette, and Frédéric Strauss. 1990. 'Entretien avec Hou Hsiao-Hsien'. Translated by Valentina Vitali. *Cahiers du Cinéma*, no. 438: 27-8.

Mi, Zou and Liang Xinhua. 1991. *Xin dian ying zhi si* [The Death of Taiwan New Cinema]. Taipei: Tonsan.

Ministry of Culture. 2007. 'Taiwan's Feature Film Production Funding Guidelines'. Bureau of Audiovisual and Music Industry Development, Ministry of Culture. Available at: <https://www.bamid.gov.tw/information_202_64362.html> (last accessed 12 November 2021).

Möller, Anna, Hans Peter Söndergaard, and Lotti Helström. 2017. 'Tonic Immobility During Sexual Assault – a Common Reaction Predicting Post-Traumatic Stress Disorder and Severe Depression'. *Acta Obstetrica Gynecologica Scandinavica* 96: 932-8.

Mora-Catlett, Juan Roberto. 1999. 'Buñuel, the Realist: Variations of a Dream'. In *Luis Buñuel's The Discreet Charm of the Bourgeoisie*, edited by Marsha Kinder, 41-59. Cambridge: Cambridge University Press.

Morice, Jacques. 2004. *Télérama* (France), 21 July.

Naficy, Hamid. 2001. *An Accented Cinema: Exilic and Diasporic Filmmaking*. Princeton: Princeton University Press.

Nagib, Lúcia. 2020. *Realist Cinema as World Cinema: Non-cinema, Intermedial Passages, Total Cinema*. Amsterdam: Amsterdam University Press.

Nicklaus, Olivier. 1998. *La Croix* (France), 25 March.

Ong, Xinhan. 2017. 'Wu Ke-Xi Furiously Shout Curse Words at the Film Director for 10 Minutes'. *NOWnews*, 4 November.

Ostrowska, Dorota. 2010. 'International Film Festivals as Producers of World Cinema'. *Cinema & Cie* X, no. 14-15 (Spring–Fall): 145-50.

Park, Je Cheol. 2013. 'The Postnational and the Aesthetics of the Spectral: Hou Hsiao-hsien's *Flight of the Red Balloon*'. In *World Cinema and the Visual Arts*, edited by David Gallagher. New York: Anthem Press.

Peng, Hsiao-yen. 2012. '*Auteurism* and Taiwan New Cinema'. *Journal of Theatre Studies* 9 (January): 125–48.

Persall, Steve. 2008. 'The Red Balloon Remake: Good, but a Snoozer'. *Tampa Bay Times*, 16 July.

Pickowicz, Paul G. and Yingjin Zhang, eds. 2020. *Locating Taiwan Cinema in the Twenty-first Century*. Amherst, NY: Cambria Press.

Qi, Long-ren. 1988. 'Tendencies of Taiwan Film Criticism – The "Audiences' Film" Criticism and the "Auteur Film" Criticism'. In *Taiwan Xindianying* [New Taiwan Cinema], edited by Peggy Chiao, 40–6. Taipei: China Times Publishing Co.

Rauger, Jean-François. 1993. 'Naissance d'une nation' [Birth of a Nation].' *Cahiers du Cinéma* 469 (June): 18–19. Translated by Valentina Vitali.

Rawnsley, Ming-Yeh T. 2013. 'Taiwanese-Language Cinema: State Versus Market, National Versus Transnational'. *Oriental Archive* 81: 437–58.

Rayns, Tony. 1984. 'Chinese Changes'. *Sight and Sound* 54, no. 1: 24–9.

Rayns, Tony, 2014. *Flowers of Taipei: Taiwan New Cinema*. Directed by Chinlin Hsieh. Taipei: Rice Flower Films. Documentary.

Remes, Justin. 2016. 'Abbas Kiarostami's *Five: Dedicated to Ozu*'. In *Slow Cinema*, edited by Tiago de Luca and Nuno Barradas Jorge, 231-42. Edinburgh: Edinburgh University Press.

Roan, Feng-I Fiona. 2021. 'American Girl Director Feng-I Fiona Roan: Interview'. Interview by Angeline Hsiao. *Harper's Bazaar*, 27 November.

Robinson, Luke. 2020. 'Midi Z, Network Aesthetics from Below, and the Cultural Politics of Taiwanese Subimperialism'. *Screen* 61, no. 1 (Spring): 98–118.

Ross, Miriam. 2011. 'The Film Festival as Producer: Latin American Films and Rotterdam's Hubert Bals Fund'. *Screen* 52, no. 2: 261-7.

Said, Edward W. 1982. 'Traveling Theory'. *Raritan: A Quarterly Review* 1, no. 3 (Winter): 41–67.

Said, Edward W. 2002. *Reflections on Exile and Other Essays*. Cambridge, MA: Harvard University Press.

Sánchez-Vidal, Agustín. 1991. *Luis Buñuel*. Madrid: Editorial Cátedra.

Sarris, Andrew. 1962/3. 'Notes on the Auteur Theory in 1962'. *Film Culture* 29 (Winter): 1–8.

Sato, Tado. 'Interview'. In *Film in Our Time: Taiwan New Cinema on the Road*, edited by Geng-yu Wang, 146–8. Taipei: Department of Cultural Affairs, Taipei City Government.

Scott, A. O. 2004. 'Like Trains, Crossing but Never Touching'. *The New York Times*, 16 October.

Shaw, Deborah. 2017. 'Transnational Cinema: Mapping a Field of Study'. In *The Routledge Companion to World Cinema*, edited by Rob Stone, Paul Cooke, Stephanie Dennison, and Alex Marlow-Mann, 290–8. New York and London: Routledge.

Shen, Kun Xian. 2018. 'Cinema of Distance: Midi Z's "Homecoming Trilogy" and the Borders of the Postcolonial and the Sinophone'. Master's thesis, National Taiwan University.

Silverman, Kaja. 1984. 'Suture'. In *The Subject of Semiotics*, 194–236. New York: Oxford University Press.

Sing, Song-Yong. 2014. *Ru jing/chu jing: Tsai Ming Liang de ying xiang yi shu yu kua jie shi jian* [Projecting Tsai Ming-liang: Towards transart cinema]. Taipei: Wunan.

Sontag, Susan. 1996. 'The Decay of Cinema'. *The New York Times*, 25 February.

Stam, Robert, Robert Burgoyne, and Sandy Flitterman-Lewis. 1992. *New Vocabularies in Film Semiotics*. New York: Routledge.

Stringer, Julian. 2003. 'Regarding Film Festivals'. PhD dissertation, Indiana University.

Stringer, Julian. 2011. 'Global Cities and the International Film Festival Economy'. In *Cinema and the City: Film and Urban Societies in a Global Context*, edited by Mark Shiel and Tony Fitzmaurice, 134-44. London: Blackwell.

Stringer, Julian. 2016. 'Film Festivals in Asia: Notes on History, Geography, and Power from a Distance'. In *Film Festivals: History, Theory, Method, Practice*, edited by Marijke de Valck, Brendan Kredell, and Skadi Loist, 34–48. New York: Routledge.

Su, Chih-Heng. 2020. 'Colour Glass Ceiling: The Life and Death of Taiwanese-Language Cinema'. *Journal of Chinese Cinemas* 14, no. 2: 76–87.
Sun, Zhi-xi. 2016. 'The Way Out for the Films of Our Generation: Failing to Succeed, Looking for the Real Way Out for Independent Films'. *Bios Monthly*, 17 May.
Taiwan Culture Portal. n.d. '2020 Program: A Transition from Taiwan New Cinema: Beyond Realism'. Available at <https://toolkit.culture.tw/en/filmtheme_60_159.html?themeId=159> (last accessed 1 August 2022).
The Economist. 1949. 'The Chinese in Formosa'. *The Economist*, 23 July.
Thompson, Kristin, and David Bordwell. 2010. *Film History*. 3rd Edition. New York: McGraw-Hill.
Tsai, Beth. 2022. '*Visage* (2009): That Obscure Face of the Muses'. In *32 New Takes on Taiwan Cinema*, edited by Emilie Yueh-yu Yeh, Darrell William Davis, and Wenchi Lin, 346-59. Ann Arbor: University of Michigan Press.
Tsai, Ming-liang. 2010a. International Film Festival at Rotterdam. Interview by Peter van der Lugt. Rotterdam. 9 December.
Tsai, Ming-liang. 2010b. *Taipei Times*. Interview by Noah Buchan. Taipei, Taiwan. 25 March.
Tsai, Ming-liang. 2011. 'On the Uses and Misuses of Cinema'. *Senses of Cinema*, no. 58 (March).
Tsai, Ming-liang. 2016. *Catalogue of Stray Dogs at the Museum: Tsai Ming Liang Solo Exhibition*. Taipei: Museum of National Taipei University of Education.
Tsai, Ming-liang. 2018. *Walker, Tsai Ming-liang*. Zhuangwei, Taiwan: Zhuangwei Dune Visitor Centre.
Tsai, Ming-liang. 2019. 'Dialogue with Filmmakers', 2019 Hong Kong International Film Festival, 22 March.
Udden, James. 2003. 'Taiwanese Popular Cinema and the Strange Apprenticeship of Hou Hsiao-hsien'. *Modern Chinese Literature and Culture* 15, no. 1: 120-45.
Udden, James. 2013. 'Taiwan New Cinema: A Movement of Unintended Consequences'. *Frontiers of Literary Studies in China* 7, no. 2: 159–82.
United Daily News. 1989. 'Beiqing chengshi can jia weinisi yingzhan wei gui' [*A City of Sadness* Attends the Venice Film Festival in Violation of Film Law], 8 August.
Uroskie, Andrew V. 2011. 'The Philosophical Toy as Model: Duchamp, Breer, and the Postwar Emergence of Cinema in the Gallery Space'. *Secuencias* 32: 34-58.
Vagenas, Maria Giovanna. 2013. 'Filmmaker Tsai Ming-liang Says His Work Should Be Appreciated Slowly'. *South China Morning Post* (Hong Kong), 27 August.
Vasudevan, Arthi. 2016. 'Café Lumière as Hou Hsiao-Hsien's Own and as a Homage to Yausjiro Ozu', *Frames Cinema Journal* 10 (December). Available at: <https://framescinema-journal.com/article/cafe-lumiere-as-hou-hsiao-hsiens-own-and-as-a-homage-to-yasujiro-ozu-2> (last accessed 2 August 2022).
Vitali, Valentina. 2008. 'Hou Hsiao-Hsien Reviewed'. *Inter-Asia Cultural Studies* 9, no. 2: 280–9.
Wang, Wan-jui. 2017. 'No Country for Young Men: DV Realism, Popular Songs and Midi Z's "Homecoming Trilogy"'. *Chung Wai Literary* 46, no. 1 (March): 147-84.
Wen, Tian-Xiang. 2002. *Guangying dingge: Tsai Ming-liang de xinling changyu* [Freeze-frame in Light and Shadow: The Spiritual Site of Tsai Ming-liang]. Taipei: Hengxing.
Wen, Tian-Xiang. 2015. Quoted in *Film in Our Time*, edited by Angelika Wang, 250–63. Taipei: Taipei City Government Department of Cultural Affairs.
Wilson, Flannery. 2014. *New Taiwanese Cinema in Focus: Moving Within and Beyond the Frame*. Edinburgh: Edinburgh University Press.
Wolff, Janet. 1985. 'The Invisible Flâneuse: Women and the Literature of Modernity'. *Theory Culture Society* 2, no. 3: 37–46.

Wu, Chia-chi. 2007. 'Festivals, Criticism and the International Reputation of Taiwan New Cinema'. In *Cinema Taiwan: Politics, Popularity and State of the Arts*, edited by Darrell William Davis and Ru-shou Robert Chen, 75–91. New York: Routledge.

Wu, Isabelle. 2007. *In the Age of Cinematic Thinking*. Taipei: Bookman.

Xu, Hui. 2014. '*Ice Poison* Has Been Chosen to Represent Taiwan in Oscars'. *Liberty Times*, 10 September.

Yap, Nicholas. 2021. '*Nina Wu*'. In *Review Online*.

Yeh, Emilie Yueh-yu. 2022. '*Dangerous Youth* (1969): Sexual Economy, Taiyu Films and Bricolage'. In *Thirty-two New Takes on Taiwan Cinema*, edited by Emilie Yueh-yu Yeh, Darrel Davis, and Wenchi Lin, 75–88. Ann Arbor: University of Michigan Press.

Yeh, Emilie Yueh-yu and Darrell William Davis. 2005. *Taiwan Film Directors: A Treasure Island*. New York: Columbia University Press.

Yeh, Long-Yan. 2017. *Tu jie tai wan dian ying shi* [Illustrating A History of Taiwan Cinema]. Taipei: Morning Star.

Yip, June. 2004. *Envisioning Taiwan: Fiction, Cinema, and the Nation in the Cultural Imaginary*. Durham, NC: Duke University Press.

Your Face & Light. n.d. Available at: <https://www.flyingv.cc/projects/22576> (last accessed 12 April 2021).

Zen, Da. 2021. 'A Review of *American Girl*: Family Drama Through Everyday Life'. *Zen Da's New Life in Dunnan*. Blog. 3 December. Available at <https://zen1976.com/american-girl/> (last accessed 16 August 2022).

Zhan, Hongzhi. 1984. 'The Past and Future of Taiwan New Cinema: One Report and Three Reviews'. *Xin shu yue kan* [New Book Monthly] 14 (November): 14–18.

Zhang, Dao-Fan. 1994. 'The Cultural Policy We Need'. In *Politics and Contemporary Taiwanese Literature*, edited by Cheng Ming-Lee, 13–23. Taipei: Shibao.

Zhang, Yingjin. 2020. 'Taiwan Film Market in the New Millennium'. In *Locating Taiwan Cinema in the Twenty-first Century*, edited by Paul G. Pickowicz and Yingjin Zhang, 21–39. Amherst, NY: Cambria Press.

Zhao, Deyin. 2015. *Ju li bindu: Zhao De-yin de dianyin rensheng jishi* [Unite, Separate, Ice Poison: Accounts of Zhao Deyin's Moviemaking]. Taipei: Tienxia Magazine.

Index

Note: 'n' indicates note.

À bout de souffle (1960), 62
A Brighter Summer Day (1991), 49, 80
A City of Sadness (1989), 9, 19, 30, 32–5, 48, 52–3, 64
A Summer at Grandpa's (1984), 32, 34, 63, 150
A Time to Live, A Time to Die (1985), 32, 34, 62
A Wardrobe in the Room (1983), 95
accented cinema, 115, 151
Address Unknown (2001), 129
affect, 13, 130, 147
Afternoon (2015), 144
All the Corners of the World (1989), 95
Amarcord (1973), 62
American Girl (2021), 149–51
Anderson, Wes, 126
Ando Masanobu, 143
anthropocentrism, 13–14, 138, 144–8
Antonioni, Michelangelo, 37, 51, 57, 97, 103
apparatus theory, 99, 101, 104–5, 147–8
Arnold, Andrea, 151
art gallery, 12–13, 55, 87–93, 100–5, 130–48; *see also* museum
Asia Society (in New York), 114
Asian Project Market *see* Pusan Promotion Plan
Assayas, Olivier, 19, 30–1, 35, 38–9, 47, 78, 78n, 83, 97
Atsuta Yuharu, 72
auteur theory, 7, 10, 40, 45, 51–4, 56–8

Bai Jing-rui, 47
Ballon rouge, Le (1956), 12, 78–9, 82–3, 86
Barthes, Roland, 90, 100, 104, 125
Baudelaire, Charles, 11, 67, 77–8

Bazin, André, 25, 53–4
Beautiful Duckling (1965), 23, 25, 139
Beijing Bicycle (2001), 50, 129
Benjamin, Walter, 53, 67n
Berlin International Film Festival, 7, 11, 29, 32, 49–50, 87n, 95–6, 98, 110, 130–3, 152
  European Film Market, 133
  Golden Bear, 49–50, 87n
  Teddy Award, 87n, 98
  World Cinema Fund, 110, 130–1, 152
Berlinale *see* Berlin International Film Festival
Bhabha, Homi, 75
Bloom, Michelle, 82, 102n
Blue Gate Crossing (2002), 50
Bold, the Corrupt and the Beautiful, The (2017), 123
Bong Joon-ho, 38
border crossing, 2, 62, 86, 117
  cross culture, 65–6, 86, 102, 135
boredom, 55, 96, 137, 147–8
Boys (1991), 95
Boys from Fengkuei, The (1984), 27, 31–2
Breton, André, 14, 147
Bride Who Has Returned from Hell, The (1965), 21
Brody, Richard, 57
Brother Wang and Brother Liu Tour Taiwan (1959), 24
Buchan, Noah, 93
Buñuel, Luis, 7, 126, 143
Burial Clothes (2013), 128
Busan International Film Festival, 108–9, 132–4
  Busan New Currents, 109
  Pusan Promotion Plan (PPP), 129, 131–4

Café Lumière (2003), 11–12, 61–77, 86
Cahiers du Cinéma, 19, 31, 33, 47, 51, 97
Canby, Vincent, 34, 49
Cannes Film Festival, 3, 7, 11–12, 29, 32, 78, 88, 91–2, 96, 108, 120, 131–3, 136, 151–2
   Cannes Cinéfondation, 131
   Marché du Film, 133
   Palme d'Or, 88
   Un Certain Regard, 108, 120, 152
Cape No. 7 (2008), 4
censorship, 12, 17, 23–4, 28, 32–3, 40–5, 110, 115, 117, 142
Central Motion Picture Corporation, 25, 27–8, 37–8, 40–3, 49
Chai Ling-ling, 53
Chang Shih-Lun, 29, 39
Chang Wen-Chin, 114
Chang Yi, 28
Chen Kunhou, 27
Chen Kuo-Fu, 28, 31, 45, 47
Chiang Ling-ching, 89–90
Chiao Peggy Hsiung-ping, 3, 10, 23, 37–58, 96n
China Times, 32, 45, 49
Chinese Taipei Film Archive, 20, 37, 52
Chinese Taipei, 6, 20, 37, 52, 112–13
Ching, Leo T. S., 75
Chion, Michel, 115
Chou Mei Ling, 98
Chu T'ien-wen, 3, 10, 12, 28, 34, 37, 39, 46, 52–3, 63, 66n
cinephilia, 7, 12, 20, 31, 35, 43n, 55, 74, 89–90, 96, 104, 138
Circle, The (2000), 129
class, 20, 25, 41, 95, 107, 114, 135
co-production, 13–14, 26, 49–50, 64, 86, 126, 130–7, 152
colonialism, 1, 6, 12, 74–7, 132
Copenhagen International Documentary Film Festival, 134
Cruel Story of Youth (1960), 22

Dai Jinhua, 64
Dallenbach, Lucien, 83–5
Dangerous Youth (1969), 22
Daughter of the Nile (1987), 32, 34, 57
Davis, Darrel William, 21, 63, 102n, 132
Days (2020), 87, 87n
de Luca, Tiago, 55, 90

de Villiers, Nicholas, 91, 102, 147
death, 43, 98
   of cinema, 90–1, 101
   of the author, 125
Deleuze, Gilles, 54–5, 96, 98
Diamond Sutra (2012), 136
diaspora, 14, 107, 110, 115, 128, 151
   qiao sheng, 110
Diaz, Lav, 90
Discreet Charm of the Bourgeoisie, The (1972), 126
disorientation, 101, 113, 127, 149
Dissanayake, Wimal, 46
Doyle, Christopher, 35
dreams, 13–14, 68, 94, 101, 104, 119, 125–6, 138, 141, 147
   American dream, 111, 150
   Taiwan dream, 2, 13, 107, 110–12
Dreyer, Carl Theodor, 103
drifting, 64, 79, 96, 100, 147–8
Du Duzhi, 28
Du Yunzhi, 44, 44n
duration, 13, 48, 54–6, 98, 125, 128–48
Dust in the Wind (1986), 47–8, 57

Easy Rider (1969), 22, 125
écriture féminine (women's writing), 12, 63
Edinburgh Film Festival, 109
exhaustion, 55, 130, 137, 147
exile, 17, 33n, 38, 47, 76, 107, 115–16

Fang, Caitlin, 150
Farhadi, Asghar, 151
Fassbinder, Rainer Werner, 87
Fellini, Federico, 62, 103
feminism, 3, 68; *see also* gender, women
Film Critics China, 41, 43, 45
Five (2003), 138
flâneur, 3, 11–12, 61–86
Flowers of Shanghai (1998), 77, 77n
Foucault, Michel, 53, 115
French New Wave, 12, 17, 22, 34–5, 39, 87–9, 96–7
Fresnoy, Le, 91
Fudaojin, 12, 107–110, 151
Fukuoka International Film Festival, 46

gay, 104
   homosexuality, 56, 97
   see also queer

gender, 2, 12–13, 63, 66n, 127; *see also* feminism, gay, queer, women
Genzken, Isa, 93
German Federal Cultural Foundation, 110
ghosts, 88, 100, 103
Global South, 110–13, 132, 137, 152
Globalisation, 8, 54, 115, 126–7
Godard, Jean-Luc, 34, 37, 51, 62, 96–7
Golden Horse Awards, 1, 46, 109
Golden Horse Film Academy, 108
Golden Horse Film Festival, 3, 11n, 19, 150
Goldsmith, Leo, 78
Good Men, Good Women (1995), 64
Goodbye, Dragon Inn (2003), 57, 100–5
Growing Up (1983), 63

Harvard Film Archive, 20
Hawaii International Film Festival, 46
He Never Gives Up (1979), 23
Healthy Realism, 9, 18–27, 45, 47
Hitchcock, Alfred, 21, 23
Ho Wi-ding, 2
Hoberman, Jim, 49, 78
Hole, The (1998), 50, 50n, 91, 95, 102
Hollywood, 5, 11n, 19, 21–3, 35, 48, 66, 95, 143n
Holt, Victoria, 21
Hong Kong International Film Festival, 13, 46, 129, 132, 134–6
  Hong Kong Film Awards, 50
  Hong Kong Asia Film Financing Forum (HAF), 134–5
Hong Sang-soo, 129
Hopper, Dennis, 22, 125
Hou Hsiao-hsien, 1–3, 9–12, 17–19, 27–9, 31–5, 39–40, 47–9, 52–7, 61–86, 108–10, 127, 138, 150
hsiang t'u literature, 18, 40, 51
Hsiao Yeh, 31, 37, 39, 46, 96n
Hsin Chi, 21–3
Hu, Brian, 5, 7–8
Huang Chun-ming, 40–2, 46
Huang Hui-chen, 98
Huang Jianye, 37, 40, 52
Huang Sheng-yuan, 139
Huasin Incident (2009), 108
Hui La Frances, 114

I Don't Want to Sleep Alone (2006), 102
Ice Poison (2014), 12, 106, 108–9, 118, 126–8

In Our Time (1982), 28, 31, 38–9, 46
Influence (Yingxiang), 10, 40, 51
installation art, 12–14, 54, 87–94, 98–102, 128–31, 138–48
Instant Fried Sauce Noodles (1981), 94
International Federation of Film Producers' Associations, 29
International Film Festival Rotterdam, 7, 46, 109, 130–1, 134, 138
  CineMart, 134
  Hubert Bals Fund, 130–1
  Tiger Competition, 109
Iordanova, Dina, 8, 132
It's a Dream (2007), 12, 90–2, 98, 100–1, 105

Jacob, Gilles, 91
Jade Love (1984), 44
Jaffe, Ira, 55
James, Caryn, 19, 34
Jarmusch, Jim, 78
Jenkins, Barry, 38
Jia Zhangke, 7, 38, 110, 129, 135, 146
Jie Jie (2016), 151
Journey to the West (2014), 136
Julé, Vincent, 79

Kael, Pauline, 51
Kaganski, Serge, 97
Kano (2014), 106
Keaton, Buster, 7, 103
Kiarostami, Abbas, 90, 138
Kim Ki-duk, 129
Ko I-cheng, 28
kominka (becoming Japanese), 75
Kon Satoshi, 7, 120
Kore-eda Hirokazu, 38, 151
Kraicer, Shelly, 46, 94
Kuomintang (KMT, the Nationalist), 9, 19–33, 41–58, 64, 75–7
Kurosawa Akira, 22, 51

L'Arrivée d'un train en gare de La Ciotat (1985), 69
La Nuit (1961), 97
labour, 8, 51, 112–13, 128, 131–2, 137, 141, 147
  and DV filmmaking, 12, 82, 107, 113–19
  exhaustion, 55, 130, 137, 147
  of production, 53, 126, 129, 131
  of walking, 128, 137
  poverty and shots, 113–19

Laclau, Matthieu, 110
Lamorisse, Albert, 12, 78
Late Autumn (1960), 66
Late Spring (1949), 68–9
Lau Kek-huat, 2
Lee Ang, 11n, 17, 28, 49, 108–9, 127, 150
Lee Chang-dong, 129
Lee Hsing, 23–5, 139
Lee Pingbing Mark, 28
Leigh Alphonse Youth (Li Youxin), 37, 43, 43n
Letters from the South (2013), 109, 128
Lewis, Oscar, 114
Li Bing, 151
Liao Qingsong, 28
Lim Giong, 110, 119
Lim Song Hwee, 7–8, 11, 54–6, 96, 117, 127–8, 136–7
Lin Sheng-wen, 109, 109n
Lin Tom Shu-Yu, 151
Lin Wenchi, 85, 102n
Lloyd, Harold, 99
long shots, 28, 36, 48, 53, 65, 70, 77, 90, 108
long takes, 11, 22, 28, 36, 48, 53–5, 64–5, 74, 79, 90, 94–100, 106, 108, 117, 127, 141
Louvre Museum (Musée du Louvre), 11–12, 87–9, 93, 102–3
Lukács, György, 53
Lupke, Christopher, 12, 63, 65

#MeToo, 3, 108, 120–1
Ma Ran, 8, 117, 127
Mandarin, 1, 20–8, 40, 44n, 47, 107n, 109, 111, 115, 149
marginalisation, 36, 45–6, 57, 77, 111, 114–5, 137, 149
Marseille International Film Festival, 136
Maslin, Janet, 34, 49
Maurier, Daphne du, 21
memory, 33, 43, 64, 91, 98, 100–2, 126, 147–8
migrants, 1–2, 6, 54, 106–15
migration, 2, 107, 114–15, 149
Millennium Mambo (2001), 110
mise en abyme, 12, 81–5
Mistress of Mellyn, 21
Mizoguchi Kenji, 103
mobility, 2, 114, 126; *see also* border crossing
movement-image, 96
movie theatres, 89–105, 130–1, 143–4

modernity, 11, 39, 67–8, 99
modernisation, 33n, 37, 62
modernism, 2, 37–8, 51
postmodernism, 54–7
Muller, Marco, 19, 30–1
Musée d'Orsay, 11, 61, 78, 83
museum, 10–13, 35, 55, 78, 83–94, 102–5, 114, 130–1, 143–6
music, 22–3, 73, 102n, 115, 119
musicals, 21, 50n, 103

New York Film Festival, 34, 49, 87n
New York Times, The, 34, 49, 65, 121
Nicklaus, Olivier, 97
Nina Wu (2019), 3, 13, 108, 110, 119–26, 151
No Form (2012), 136, 136n
No No Sleep (2015), 129, 136, 142–3, 147
noises, 64, 104, 119–20, 125
soundtrack, 20, 22, 119
see also music
nostalgia, 2, 35, 68, 95, 98, 102, 116, 146
nouvelle vague *see* French New Wave

Oasis (2002), 129
Oiticica, Hélio, 7, 145–6
Orientalism, 2
Oshima Nagisa, 22
Oyster Girl (1963), 23, 25
Ozu Yasujiro, 34, 55, 61–74, 86, 151

Paloma Blanca (2006), 108
Panahi, Jafar, 129
Panopticism, 115
Park Chan-wook, 135
Park Je Cheol, 80
Pasolini, Pier Paolo, 57, 103
pastiche, 73, 78
Peckinpah, Sam, 57
Peng Hsiao-yen, 44n, 45, 47
Perfect Blue (1997), 120
performance, 27, 49, 55, 62, 87n, 94, 97, 103, 118, 123, 128–43
Persall, Steve, 78
Platform (1998), 129
Polanski, Roman, 57
Poor Folk (2012), 1, 108
postcolonialism, 1, 6, 8, 62, 73–7, 86, 88, 99
poverty, 108, 113–19, 145
Psycho (1960), 23
Puppetmaster, The (1993), 34n, 64, 80

qiong yao, 26–7
Quatre cents coups, Les (1959), 88–9
queer, 2, 98–9, 147; *see also* gay

Rayns, Tony, 19, 30–1, 36, 39, 46
realism, 2, 5, 17, 25, 53–4, 57, 71, 113–17
   neorealism, 17, 25, 36, 57
   see also Healthy Realism
Rebecca, 21
Rebel Without a Cause (1955), 95
Rebels of the Neon God (1992), 88n, 95, 97
recycling, 13, 90, 93, 105, 144, 146, 148
reflexivity, 81–2, 100
Reichardt, Kelly, 138
Remes, Justin, 138, 144
Resnais, Alain, 37, 51, 97
Return to Burma (2011), 108–9, 111–12, 116n
Reynaud, Bérénice, 46
Rice Dumpling Vendors, The (1969), 23
River, The (1997), 56
Road to Mandalay, The (2016), 109–10, 126n, 152
Roan Feng-I Fiona, 149–51
Robinson, Luke, 2, 107, 112, 127
Ruiz, Raúl, 78
Russian Ark (2001), 94
Ryu Chishu, 72

Safety Last! (1923), 99
Said, Edward, 116
Sand (2018), 136
Sandwich Man, The (1983), 39–40
Sarris, Andrew, 45, 51
Sato Tado, 28, 46
Scott, A. O., 65
Screen Tests (1964–6), 57, 130
Sherlock Jr. (1924), 103
Shochiku Studio, 61, 64–6
Shu Kei, 30, 46
Sight and Sound, 30, 34
Sing Song-Yong, 54, 56–7
Sissako, Abderrahmane, 152
Skywalk Is Gone, The (2002), 91
Sleep (1964), 57
sleep, 13–14, 69, 88, 98, 128–48
Sleepcinemahotel, 138
Sleepwalk (2012), 136
slow cinema, 3, 10, 40, 54–5, 90, 96, 109–10, 127, 136–8, 147, 150
   aesthetics of waiting, 34, 55, 79, 96, 137, 147
   discourses, 54–7, 96–7

   duration, 13, 48, 54–6, 98, 128–48
   languid, 34, 67, 69, 77n, 79
   movement, 10, 40
   slow walks, 55, 128, 136–7, 141
   slowness, 3, 40, 54–8, 136–7, 143, 147–8
   stillness, 56, 137, 147
   see also long takes
Slow Walk, Long March, 13, 87n, 128, 137; *see also* Walker
Small Talk (2016), 98
Snow, Michael, 91
Soderbergh, Steven, 126
soft power, 5, 7
Sokurov, Alexander, 94, 138
Sontag, Susan, 90
sound, 28, 42, 44n, 57, 64, 67, 69, 104, 109–10, 117, 119–27, 145
   soundscape, 11, 13, 115, 119–27
spectatorship, 13, 67, 101, 130, 138–48
Spider Lilies (2007), 98
Still Life (2006), 146
Story of a Small Town, The (1979), 23
Stray Dogs (2013), 87n, 88n, 106, 144–6
Sundance Film Festival, 50, 131
surrealism, 13, 120, 125

Taipei Fine Arts Museum of Taiwan, 92
Taipei Story (1985), 80, 150
Taiwan Black Movies, 26–7
Taiwan Film Festival Edinburgh, 20
Taiwanese-dialect films *see* taiyupian
taiyupian, 9, 17–37
Tan Chui Mui, 128
Tarkovsky, Andrei, 103
Tarr, Béla, 55, 90, 138
Taste of Apples, The, 40–3
Terrorizers, The (1986), 57
The Perfumed Hill, 152
Theatre in the Boiler Room: Art Installation, The (2011), 93
Theatre Quarterly (Juchang), 10, 40, 51
Third cinema, 5
Three Continents Festival (Festival des 3 Continents), 31–2
   Golden Montgolfière, 32
Timbuktu (2014), 152
time, 14, 54–5, 58, 67, 74–5, 79, 80, 86, 93–4, 99–101, 105, 126, 128, 132, 137, 141, 145, 147
   and space, 86, 94, 100–1, 105, 137

clocks, 83, 93, 99
temporality, 55, 61–2, 67, 73–6, 101, 105, 147
see also duration
Tokyo International Film Festival, 49, 95, 132, 134, 150
  Tokyo Film Creators' Forum, 134
Tokyo Story (1953), 65–6, 73
Tokyo-Ga (1985), 72–3
Toronto International Film Festival, 32n, 132
trains, 64–77, 119, 125
transnational cinema, 7–9, 22–3, 64–6, 102–5, 151–2
Tribeca Film Institute, 131
  Latin American Media Fund, 131
Tropicalia (1966–7), 145
Truffaut, François, 7, 34, 37, 45, 47, 87–9, 96–7, 102n, 103
Tsai Chin, 80
Tsai Ing-wen, 111
Tsai Ming-liang, 1–2, 10–17, 50, 54–7, 61, 87–105, 128–48
Tseng Chuang-hsiang, 40
Two Women in Combat (1972), 93

Udden, James, 39, 62
United Daily News (Lian he bao), 32, 40, 43
Uroskie, Andrew V., 101

Valck, Marijke de, 8, 133, 136
Vallotton, Félix, 83–5
Valsamis, Giorgos, 150–1
Venice Biennale, 13, 92, 136
Venice International Film Festival, 7, 9, 11, 29–30, 32, 87n, 96, 132
  Golden Lion, 9, 30, 32
Vicki's Hat, 40
Village Voice, 49, 78
Viola, Bill, 91
Visage (2009), 12, 50n, 88–90, 102–5, 146
Vitali, Valentina, 35, 74n
Vive l'amour (1994), 97–8
Voyage du ballon rouge, Le (*Flight of the Red Balloon*, 2007), 11–12, 61–4, 78–86

Walker (2012), 128–9, 136
Walker (2012–continuing), 13, 87, 128, 130, 136–41, 147–8; *see also Slow Walk, Long March*

Walking on Water (2013), 128, 136
walking, 11, 61, 67, 69, 77–8, 86, 87n, 125, 128–30, 137, 145–6
Wan Ren, 28, 40–2
Wang Bing, 38
Wang Shin-Hong, 109n, 111–12
Wang Tong, 1, 28
Wang Wan-jui, 115
Wang Xiaoshuai, 50, 129
Warhol, Andy, 57, 93, 130
Warriors of the Rainbow: Seediq Bale (2011), 4
Wayward Cloud, The (2005), 50n, 91
Wedding Banquet, The (1993), 49
Weerrasethakul, Apichatpong, 7, 38, 110, 129, 135, 138
Wei Te-sheng, 4
Weinstein, Harvey, 119–20
Welles, Orson, 103
Wenders, Wim, 7, 57, 72–3
What Time Is It There? (2001), 61, 88, 91, 98–100, 105, 146
White Terror, 33
Wilson, Flannery, 80
Wolff, Janet, 67
Woman is the Future of Man (2004), 129
women
  critics, 3, 10, 38–58
  film directors, 98, 128, 138, 149–51
  screenwriters, 3, 10, 12, 28, 37, 39, 63, 66n, 119, 125
  see also écriture féminine
Wong Edmond, 30, 96n
Wu Chia-chi, 36
Wu Isabelle, 85
Wu Ke-Xi, 3, 108, 109n, 118–25
Wu Nien-Jen, 28, 39, 46

Yang Edward, 1, 11, 17–18, 27–9, 35, 46, 49, 80, 138, 150
Yang Shi-chi, 10, 39–45
Yang Ya-che, 123–4
Yeh Emilie Yueh-yu, 21, 23, 63, 102n, 132
Your Face (2018), 87, 130

Z. Midi (Zhao Deyin), 1–3, 10–13, 71, 106–29, 151–2
Zhan Hongzhi, 43, 52
Zhang Yimou, 34, 49

EU representative:
Easy Access System Europe
Mustamäe tee 50, 10621 Tallinn, Estonia
Gpsr.requests@easproject.com